Managing Privacy

Managing

Information Technology

Privacy

nd Corporate America

H. Jeff Smith

The

University

of North

Carolina

Press

Chapel Hill

and London

Manufactured in the United States of America

The paper in this book meets the guidelines for permanence and
durability of the Committee on Production Guidelines for Book
Longevity of the Council on Library Resources.

Library of Congress Cataloging-in-Publication Data
Smith, H. Jeff.
    Managing privacy : information technology and corporate
America / by H. Jeff Smith.
        p.   cm.
    Includes bibliographical references and index.
    ISBN 0-8078-2147-0 (cloth : alk. paper).
—ISBN 0-8078-4454-3 (pbk. : alk. paper)
    1. Privacy, Right of—United States.   2. Computers—United
States—Access control.   3. Records—United States—Access
control.   I. Title.
JC596.2.U5S64   1994
323.44'8—dc20   93-33334
                        CIP

Portions of this book appeared in a different form in H. Jeff Smith,
"Privacy Policies and Practices: Inside the Organizational Maze,"
Communications of the ACM 36, no. 12 (December 1993): 105–22.
Some brief passages also appeared in a different form in Frank V.
Cespedes and H. Jeff Smith, "Database Marketing: New Rules for
Policy and Practice," *Sloan Management Review* 34, no. 4 (Summer
1993): 7–22.

98   97   96   95   94   5   4   3   2   1

To Margaret,

for her constant

love and support

Contents

Tables and Figures

Tables

Figures

Acknowledgments

My research into the subject of information privacy began while I was a doctoral student at Harvard Business School. While this book includes much new, additional research, it had its origins in my doctoral thesis. For that reason, I would like to thank Professor Warren McFarlan, who served as my thesis committee chairman, as well as Professors Tom Piper, James McKenney, and Jane Linder, the other members of my committee. Their tireless reading of successive drafts, their insightful comments, and their constant encouragement were all appreciated.

I would also like to thank many other members of the Harvard Business School community. Other faculty members offered comments and assistance, and my fellow doctoral students were a source of consistent good humor and moral support. I am especially appreciative of the financial support provided by Harvard Business School for travel and survey administration expenses involved in the first phases of the study.

Of course, this study would not have been possible without the kind cooperation of the organizations that participated. I will be forever indebted to these organizations for granting me access to their employees and operations. To all the individuals who spent time with me, I offer my thanks.

I would also like to thank my colleagues at Georgetown School of Business for their support and encouragement. John Dealy is gratefully acknowledged for his support of the research in its later stages. And to David Flaherty of the University of Western Ontario, a special note of appreciation for prodding me to extend my earlier work.

I am very grateful to those who read and offered helpful comments on drafts of all or part of this manuscript: Peter Berge, Mary Culnan, Dorothy Denning, David Flaherty, Bob Gellman, John Hasnas, Ernie Kallman, Mark Keil, Jane Linder, Warren McFarlan, Bill McHenry, Jim McKenney, Gary Marx, Keri Pearlson, Craig Smith; several anonymous industry observers; and the anonymous reviewers selected by the University of North Carolina Press. In addition, I especially appreciate the help of LuAnn Hartley, who spent long hours in front of her computer helping me to finalize the manuscript. And of course I appreciate the support and expert administrative assistance of the University of North Carolina Press management and staff.

Finally, I would like to thank my family and friends for their patience, support, and love during this endeavor. I will not attempt to list names, but you all know who you are.

Abbreviations

ACLI	American Council of Life Insurance
ACM	Association for Computing Machinery
AG	Attorney General
AIDS	Acquired Immune Deficiency Syndrome
ATM	Automated teller machine
CD	Certificate of deposit
CD-ROM	Compact Disk–Read Only Memory
CIO	Chief Information Officer
DIB	Data Inspection Board (Sweden)
DMA	Direct Marketing Association
EC	European Community
EFT	Electronic Funds Transfer
EFTA	Electronic Fund Transfer Act of 1978
ERISA	Employee Retirement Income Security Act
FASB	Financial Accounting Standards Board
FCC	Federal Communications Commission
FCRA	Fair Credit Reporting Act of 1970
FDIC	Federal Deposit Insurance Corporation
FTC	Federal Trade Commission
GAAP	Generally accepted accounting practice
GAPP	Generally accepted privacy practice

HEW	U.S. Department of Health, Education, and Welfare
HIAA	Health Insurance Association of America
HMO	Health maintenance organization
I/S	Information systems
LAN	Local area network
MassPIRG	Massachusetts Public Interest Research Group
MIB	Medical Information Bureau
NAIC	National Association of Insurance Commissioners
NCOA	National Change of Address
OCC	Office of the Comptroller of the Currency
PC	Personal computer
PPO	Preferred provider organization
PPSC	Privacy Protection Study Commission
T&E	Travel and entertainment

Managing Privacy

Chapter 1

Privacy in the 1990s

It is inevitable that personal privacy will be one of the most significant pressure points in our national fabric for most of the 1990s. Advancing technology, depersonalization of the workplace and other social environments, a growing popula-tion . . . all can be expected to create a greater personal need for a sense of space and dignity.
—Erwin Chemerinsky[1]

For very little cost, anybody can learn anything about anybody.
—R. E. Smith[2]

Computers and telecommunication networks are at once effi-cient expediters, sources of storage for vast amounts of information, and bases for significant strategic benefits in commercial enterprise. With these benefits, of course, come some societal issues—most notably, the effects of these vast amounts of information on institutions and individuals. As with any new tech-nologies, the absorption of computers and telecommunication networks into our societies has created an area of ambiguity—a space in which there are often no explicit or agreed-upon specific rules with respect to appropriate and inappropri-ate behaviors.[3] The technologies enable new applications, many of which were not feasible or economical before the innovation. With the new applications come significant policy questions at both corporate and public levels.

One of the most important areas for such debate is information privacy—a condition of limited access to identifiable information about individuals.[4] On an almost weekly basis, one can find new examples of the growing concern regard-ing the collection, use, and protection of personal information in the United States. For example:

• Executives of Lotus Development Corporation and Equifax Marketing Decision Systems canceled the release of a proposed product called "Lotus MarketPlace: Households" in the wake of an unprecedented storm of consumer protest regarding its alleged invasion of consumer privacy. The product would have provided operators of small businesses with information regarding American households, in compact disk–read only memory (CD-ROM) form, to be used in targeted marketing campaigns. After a number of negative news articles appeared in the press, the product began to receive legislative scrutiny, and a grass-roots protest campaign began. After over thirty thousand consumers requested that they be deleted from the database, the project was canceled.[5]

• The *Wall Street Journal* reported that the Blockbuster Video chain was planning to sell mailing lists of its customers, categorized according to the types of movies they rented. After a strong negative reaction from the chain's customers as well as much additional media scrutiny, Blockbuster's chairman announced a few days later that a vice president "misspoke" when discussing the plan with the *Wall Street Journal* reporter.[6]

• A consumer foods company used information from redeemed coupons and rebate forms to create a database for targeted marketing. It was assailed in a national consumer publication with the headline "Smile—You're on Corporate Camera!"[7]

• The three major credit bureaus used some pieces of information from their credit files to create new databases, from which mailing lists of names and addresses were sold for targeted marketing purposes. Privacy advocates have voiced serious concerns about the practice, which has become a pivotal point in congressional debates about credit-reporting laws.[8] The concerns have also prompted a number of changes in the industry: in July 1991, six states sued one of the credit bureaus (TRW Credit Data) for, among other things, "violating consumer privacy"[9] by "illegally selling sensitive data to junk-mailers."[10] In August 1991, after discussions with the New York attorney general's office, another of the credit bureaus (Equifax) announced its intention to discontinue the sale of such lists.[11] Then, in early 1993—as part of an agreement with the Federal Trade Commission (FTC)—TRW agreed to a policy similar to Equifax's. As of this writing, the third credit bureau (Trans Union) has lost a court case challenging the FTC position. However, Trans Union may appeal the ruling.[12]

• A number of consumer goods companies have expanded their toll-free 800 customer service lines so that they intercept the phone numbers, names, and addresses of callers. These systems provide the companies with records of loyal customers who call for spare parts or recipes. The practice has come under attack from privacy advocates; in a recent issue of *Privacy Journal*, the companies' actions were described under the heading "Zooming In on You."[13]

Often, because of the changing marketplace and increasing speed of technological change, executives must make decisions regarding new uses of personal information while there is still much ambiguity regarding proper and improper practices. Later, executives often find themselves facing societal anxieties about privacy in two different forms: 1) public opinion backlashes against various computerized processes and 2) a tightened legal environment with additional governmental control.

But the executives are certainly not without blame. This study relied on interviews with executives and managers in three banks, three insurance organizations, and one credit card issuer; interviews with privacy and consumer advocates; interviews with consumers themselves; interviews with industry observers; and on a written survey of employees in several organizations. The study reveals that in many industries, executives are afraid to confront the issue of information privacy—so much so that they go to extensive lengths to avoid the topic's discussion and investigation. And when executives do confront the issue, it is almost always in a reactive and not a proactive manner, primarily because the decision-making process is a cyclical one. A period of "drift," in which executives rely on middle management to create new practices, is followed by some external threat—a disturbance, usually through legislation or the media—that shocks the corporation into an official response. Then, the totality of practices is considered formally in an official policy-making exercise. In the case of an extreme and immediate external shock (e.g., AIDS in the insurance industry), the industry as a whole creates a policy to which individual firms then react.

Because of the executives' refusal to confront the information privacy issue in a proactive manner, several negative phenomena may occur:

• Especially during the policy drift stage, individuals in the corporations frequently experience a great amount of emotional dissonance. Their own values regarding uses of personal information are often at odds with those of their corporation. They usually resolve this discrepancy by subjugating their own values to the corporation's and by rationalizing their misgivings.

• There is a distinct lack of leadership with respect to privacy issues at both corporate and internal levels. At a corporate level, very few executives indicate a desire to become leaders in privacy issues within their industries. They prefer to wait for others to establish the guidelines and rules. Internally, the organizations' information systems (I/S) executives—who are often in the best position to understand the totality of the organization's information—adopt particularly subservient roles in most privacy discussions. They do not see themselves as the corporate leaders on information privacy issues.

• The corporations seem most likely to formalize their policies for information handling if the *type of information* they handle is particularly sensitive (e.g., medical information). When the information is apparently less sensitive (e.g., financial information), policies are less formal. But, regardless of the content of the official policies, employees report much dissatisfaction with actual practices inside the corporation.

• For several reasons—executives' intentional hiding of their policies and practices, inaccessible information conduits, lack of forcefulness on their own parts—consumers tend to be quite uninformed regarding the actual policies and practices of industries with which they deal regularly. When they learn of the practices, they often become angry and call for legal intervention. Quite often, corporations and consumers disagree about the intended purpose of information collection and use.

These findings about corporations' handling of information privacy issues should be troubling to the growing "privacy coalition" in America—those individuals, advocates, organizations, and legislators who are concerned about the threats to personal privacy in today's society. If public opinion polls are any indication, the size of this coalition is becoming quite large. Consider the results of seven public opinion polls from 1977 to 1992. Respondents who answered either "very concerned" or "somewhat concerned" to a general question about personal privacy are shown in Figure 1.1.

Why might the public's concern have become so large in this recent time frame? The best explanation is that the media has devoted an increasing amount of attention to the issue of information privacy, and consumers are slowly becoming more aware of how information is being used. Alan Westin, a professor at Columbia University and an academic adviser to the 1990s opinion polls, cited "feature articles in *Business Week*,[14] *U.S. News and World Report*, the *Washington Post*, the San Francisco *ExaminerChronicle*, the Dallas *Morning News*, and

Figure 1.1. Public Opinion Polls

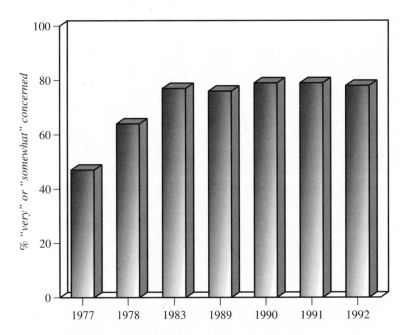

Source: For years other than 1989, the sources for the percentages are Equifax Inc., *The Equifax Report on Consumers in the Information Age*, conducted by Louis Harris and Associates and Dr. Alan Westin (1990); and Equifax Inc., *Harris-Equifax Consumer Privacy Survey 1991* and *Harris-Equifax Consumer Privacy Survey 1992*. (Equifax data appear courtesy of Equifax Inc., 1600 Peachtree Street, Atlanta, Ga. 30302.) The source for the 1989 percentage is Cambridge Reports, *Technology and Consumers: Jobs, Education, Privacy* (1989), Bulletin on Consumer Opinion no. 157. The same question—"How concerned are you about threats to your personal privacy in America today?"—was administered in the 1978, 1983, 1990, 1991, and 1992 polls. The 1989 Cambridge Reports question asked, "How concerned are you about the invasion of your personal privacy in the United States today?" The 1977 question (which was reported in the 1990 Equifax summary) asked, "Now some people tell us they are concerned about what's happening to their personal privacy—the right to live their own life without others knowing more about it, or intruding into it, more than is absolutely necessary. I'd like to know if you've ever thought about that. [How concerned are you] about the loss of personal privacy?" Options of "very concerned," "somewhat concerned," etc., were provided.

USA Today, and . . . network TV programs such as the NBC 'Today' show"[15] as contributing to the increased public awareness. Other television programs across the country have also addressed the privacy issue. The program "Evening Magazine" did an extensive exposé that was shown on many television stations,[16] many local television stations have followed suit with their own stories,[17] and syndicated "talk shows" (e.g., Oprah Winfrey's) have also featured discussions about privacy in various contexts. Other publications with more limited circulation (e.g., *Computerworld*) have also addressed the topic.[18] A book entitled *Privacy in America* was released in 1989 with extensive publicity,[19] and a 1992 synopsis of an investigative reporter's success in buying personal information— Jeffrey Rothfeder's *Privacy for Sale*—received much public attention.[20] In short, both the print and broadcast media have fueled the privacy fire, and the strong public concern regarding privacy undoubtedly reflects the media's influence. This media attention can be expected to continue into the foreseeable future.

Consistent with the media attention, in the early 1990s corporate practices are also receiving much scrutiny from legislators and law enforcement officials. The credit-reporting industry has garnered much of the attention: prodded by a number of quite visible industry and corporate gaffes, including the incorrect misreporting of tax payments as tax liens for the entire town of Norwich, Vermont,[21] the Federal Trade Commission forced TRW into an out-of-court settlement regarding its practices of data collection, storage, and use. This settlement was reached only a few weeks after the company announced—just before Congress began hearings on the industry's practices—that it would begin giving individuals free annual copies of their own credit reports.[22] Amendments modifying the Fair Credit Reporting Act, which would give consumers some additional rights in the new "information age," are—as of this writing—winding their way through Congress with a high probability of passage, according to the bill's backers.[23] And, as noted in the introductory example, the sale of mailing lists from credit reports continues to generate much legal controversy and confusion. In other industries, Caller Identification and Automatic Number Identification technologies have seen disparate state legislation in several locales. American Express has agreed with the state attorney general of New York to begin notifying its cardholders that the company sometimes profiles them based on their purchases and sells lists based on those profiles.[24] And, in another development related to targeted marketing, a federal telemarketing law (the Telephone Consumer Protection Act) was signed in early 1992. Although its full effects are unclear as of this writing—in fact, one of its provisions regarding automated dialers has been struck down in court[25]—the Federal Communications Commission (FCC) was to study various systems for controlling telemarketing calls to individuals who do not want to receive them and to implement the system deemed most effective.[26]

Driving Forces

Why are consumer concerns on the rise, fueled by the media? Why is legislative scrutiny increasing? What is driving this growing focus on privacy? As Richard Mason notes,[27] the forces are twofold: 1) new technological capabilities make new applications possible, and 2) the value of information is increasing.

Technological Factors

There are several technological drivers fueling perceptions. Increasingly, data are available in a computerized format in addition to—or instead of—a paper format. The business world of the 1950s was one of filing cabinets filled with carbon copies. In the 1990s, the filed documents are also stored on a computer disk drive in a digital form, and many business transactions are now being handled exclusively in an electronic format. Some speak of a "paperless office," in which all communications and data are exchanged electronically. While still a futuristic objective for most organizations, such an approach is becoming more and more possible as computer technology improves. But with this movement toward computerization—viewed by most Americans as a source of increasing efficiency—comes a concern that privacy is harder to maintain in a computerized environment. In a 1992 opinion survey, for example, 79 percent of Americans agreed that "computers have improved the quality of life in our society." In the same survey, though, 68 percent of Americans agreed that "the present uses of computers are an actual threat to personal privacy"—a sharp increase from 1974 and 1978, when only 38 percent and 37 percent of Americans, respectively, felt this way.[28]

It is becoming much easier to join data items from disparate sources and to draw inferences from the compiled data package. Enabled by the development of relational database techniques and structured query languages, organizations are no longer constrained by traditional dependencies of computer programs on the programs' unique (and often inconsistent) data structures. Now, organizations can pull data from numerous sources—both internal and external to the firm—and can create a much more powerful information package. But this package also carries the burden of heightened privacy concerns, since the collected data package is often perceived as more intrusive than the disparate data elements taken by themselves.

Telecommunications capabilities are breaking down the data boundaries between organizations. With the advent of wide-area networks (WANs) and value-added networks (VANs), organizations are finding that it is increasingly easy to share data among themselves. This has led to a number of powerful, strategic applications at an interorganizational level.[29] Indeed, an organization's existence as an "island" of computing—efficiently automated within itself but disconnected from the outside world[30]—is quickly becoming a concept of the past. Instead, many members of the business and political communities are embracing the objective of a high-speed "information highway," which will connect both public and private entities.[31] But with this inevitable exchange of data across organizational lines comes a greatly increased privacy threat. Control over personal data is quickly lost, and problems with data errors are quickly exacerbated as the data jump from one computer to another.

During the last decade, phenomenal improvements in the computing price/performance ratio have enabled organizations to "downsize" their computing. Applications that once ran on mainframe computers are increasingly being found on personal computers (PCs) at individuals' desks, and data are now being stored on individuals' hard disk drives and on local area network (LAN) file servers.[32] This decentralized approach to computing has enabled many new applications with demonstrable benefits to the business community.[33] But with this downsizing trend come many challenges to privacy, as it is much harder to maintain the security and integrity of data that are managed in a decentralized manner. When all the computing resources and data were under the control of a centralized data processing department, requests for data access and modification were centrally controlled. As responsibilities for data management are pushed downward in the organization, control is similarly diffused.

Increasing Value of Information

At the same time, the value of information is increasing as decision makers discover new ways to use information for strategic advantage—especially in the marketing of services and merchandise, as targeted "micromarketing" becomes the norm.[34] Instead of the traditional, one-to-many approach—in which a single advertising campaign was utilized for all potential buyers—targeted marketing utilizes a one-to-one approach. This specialization moves the market closer to what has been called the "segment of one," targeting specific products to smaller and smaller segments.[35] Thus, instead of the traditional marketing approach—media advertising or mailings to large lists—this approach aims at narrower targets. Such micromarketing often entails a telemarketing campaign or a mailing to a quite limited list chosen for its specific characteristics. Targeted marketing improves the efficiency of marketing distribution channels. But, of course, to market to specific individuals, companies must store and share information about those individuals. It is this process that comes under much scrutiny.

In fact, many of these uses of information were theoretically possible in earlier days; however, technological constraints made the applications either impossible or prohibitively expensive. With the increase in processing speeds and the decline in storage costs during the last decade, the applications have become feasible. As an example, consider the use of credit card holders' purchase histories in targeted marketing activities. The purchases that a cardholder makes, over time, are scrutinized to determine the cardholder's tendencies, and a market profile of the cardholder is created. In theory, it would always have been possible to categorize cardholders according to their purchase histories using manual methods; however, the cost would have been so great as to negate the benefits of such a project. With improved technology, such a project becomes a viable one for companies to pursue.

Legal Domain

One might ask, in such an environment of ambiguity, increasing consumer concerns, media exposure, and legislative scrutiny: doesn't the law protect us from privacy violations? Isn't the executives' duty simply to follow the legal proscriptions for their industry? Doesn't the fact that legislators are paying more attention indicate that a societal solution is forthcoming soon? Unfortunately, history reveals that the U.S. legislative agenda and privacy have a reactive, "bits and pieces," up-and-down relationship. The development of appropriate laws has occurred in a piecemeal fashion, with legislation targeted to a specific problem that has, for one reason or another, caught lawmakers' attention. For example, in 1988 Congress was outraged to find that a Supreme Court nominee's video rental records were legally released to a newspaper reporter. Sensing a future trend that could affect themselves as well as other Americans, they quickly passed the Video Privacy Protection Act (often called the "Bork Bill," in honor of the Supreme Court nominee). Yet many other issues of similar or greater weight—for example, records of one's purchases—have never received federal legislative attention, because until quite recently there has not been a perceived "crisis."[36] No cohesive framework has ever been created. Furthermore, even the legislative attention that privacy has received has been of a cyclical nature: the focus tends to ebb and flow. Neither executives nor members of the privacy coalition can rely on the present U.S. law to resolve the majority of privacy disputes. For example, the dilemmas suggested by the introductory examples cannot, in general, be resolved through current U.S. federal law. (The uses of information in the above examples could all be argued to be legal at the times they occurred, even though they have resulted in negative consequences for individuals and/or corporations.) Although a number of privacy laws have been passed, they do not address the issues in a cohesive fashion; rather, they form a patchwork quilt. Thus, as changing technologies and social conditions require new corporate policy decisions, executives often must make decisions years before the courts and lawmakers offer guidance, and the privacy coalition must deal with those decisions without clear legal guidance or a mechanism for resolving disputes.

1960s: A Growing Awareness

The U.S. history of legal attention to privacy concerns is not a consistent and smooth tale. The privacy advocates' arguments began in the mid-1960s, when several factors came together to create an awareness of privacy concerns: 1) the first commercially successful computer, the IBM 360; 2) the increasing proliferation of the social security number as a personal identifier; 3) a general societal mistrust of government, fueled by the Vietnam War; and 4) a proposal for a National Data Center to combine various federal agencies' databanks in a central repository.

1970–1977: Legal Responses

Largely in response to the increasing consumer concerns raised by the privacy advocates, the early 1970s saw a strong federal focus on information privacy. In 1973, a study by the U.S. Department of Health, Education, and Welfare (HEW) recommended a legal structure based on a set of "Fair Information Practices" (see Figure 1.2).

During the same time period, a substantial number of privacy laws were passed, starting with the Fair Credit Reporting Act in 1970 and including the Privacy Act of 1974. Most of these laws focused on the government's use of information—the most salient concern during those years. The Right to Financial Privacy Act (1978), for example, was a response to a 1976 Supreme Court Case

Figure 1.2. 1973 Code of Fair Information Practices

- There shall be no personal data record-keeping systems whose very existence is secret.
- There must be a way for a person to find out what information about the person is in a record and how it is used.
- There must be a way for a person to prevent information about the person that was obtained for one purpose from being used or made available for other purposes without the person's consent.
- There must be a way for a person to correct or amend a record of identifiable information about the person.
- Any organization creating, maintaining, using, or disseminating records of identifiable personal data must assure the reliability of the data for their intended use and must take precautions to prevent misuses of the data.

Source: United States Department of Health, Education, and Welfare, *Records, Computers, and the Rights of Citizens: Report of the Secretary's Advisory Committee on Automated Personal Data Systems* (Washington: U.S. Government Printing Office, 1973), as presented in "The CPSR Newsletter" (Computer Professionals for Social Responsibility, Palo Alto, Calif.), vol. 7, no. 4 (Fall 1989): 16.

(*United States v. Miller*) that had clipped bank customers' rights with respect to government access to their banking records.

In 1977, the Privacy Protection Study Commission (PPSC) was appointed to examine the status of privacy protection as it had evolved since the 1973 HEW study. This group called for a number of additional legislative remedies that had not been considered by the earlier laws. Ironically, although there was great societal concern regarding the linking of files on mainframe computers during this time frame, the limits on technological capabilities made such linkages few in number. In fact, merely *accessing* the data was quite difficult on most mainframes, as access was application-bound, and database management concepts had not yet been widely embraced.

1977–1986: A Quiet Decade

For several reasons, the PPSC recommendations were ignored by Congress, and the next decade passed with very few legislative attempts to confront privacy issues. To some degree, the Carter administration can be faulted for a weak initial response. David Flaherty has noted that

> the recommendations of the [PPSC] had little direct impact on the public or private sectors, except for the considerable number of voluntary improvements that took place as a result of its extensive hearings. These weak results were part of the failure of the Carter administration to settle its own privacy agenda and then sell it to Congress. The so-called Carter Privacy Initiative, sent to Congress on April 2, 1979, was ill-fated. . . . Although major hearings took place, almost no legislation was enacted before the 1980 electoral defeat of Carter.[37]

As the more conservative Reagan administration took office, privacy laws were widely viewed as anti-business and thus ran counter to the pro-business sentiment of the times.

After 1986: A Reawakening

In the late 1980s, however, the legislative pendulum began to swing in the opposite direction. Privacy issues began to regain momentum. Relational database techniques, personal computers, and expanded telecommunications networks made information more readily available. In addition, faster processing speeds and cheaper storage costs made many new applications feasible. As corporations and the government began to take advantage of these new technological possibilities, privacy advocates began to attract the attention of legislators—whose view was beginning to shift somewhat from the pro-business attitude of the early 1980s.

Action started at the state level, but by the end of the 1980s, three major federal laws and a few minor laws had been passed, and several others had been considered in the 99th, 100th, and 101st Congresses. One that could have had significant commercial impacts—the creation of a federal Data Protection Board —was proposed in all three Congresses and reintroduced in 1993.[38] Governmental activities continued to receive a moderate amount of scrutiny (one of the major laws dealt with government agencies' sharing records to catch welfare cheats), but another shift was also becoming evident: commercial activities— especially in the financial industries—were receiving increasing attention from the legislators.

This new focus on commercial activities has been and will continue to be quite jarring for many industries that have escaped scrutiny for many years. Because corporations in these industries have operated in the darkness of data processing shadows, Americans are relatively uninformed about their activities, and this situation could eventually lead to some economic as well as legal challenges. For example, most of the consumers interviewed as part of this study were poorly informed as to how companies were using information about them. As they learned about these uses, many became angry and called for legal responses—even when it was pointed out that they often received personal benefits from those uses of information. As the media focus educates the consuming populace—if this focus group research is any indication—corporate decision makers may find themselves facing a consumer backlash in addition to the legislative response.

This consumer backlash could result in economic pressure against corporations that are seen as violating privacy. Such pressures are already being seen in an elementary form in the credit card industry, where one large bank recently advertised a new "Privacy Protection Plan" for its credit card holders. It promised that it would "never give your name to one of those telemarketing firms." In a similar vein, one large long-distance telephone carrier, MCI, introduced a "Friends and Family" promotion, under which members of a "calling circle" received a discount when they all became MCI customers. But its chief competitor, AT&T, has responded with a set of television commercials deriding the MCI plan as invading individuals' privacy.[39] Such campaigns based on the theme of privacy may well become more frequent in the next few years, and consumers will likely respond. So, in addition to a legal backlash, an economic backlash also appears to be brewing.

Today's Privacy Environment

The two drivers—new technological capabilities and the increasing value of information—have created an environment in which consumers' privacy awareness is quite high. Media attention is increasing, also, at a time when the "ebb and flow" of legal attention finds privacy concerns in an "up" cycle. In addition, a great amount of pressure for new privacy laws may be exerted by the European Community (EC) by the mid-1990s. The EC is drafting a set of uniform privacy laws that are more restrictive than those in the U.S. The most troubling issue for U.S. companies will be the EC laws' possible prohibitions against data exchanges with countries where laws are perceived to be weaker. Thus, if it wants to trade with EC members, the U.S. might have to acknowledge the more rigorous constraints of the EC, or at least show that its privacy environment is improving in some structural way.[40] Fueled by these multiple factors, the acceleration of the cycle seems to be increasing.

What is the probable path for the next decade? At this juncture, the U.S. privacy environment is at a crossroads. The most likely path for the next few years—the one that will come to pass if corporate decision makers continue in their present modes of operation—is one in which federal privacy laws restricting commercial activities will be passed at an increasing rate. It is not clear, though, that this scenario will actually result in a stronger privacy environment; rather, it may simply represent an excessive reliance on a "regulatory fix."[41] If past experience is any indication, the laws will be of a reactive and narrow nature, protecting individuals in some small areas while leaving other areas largely untouched. So, while the number of laws will be greater, they will not necessarily represent an overall increase in personal privacy.

Yet there are several attractive alternatives to this path. The best holds meaningful roles for corporations, industry associations, consumers and their advocates, and the federal government. This book informs all the players but is specifically addressed to 1) corporate executives who wish to avoid future privacy problems and 2) members of the privacy coalition—concerned consumers, advocates, and informed legislators—who recognize a need for change in the way our society handles privacy issues. Chapter 2 details the study itself, with a special focus on the industries and their characteristics. Chapter 3 considers the corporations' decision-making process for privacy matters, with all of its reactivity and the attendant problems. Chapter 4 reports on some of the consequences of this hackneyed decision-making process: the misaligned policies and practices for handling personal information. Chapter 5 then moves outward and explains much of the contention, by comparing the perceptions of individuals *inside* the corporation with the consumers and advocates *outside*. Chapter 6 considers the real driver of all the study findings: ambiguity in the privacy domain. Finally, in chapter 7, the problems are addressed with a set of recommendations. It will become evident that the best solution to U.S. privacy problems comes not exclusively from federal laws but also from a consistent focus on privacy at both public and executive levels.

Study
Background

Because they were viewed as being most likely to have confronted information privacy issues, relatively large organizations that regularly handled personal information were chosen for the study. The organizations were:

- Banks A, B, and C, which provided checking, saving, and loan services to their retail customers. Thus, they regularly handled personal financial information of various types. (This study did not consider commercial banking.)

- CredCard, which issued credit cards, processed transactions, and engaged in various marketing programs to both current and prospective cardholders. In its credit activities, CredCard handled a large amount of personal financial information regarding applicants and cardholders. It also handled a large number of monthly purchase transactions, which gave it access to substantial information about its cardholders' purchase histories.

- LifeIns, a life insurance organization. In the course of underwriting life insurance policies, LifeIns gathered a large amount of medical information regarding applicants. It also shared medical information with the Medical Information Bureau (MIB), an industry database.

- HealthIns A and B, which provided medical insurance. These organizations handled extensive amounts of personal medical information in the course of processing health claims. Also, for individual applicants (those not in employer-sponsored group plans), some amount of information was collected during the underwriting process. During this process, the underwriting organization evaluated the health history of the applicant and determined whether the policy should be approved, denied, or approved with certain restrictions.

The study's objective was to determine 1) how organizations created their policies with respect to using personal information and 2) how those policies were translated into organizational practices. Most of the data in the study were gathered through extensive interviews at all levels of the organizations. A written survey was also administered to a sample of employees at Bank A, CredCard, LifeIns, and HealthIns B.

Some additional interviews were also conducted to gather other opinions regarding the corporate policies and practices. These interviews included:

- Consumer and privacy advocates, who were concerned about uses of personal information in various industries and contexts;

- Medical doctors, who often dealt with insurance companies;

- A hospital medical records director, who also dealt with insurance companies;

- A hospital's chief executive officer (also a physician);

- Lawyers who had represented gay and lesbian clients in AIDS-related matters, as well as two advocates who had been involved in protests regarding AIDS testing;

- The president of MIB;

- Observers in each industry—for example, consultants, trade association representatives, former industry executives, etc.; and

- Individual consumers, some of whom were interviewed in a series of focus groups, others individually.

Almost all organizations and individuals in this study were promised absolute anonymity in their comments and survey responses. Only in very unusual situations where the unique nature of an organization precluded such anonymity (e.g., MIB) were interviews conducted "on the record," and this was done with the interviewee's understanding and consent. See the Appendix for additional detail regarding the study's methodology.

Before discussing the policies and practices at the sites, it will be helpful, in defining the context for the ensuing discussions, to consider a brief overview of the environment in each industry: retail banking, insurance (health and life), and credit cards.[1] I will describe the business flow in each industry, paying careful attention to the various "stakeholders." Ed Freeman defines a stakeholder as "any group or individual who can affect or is affected by the achievement of the organization's objectives."[2] Certainly, the corporate shareholders, as a group, are one stakeholder. But, depending on the industry structure, there can be many others: for example, customers, suppliers of one sort or another, shared database units, etc. As organizations embrace new technologies, the stakeholders can be instrumental in determining the success or failure of a particular implementation. Therefore, for each industry, a "stakeholder map" is presented; this map defines the parties who are most affected by the decisions in the corporations, particularly as they relate to economic conditions and information flow. The industry background discussions also include some summary statistics for the industry and, to the extent possible, the particular sites of this study. (Note, however, that some of the characteristics of this study's sites must be omitted to preserve their anonymity.) Each section also includes a very brief overview of the regulatory environment for privacy in the industry and a few comments regarding the level of technological sophistication in the industry's corporations.

Retail Banking

Most Americans are familiar with the retail banking (sometimes called "consumer banking" at the branch level) relationship, since they encounter it on a regular basis while managing their own financial matters. In fact, almost 90 percent of U.S. households have accounts with banks.[3] In general, retail banking offers checking (sometimes called "demand deposit") accounts; savings accounts; personal and home loans; credit cards; certificates of deposit; and money market accounts.[4] The focus of these services is the individual consumer, in contrast to commercial banking, where the focus is a business customer.

Banks make money from retail customers by 1) charging interest on loans; 2) investing customers' deposits in profitable ways, and keeping the profits in excess of what is returned to the customer via interest; and 3) charging fees for some services. Banks are increasingly finding that service charges, which can be levied on many transactions such as automated teller withdrawals, are a lucrative source of funds.[5] The trend is for banks to package as many of their services as possible into one consolidated product, so that they can have "all in one" accounts[6] that lock their customers in. Thus, a customer might find that checking, savings, money market, and loan services were all available in a single product offering, with consolidated statements tying all the services together. Bankers hope that such consolidated offerings will increase the number of customers who give all their business to a single bank.

Bankers are paying more attention to retail banking than they did a few years ago—it now accounts for about 60 percent of the capitalization of the largest bank holding companies[7]—mainly because of "regional banking," which was outlawed for many years by the 1933 McFadden Act, which prohibited mergers across state lines. But in 1985, the U.S. Supreme Court upheld the states' rights to determine whether or not their banks could expand across state lines. Since then, the biggest states have all enacted some form of interstate banking legislation, creating "superregional" banks like Banc One Corp. and NationsBank.[8] Increasingly, banks are merging, and the industry is consolidating into a number of large, regional banks that have large numbers of branches spread across several states. In some cases, these superregionals are growing to be as large as some of the "money center" banks, primarily New York–based megabanks that traditionally handled much commercial and international business. With these consolidations comes a reduction in the number of banks nationally. A 1990 study observed:

> Between 1975 and 1989, the number of . . . banks fell about 13 percent, to 12,706 from 14,629. Many in the banking community feel that the continuation of this trend is inevitable, and that by the year 2000 another 20 percent will be digested by larger banks. . . . The advantages of size include the ability to offer a full range of sophisticated services, which often rely on expensive state-of-the-art computer systems that only the largest banks can afford.[9]

Also prodding banks to place a greater focus on retail banking is the dismal performance, nationally, of commercial lines of banking. The late 1980s saw a collapse of the commercial real estate market, a trend that began in New England and then spread outward. This collapse, plus some mismanagement, led to the demise of several large banks and "thrifts" (savings and loan associations). Increased governmental regulation and supervision of lending has been the result, with some arguing that regulators have become too conservative in their interpretations. In this time of poorly performing commercial accounts, many banks have refocused their energies on their retail operations. Citicorp—the nation's largest bank of the early 1990s[10]—was one of the first to take the plunge, announcing in 1987 that it was creating an "Individual Bank," from which Citicorp expects to reap 60 to 70 percent of its earnings.[11] Numerous mergers have created a consolidated regional banking picture; Table 2.1 lists some representative entries.

To one degree or another, each of the banks in the study could be called a "regional bank." Bank A, with well over $20 billion in assets, was the largest of the three. Bank B, with revenues of over $1 billion per year, was somewhat smaller than Bank A but still a large regional player. Bank C, the smallest of the three, could be called either a "large local bank" or a "very small regional." With over 1,000 employees and over $3 billion in outstanding loans, it had a growing presence in its local area and region.[12] All three of the banks had thriving retail businesses with numerous branches.

One of the biggest challenges facing the banks in this study—as well as other retail bankers—is the negative trend in consumers' willingness to place their investments with banks, since there are many other attractive alternatives (e.g., mutual funds, tax-exempt or commercial bonds) available. In fact, the growth rate of household deposits into banks declined from 9.9 percent between 1979 and 1984 to only 5.9 percent between 1985 and 1989. At the same time, mutual fund deposits have been growing at 21 percent per year, nongovernment bonds at 16 percent, government bonds at 13 percent, and investments in equities (stocks) at 10 percent. On the credit side, consumer lending is shifting from past years' closed-ended form of lending ("Can I borrow $800 to buy a refrigerator?") to the open-ended lines of credit more commonly in use today.[13] In addition, home equity loans are exceptionally popular.[14] However, almost all Americans continue to have a relationship of one form or another with a retail bank, even if it is only a fee-based checking account. Bankers' challenge, then, becomes the conversion of these customers into better-rounded ones.

The most common reaction to this challenge has been market segmentation and product differentiation. Often, banks rely on "cross-selling" to accomplish this feat, by offering existing customers products and services that are compatible with those they are already buying from the bank. Some banks take this one step further by segmenting their market based on life-style factors. For example, one Colorado bank has broken its customer base into forty-eight life-style segments and is selling different products to the different segments (e.g., individual retirement accounts to younger customers).[15] As we will see later, this approach was being attempted to some degree by the banks in this study, and it had significant implications for their privacy policies and practices.

Table 2.1. Representative Regional Banks

Regional bank	Revenues ($ mil; 1989)	Revenue growth rate (1984–89)	Loans ($ mil; 1989)	Deposits ($ mil; 1989)
Amsouth Bancorp	399	12.2%	5,812	6,672
Barnett Banks	1,542	16.7%	23,364	25,056
Bank of Boston	2,072	11.5%	26,297	28,697
First Interstate	3,660	8.6%	38,702	46,467
First Wachovia	1,191	19.5%	15,297	17,387
NCNB Corp.	2,402	28.5%	34,719	48,576
Northern Trust	604	13.4%	5,660	7,039
Security Pacific	4,873	15.3%	61,728	52,630
Shawmut National	1,343	30.2%	19,646	18,765
Suntrust Banks	1,819	27.4%	21,380	24,962
Wells Fargo & Co.	2,963	16.3%	41,727	36,430

Source: Information selected from *Industry Surveys* (July 26, 1990): B48–B55. Only a small subset of the data and bank entries are depicted here; interested readers should see this source for more information.

Stakeholder Map

Retail bankers have stakeholders not only in their own operations but in several interlocked relationships. Banks, like any other businesses, have their shareholders and employees as stakeholders. In addition, their retail customers and the communities in which they live—which can be affected by banks' commitments to civic affairs as well as by their lending and investment practices—have stakes in the banks' operations. Retail banks also deal with a number of nonbanking financial organizations (e.g., stock brokerages, large commercial lenders) when they enter the national and international capital markets. They also deal with other banks, as funds are transferred between them. For example, when checks written on one bank are presented to another bank for payment, a transfer of funds (and, in most cases, the physical check itself) must be exchanged. (Note that one "bank" that also acts as an important stakeholder is the regional Federal Reserve Bank, through which currencies are exchanged.) Increasingly, the exchanges between banks are being accomplished through electronic means, so that payments are often exchanged through Electronic Funds Transfers (EFTs) rather than traditional paper documents. There is an extensive set of protocols for

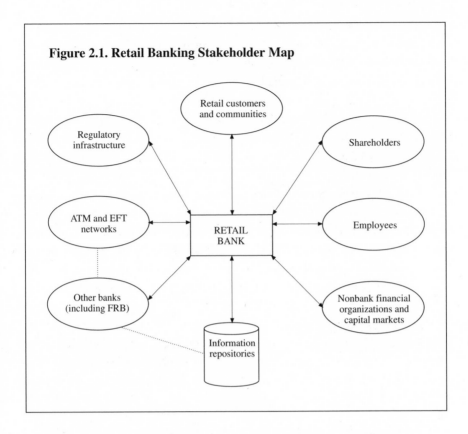

Figure 2.1. Retail Banking Stakeholder Map

assuring security in these electronic exchanges. In addition, through the growing number of Automated Teller Machine (ATM) networks, banks are tying together in regional exchanges so that their customers can use their ATM cards at banks other than their own. Retail banks also exchange data with a number of information repositories such as credit bureaus (the largest are Equifax Inc., TRW Credit Data, and Trans Union, but there are hundreds of smaller, localized bureaus) and sellers of database marketing file enhancements (e.g., income estimates for a bank's customer set, which the bank would purchase from one of these repositories).

Finally, the banks must deal with the "regulatory infrastructure," which also acts as a stakeholder in their decisions. Most bank regulation is in the form of federal oversight to ensure that banks are solvent. The Federal Deposit Insurance Corporation (FDIC) insures customers' deposits in the event that banks fail; when that happens, the FDIC will seize a bank and provide protection for the customers. The job of examining banks' operations falls to the Office of the Comptroller of the Currency (OCC),[16] which is often known to question banks' categorizations of their loans (i.e., whether or not payment is "doubtful"), which can lead to a determination of insolvency. The Federal Reserve Board will issue policy statements regarding banking practices, and the Securities and Exchange Commission (SEC) addresses those issues related to the sale and transfer of securities. In addition, the FDIC, which will bear the financial brunt of a bank's insolvency or mismanagement, raises allegations against banks' officers and directors; for example, the FDIC is known to raise issues of inadequate procedures for underwriting (determining the risk of) loans and investments; failing to establish adequate loan loss reserves; conflicts of interest in loan arrangements; and kickbacks, undisclosed commissions, etc.[17] When the regulatory agency (e.g., OCC, FDIC) makes an allegation of impropriety, banks have two responses: 1) to sign a consent order, judgment, or agreement, or 2) to respond to the agency's formal notice of charges in an administrative or judicial proceeding, which will be heard by an independent judge. Individuals, and the bank itself, may be subject to civil money penalties.[18]

From the perspective of economic profitability and information exchange, then, each of these parties is a stakeholder to the bank's decisions. When the bank changes its policies or practices, there is a high probability that one or more of the stakeholders will be affected in some way.

Privacy Regulation

While banks are some of the most highly regulated institutions in the U.S., most federal banking regulation has focused on issues related to solvency and to fairness in lending (e.g., Equal Credit Opportunity Act, Truth-in-Lending Act) rather than on privacy concerns, per se. Even so, some of the lending regulations offer a measure of privacy protection through disclosure and due process provisions. A few laws prohibiting certain uses of confidential information have been enacted. In addition, many privacy regulations for bank records revolve around the banks' relationship to the government, particularly as it performs investigations of illegal activity. And, as technological innovations have led to more and more banking processes being conducted through electronic means, some laws have touched on the protection of information in computers and networks. It is in these four areas—lending, transfer of confidential information, governmental access to records, and computerized information—that most of the banking privacy regulation has been formed.

The lending regulations fall for the most part under the Fair Credit Reporting

Act (FCRA) of 1970, the first major federal law that addressed privacy, which was passed as a response to allegations of abuse and nonresponsiveness by credit bureaus. Although amendments to the FCRA were being considered by Congress as of this writing, its basic protections have been unchanged for the last two decades. Primarily, the FCRA creates responsibilities for both preparers of credit reports (the credit-reporting agencies) and the users of the reports (banks and other lending institutions), although the latter's responsibilities are weaker than the former's. Only certain uses of credit reports are approved (credit review, insurance underwriting, governmental licensing, or employment purposes, or "a legitimate business need" in connection with "a business transaction involving the consumer"). Time limits for the retention of negative information are established; and consumers are granted access to their own files, the ability to request an investigation of any information they believe to be incorrect, and the right to include a statement disputing any information. Users of credit reports (e.g., banks) must notify consumers of adverse action taken on the basis of the reports. There are three methods for enforcing these rules: 1) civil liabilities through private legal actions; 2) some criminal liabilities for willful violations; and 3) administrative enforcement through the FTC. The FTC issues interpretations of the FCRA, but they are only advisory, as it does not have the legal right to create enforceable regulations.[19]

Banks' protection of confidential information has been addressed in two particular situations, both of which most often affect commercial customers but could, on occasion, affect retail customers as well. First, an OCC regulation and a Federal Reserve Board policy statement have forced banks to create what is usually called a "Chinese Wall" between their trust departments and loan departments. This barrier prohibits the investment of trust funds based on some inside information, which would be known to loan officers. Second, a number of cases have generally prohibited a bank from communicating confidential information about a company that is being targeted for a takeover to a company that is trying to acquire it.[20]

The most active area of banking privacy regulation relates to the release of customer information to governmental authorities. This regulatory quagmire dates back to the 1960s, when Congress and federal agencies realized that large amounts of unreported income, as well as the proceeds of criminal activity, were being moved to countries with greater confidentiality in banking records than the U.S. (e.g., Switzerland). Ironically, a trend furthered by increasingly technological capabilities in the banking industry—a reduction in paper record-keeping regarding checks and other transactions—began to frustrate investigative efforts, which traditionally had relied on these records as an important source of evidence. The result was the passage of the completely misnamed Bank Secrecy Act of 1970, which provided not for customers' secrecy but, instead, the legally mandated retention of their records and the creation of reports that have "a high degree of usefulness in criminal, tax, or regulatory investigations or proceedings." The act gave the secretary of the treasury broad powers to force banks to keep records of all transactions, to require the reporting of transactions over certain dollar amounts, etc. Additional requirements and responsibilities were mandated by the Anti–Drug Abuse Act of 1988 (e.g., no bank may sell a cashier's check for over $3,000 without proper identification).[21] The Bank Secrecy Act was upheld by a 1974 court challenge in *California Bankers Association v. Schultz*,[22] but two cases in 1976 became the real turning points in the privacy arguments: in *United States v. Miller*, the Supreme Court ruled that a bank customer had no Fourth or Fifth Amendment interest to assert when the government demanded access to records an organization maintains about him or her;[23] in *Fisher v. United States*, the Supreme Court held that an individual had no Fifth Amendment right to protest an order to his attorney to produce records of his financial affairs, which had been constructed by his accountant.[24] In short, the legal wall of financial privacy was clearly crumbling.

In response to the problems created by the Bank Secrecy Act and the ensuing court decisions, two pieces of legislation restored a bit of financial privacy for citizens during the 1970s. The Tax Reform Act of 1976 and the Right to Financial Privacy Act of 1978 both require the federal government to provide individuals a notice of a summons before seizing records from financial institutions, and there is a "waiting period" during which the individual can challenge the release of the records through legal action (except in the case of search warrants). While there has been some ambiguity in certain areas (for example, what constitutes a "financial institution"?),[25] the two laws generally provide individuals with a reasonable amount of due process regarding confidentiality in their financial records.

As computers and networks have become more and more prominent in financial dealings, a few laws have addressed their specific implications for financial privacy. The Electronic Fund Transfer Act (EFTA) of 1978 gave the Federal Reserve Board the power to issue regulations regarding electronic fund transfer, or EFT, systems. Its Regulation E, which became effective in 1979, provides for the issuance of plastic cards and other access devices for EFT systems (including ATMs); regulates the liability of consumers for unauthorized transfers of funds; and describes procedures for handling errors, etc. (In addition to this federal law, several states have enacted their own laws regarding EFT systems and ATMs, and they preempt the EFTA *if* they provide for a greater level of consumer protection than the EFTA.) Also, the Electronic Communications Privacy Act of 1986 addresses the interception of wire, oral, and electronic communications, which would often include financial data transfers, and prohibits "eavesdropping" on those transmissions. Finally, the Comprehensive Crime Control Act of 1984 and the Computer Fraud and Abuse Act of 1986 address unauthorized access of computer systems[26] and the theft of information from computers.[27] While these laws were not written with only banks in mind, their implications for financial institutions and network transmissions are clear.

In these four areas—lending, transfer of confidential information, governmental access to records, and computerized information—some federal privacy regulation that applies to banking has been enacted. However, as this study will show, many other areas remain unregulated under federal law, especially where different uses of customer records (e.g., in marketing) or access authorities (e.g., tellers being allowed to see loan information) are concerned. Thus, banks—while coming under extensive regulation in most areas—do have some latitude with respect to some areas of privacy.

Technology

Banks' use of technology has traditionally been transaction-based; that is, computers and networks have been used to process specific transactions such as deposits or withdrawals. The focus has been on efficiency in the operational processes: handling more transactions, more quickly, with fewer employees. Decision making has always been left in the hands of the bank's officers; computers were viewed as workhorses programmed to handle the "back office" tasks.

To a great degree, this scenario is still an accurate one in the early 1990s. A number of technological breakthroughs have enabled EFT and ATM networks, so that today's "retail EFT family comprises ATMs and derivative products such as inquiry terminals, pure cash dispensers, and couponing devices (such as those used to dispense airline tickets); EFT/POS [point-of-sale]; and home banking including PC-based services and telephone bill payment."[28] The ubiquitous ATM card now has a place in the average American's purse or wallet,[29] and a number of banks have begun dabbling in POS systems, through which merchants accept either an ATM or debit card for payment of purchases; an EFT transaction handles the virtual paperwork. Numerous banks (including at least one in this study) have instituted telephone inquiry and transfer systems, through which individuals can call the bank on a touch-tone phone, check their balances, and even transfer money between accounts. Home banking, through which customers use their personal computers and telephones to instigate EFT transactions from home, has been slow to catch on in the U.S., although it has had more success in some other countries, like Spain. Some banks (including at least one in this study) have tested telephone systems that take advantage of technology to provide "immediate gratification" for customers, who can qualify for loans by using their touch-tone keypad.[30]

Perhaps the greatest thrust of technological sophistication in banking (and at the banks in this study), however, is that being directed toward the retail branches. While most bank branches, in addition to managers, have tellers and platform personnel (sometimes called "customer service representatives" or "personal bankers"), most customers interact only with tellers—surveys show that 90 percent of customers never speak with anyone else[31]—and use the platform personnel only to open or close accounts, apply for loans, take out certificates of deposit (CDs), etc. But the branches have traditionally been the last to get technological attention, with most of the technology being thrust upon the back office operations, where gains in efficiency could be more easily measured. One observer recently noted that "inferior and haphazard service contributes to why banks barely edge out insurance companies as the industry least responsive to customers, according to customer surveys."[32] In order to improve the efficiency of their branch personnel and to improve customer service, banks are investing great sums in giving computerized access to both tellers and platform personnel. In many cases, these employees are being equipped with personal computers, although many argue—and some experiences at Banks A and B bear them out —that well-connected "dumb terminals" can often accomplish just as much.[33] These computer applications usually speed up the processes already in place in the branch (e.g., opening a new account) and give the personnel easier access to consolidated customer information (e.g., all the customer's accounts tied together on one computer screen).

However, some banks are now taking their use of computers one step further— beyond transaction processing and into the realm of expert systems. Expert system technology provides reasoning capabilities in a computer system, so that the computer can assist with judgment calls that would previously have been made only by a human. Some are being used to recommend new banking products for customers based on their profiles (Bank B was testing a prototype of this type of system), while others are trying to augment their loan officers' judgment with expert systems applications (under consideration, but not implemented, at Bank B).

Some banks (although none of those in this study) are using expert systems to handle most of the loan applications from car dealers automatically through a special on-line system.[34]

Banks are increasingly including additional demographic information about customers in their files, since these data can be of great use in targeted marketing activities, whether in combination with expert systems or under more traditional information systems paradigms. Such information could be gathered 1) in the normal course of doing business (from, for example, loan applications); 2) from questions posed directly to the customers while they were being serviced (including matters like whether the customer owned a home, rented, or lived with parents; the number of persons in the household by age category; the highest level of education completed by the household members; the household income; and sources of income); or 3) from outside vendors who specialized in sales of such information. At the time of this study, Bank A was increasing its use of information from the first source and was considering the third source. Bank B was embracing all three sources, with a special focus on the second as it implemented an extensive platform automation system. Bank C was focusing most on the first source.

Almost all of the customer information at the banks in the study was stored in computerized form. There were a few exceptions, however; some of the loan application information was, at the time of the study, being handled only in hard-copy form at Bank A. This procedure reflected not a privacy concern but rather a technological constraint. In fact, there was a plan to enter more of these data into the computer in the future, since it would benefit the marketing efforts. The data storage at one of the banks was typical: approximately 35,250 characters per customer account.

Insurance

This section describes both life and health insurance, since most industry analyses include both, and since most life and health insurance companies handle both. Americans' involvement with the insurance industry is far-reaching: 81 percent of all U.S. families have at least one member covered by life insurance,[35] and about 76 percent of individuals are covered by private health insurance with commercial insurance companies, Blue Cross and Blue Shield plans (nonprofit), self-funded employer plans, and/or prepayment plans like health maintenance organizations (HMOs).[36] When governmental coverage is added in, the health insurance figure rises to about 86 percent.[37] Thus, the average American has some association with life or health insurance in one capacity or another.

Insurance coverage has traditionally entailed the assumption of risk by the insurer, for which the insured pays a premium. (As we will see below, some health "insurance" plans are now changing this traditional approach.) In the case of life insurance, the insured pays a premium in exchange for a promise of payment on the occasion of death; in the case of health insurance, a premium is exchanged for the promise of coverage for health care, from a doctor, hospital, or other provider. Policies can be purchased either by individuals or as part of a group plan. If purchased by an individual, as about 60 percent of life insurance policies[38] but only 19 percent[39] of purchased health insurance policies are, the policy will normally be underwritten by the insurer to determine—based on the individual's previous health history, life-style factors, etc.—the level of risk involved, whether or not the policy should be issued, and, if so, what premium should be charged. To determine such a risk, one's medical history would be examined, a medical examination might be ordered, etc. A higher risk will result in either a higher premium or the rejection of an application. If the policy is purchased as part of a group plan, individual underwriting is not normally performed, since the cost and loss structure is computed for the group as a whole and not for the individuals. For example, if an employer buys health insurance in a group plan for all its employees, the premium is determined by the cost of health care for the overall group and not for any particular individual. If the group as a whole incurs unusually high health care costs, the premium for the group might be raised the next year. However, no single individual's premium would be raised because of his or her health care expenses in a group plan. Similarly, group life insurance is normally issued without underwriting for any particular individual.

Insurance companies make money by 1) charging premiums that exceed their losses for claims and 2) placing that surplus into investments that yield a positive return. For both life and health insurance, success in the first category comes from solid underwriting in which risks are accurately classified and appropriate premiums charged. Particularly with life insurance, where premiums are often paid for many years before a claim is ever filed, the ability of an insurer to master the second category—choosing appropriate investments—becomes a major source of competitive advantage. Unfortunately for many insurers, the collapse of several real estate markets in the late 1980s and early 1990s—markets in which they had made substantial investments—has depressed their investment portfolio value and returns. This situation has led to the insolvency of a few insurers; however, the industry as a whole still seems reasonably healthy.[40]

The most important trend in the insurance industry in the early 1990s is the wild escalation of health care costs, resulting in increased premiums, reductions in covered services, and attempts by insurers to manage the expenditures being made on behalf of policyholders. Medical care costs are climbing at a rate four times that of inflation[41] and now amount to more than one-third of the profits of the nation's manufacturers.[42] Annual health care cost increases for employers— the source of health care coverage for 81 percent of those who have it[43]—have recently been in the range of 30 percent, with even higher percentages for firms of certain sizes in some industries.[44] Health insurers are, to a great degree, merely passing on the rising costs of care in their premiums. The causes of the increasing costs are not immediately clear, although it has been convincingly argued that improvements in medical technology, which aid in both diagnoses and treatments, are the primary cause "of the quadrupling of per capita health care costs between 1970 and 1986," according to Burton Weisbrod. In an essay summarizing the situation Weisbrod explains that "if a previously untreatable condition becomes treatable, a possible outcome is that an individual could encounter a larger, but unpredictable, medical care expense for treatment than was previously the case."[45] The impact of these rising health care costs has not been felt as much in the life insurance business, since payments are made only in the event of death. But on the health insurance side, the entire structure of the industry is changing.

One response to these increasing health care costs has been the increased management of costs by insurers. Two decades ago, the role of an insurer was a mechanical one: claims were received, routinely approved, and paid. But, increasingly, health insurers are adding a component of "managed care" or "utilization review" to evaluate claims for the appropriateness and intensity of the treatment. Many are adding requirements for preapprovals before hospital stays are initiated, and many procedures that were previously done on an in-patient basis are now being handled on an out-patient basis. Many health care providers resent the "intrusion" and additional paperwork generated by these reviews, and many patients complain that insurers are denying them their rightful benefits. Furthermore, some observers question whether, when the additional overhead of the review process is factored in, the reviews even save any money.[46] However, from the perspective of many health insurers, this step is a necessary though imperfect one in reducing the spiraling health care costs.

Utilization reviews can be either prospective (pretreatment) or retrospective (posttreatment). Prospective reviews are conducted when subscribers (the individuals who are insured) or health care providers call the health insurer before a procedure is performed; such inquiries are required under many health care agreements. The insurer can then request additional information before approving the procedure or an alternative. During a subscriber's treatment, both Health-Ins A and HealthIns B were taking a more active role in managing the length and type of treatment provided. This management often entailed hospital visits from the health insurer's nurses, at which time treatment records would be reviewed. The vice president of utilization review at HealthIns B explained:

> For about half the accounts, there is a requirement that, before being admitted to the hospital on an elective basis, the subscriber, the hospital, or the physician, must contact us by telephone to describe the circumstances and to get approval for admission. A nurse contacts the doctor or goes to the hospital for more information. Eligibility is checked as well as the patient's complaints, the medical history, and the diagnoses. The key determination on our part is: should the service be rendered and in what setting (e.g., in-patient versus out-patient)? The information that is collected is stored in a computer database using diagnostic codes.

In addition to the prospective reviews before subscribers received treatments, a strong focus is being placed on retrospective reviews of care providers (e.g., doctors, psychologists, social workers, chiropractors, midwives, etc.). Reports that detailed "outliers" for various services (providers responsible for a large number of claims) were produced on a regular basis at HealthIns A and B. If a reviewer deemed it worthwhile, the provider would be asked for extensive information on several of his or her patients (at HealthIns B, the usual number was eighteen), and the patients would often be surveyed to verify the service. If extensive problems were found, the situation could be referred to a peer review panel consisting of other providers. Usually, the review simply resulted in an educational meeting with the provider. The intent of the retrospective review was not to disallow subscribers' claims; rather, it was to investigate the treatment patterns of particular providers.

In addition to the increased review of claims, another growing response to this crisis in health care costs has been the creation of alternative sources of health care protection. The traditional model, under which an employer (often in combination with an employee's contribution) paid a premium to an insurer, who then indemnified the employee against any health costs, is a declining one. It is being replaced by 1) "self-insurance" plans, under which an employer bears the health care risks, while the insurer just handles administrative paperwork, and 2) alternative health care systems, such as "health maintenance organizations" (HMOs) and "preferred provider organizations" (PPOs), under which a flat fee entitles individuals to unlimited care in a managed system. The self-insurance option is growing so quickly that in 1991, the number of surveyed employers who reported that they had chosen that option stood at 65 percent, a figure that had increased quickly from only 46 percent in 1986.[47] Self-insurance plans can be administered either with or without a "stop-loss" provision, under which the insurer would bear the risk of any catastrophic claims over a predetermined amount; while such a provision limits an employer's liability, it also carries a risk premium. (Forty-six percent of employers in the 1991 survey had selected the stop-loss provision, and 19 percent were self-insured without such a provision.[48]) Both HealthIns A and B provided traditional indemnified coverage as well as administrative services for self-insured plans—with and without a stop-loss provision—and the latter represented almost 60 percent of new business at HealthIns A. Both companies also provided individual (nongroup) coverage for some individuals, although such coverage represented a very small portion of their overall business portfolio. (As the regulation section will show, the distinction between indemnified and self-insured plans is an important one with respect to privacy in the insurance relationship.)

HMO enrollments, another alternative source of health coverage, grew very quickly during the 1980s but have leveled off during the 1990s. During the mid-1980s, growth rates of 15 to 20 percent per year were common, but the figure was down to 4.9 percent in 1990.[49] Some additional alternatives are growing in popularity in the early 1990s: "open-ended" HMOs, which allow individuals to go outside the network for treatment but at a lower level of coverage, and PPOs, under which individuals have even more say in which providers they visit.[50]

One other reaction to the health care cost crisis has occurred at a political and legislative level. With thirty-four million Americans lacking health insurance—a figure up 15 percent since the 1970s[51]—it is common to hear observers refer to the "crisis in health care." During the 1988 presidential campaign, Democrat Michael Dukakis made health care coverage a major campaign issue; the issue arose again in the 1992 campaign, and the Clinton administration, as of this writing, is sponsoring a large-scale task force to study the problem and recommend a new system. Congressional approaches to solving the problem have varied in the past, not surprisingly, along partisan lines. Senate Democratic leaders have heralded a "play or pay" plan, introduced in June 1991, which would guarantee health coverage to every American; employers would either provide the coverage or pay a 7.5 to 8 percent payroll tax, from which the government would fund a federal program.[52] President Bush rejected the "play or pay" concept, instead calling for health insurance networks—nonprofit voluntary membership organizations—that would assist smaller businesses in their quest for group health in- surance. In addition, Bush's plan would have created some tax incentives through a health insurance tax credit and deduction for moderate and low-income fami- lies.[53] Other legislators have favored a plan more like the nationalized Canadian health care system; the Comprehensive Health Care Act, sponsored by Rep. Mary Rose Oaker (D-Ohio), takes that approach.[54] The issue currently remains unre- solved. However, a member of the Senate Finance Committee said in 1991 that Congress "will reform the health insurance industry in the next two years."[55] Re- gardless of the approach chosen, it is clear that some changes in the industry in- frastructure can be expected in the near future.

Although many factors are creating pressure on the life/health insurance in- dustry and are suggesting that changes are imminent, the industry remains rea- sonably profitable for most firms. Premiums continue to grow each year, albeit at slower rates than in the recent past.[56] The industry is large and fragmented, with over 2,200 competitors,[57] so there is room for many "niche" players. However, the industry is also reasonably stable, especially at the top: while the rankings of the ten leading premium writers have shifted over the past ten years, the members of that group remain relatively unaltered.[58] A number of representative firms, list- ed in order of declining size based on their premiums, are profiled in Table 2.2.

LifeIns and HealthIns A were sister organizations, owned by the same parent company. Between them, their 1990 premiums exceeded $2 billion, making the parent company one of the country's thirty largest. And, with over $300 million in 1990 premiums coming from health insurance, HealthIns A was one of the top forty national health insurers. HealthIns B wrote a large amount of health insur- ance but did less business in other lines. HealthIns B would be considered a medi- um-sized, "top 125" company.[59]

Stakeholder Map

Although there are a few differences between the life and health insurance indus- tries, their stakeholder structures are remarkably similar, as shown in Figure 2.2.

As with all industries, the insurance companies' employees form an important stakeholder unit, since corporate decisions affect them directly. A curious phe- nomenon in this industry is the relationship with shareholders: some insurance companies have shareholders in a traditional sense, but others do not, instead returning their profits as dividends to their policyholders. And, in the case of the Blue Cross/Blue Shield units, which sell primarily health insurance, there are no profits, per se, since business is done on a nonprofit basis. Financial organiza-

Table 2.2. Representative Insurance Firms

Company	Total 1990 premiums ($ mil)	% increase over 1989	1990 rank	1990 accident and health premiums[1] ($ mil)
Prudential Insurance	24,108	11.9	1	5,841
Metropolitan Life Insurance	19,531	28.5	2	2,119
Equitable Life Assurance	4,034	−12.9	13	248
Transamerica Occidental Life	1,566	5.2	40	51
Time Insurance	763	3.8	73	686
Arkansas Blue Cross and Blue Shield	373	6.6	133	373[2]
Woodmen Accident and Life Insurance	101	−17.9	302	74

Source: Representative data taken from "The 500 Leading Life Companies in Total Premium Income," *Best's Review* (July 1991): 19–24; and "Accident and Health Insurance—1990," *Best's Review* (December 1991): 60–66.

1. A part of "Total 1990 premiums"; the larger category also includes life insurance premiums.

2. Blue Cross and Blue Shield organizations (known in the industry as "the Blues") offered only health insurance on a nonprofit basis; hence accident and health premiums in this case equal total premiums.

tions and capital markets make up another stakeholder unit, since insurance companies invest many of their funds in various debt and equity vehicles. Other insurance companies have an important stake in particular companies' decisions, especially in cases involving "co-insurance," where individuals have health insurance with more than one carrier—a situation that requires some coordination of benefits.

Insurance companies share some information in industry-wide repositories. The largest is the Medical Information Bureau (MIB).[60] Organized in 1902, MIB is a nonprofit incorporated trade association of about 750 life insurance companies formed to conduct a confidential exchange of underwriting information among its members as an alert against fraud. Member companies are required to report a brief, coded resume to MIB of the relevant results of the underwriting evaluation made at the time of application. Medical conditions are reported by using one or more of about 210 codes. Nonmedical conditions are reported by using one or more of five codes. Such nonmedical conditions might include adverse driving records, hazardous sports, or aviation activity as confirmed by the

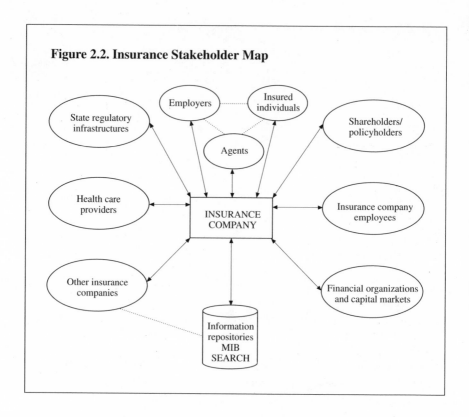

Figure 2.2. Insurance Stakeholder Map

applicant or by official records. Member companies are not allowed to report information or action on claims made on life, health, or disability insurance.

Under the terms of the MIB constitution and agreements with member companies, MIB information cannot be used as a basis for establishing an applicant's eligibility for insurance. MIB information is to be used only to alert members to the possible need for further investigation. An MIB disclosure statement is required in any application process in which information might be shared with MIB. MIB reports are used much more often with respect to life insurance than to health insurance underwriting decisions.

While MIB is used only for underwriting decisions, a second database—SEARCH, a for-profit enterprise operated by Equifax Inc.—had been available until September 1992 for the exchange of claim information among health insurers. Insurers would report basic information about individuals' claims (name, address, amount of claim, etc.), and other insurers were able to query the database to see whether their customers were also filing claims with other insurers. However, since the database contained no information about specific diagnoses or treatments, it operated more as a flag for further investigation than as a source of information itself.[61] The SEARCH database was not used very widely in the health insurance industry; one observer estimated that fewer than 15 percent of filed claims were represented in its files.

Health care providers (e.g., doctors, hospitals) serve as another stakeholder. Particularly for health insurance claims, these providers are responsible for giving health insurers the necessary information to support charges and to defend them as necessary and appropriate. This responsibility has led to a great increase in both paperwork for providers and tension between the providers and insurers. Regulators also serve as another source of tension in the industry, which—unlike banking—is regulated almost solely at the state level. Each state has its own insurance commission and set of regulations. One duty of these regulators is the assessment of the insurers' loss reserves, which are set by statutory limits to ensure solvency. In addition, regulators often address the claims processing procedures for both life and health policies. The varying regulations and regulatory structures from state to state can create some confusion for insurers that sell policies in a number of different states. This situation also causes problems for some individuals in states where insurers become insolvent, since the "safety net" for insurance company insolvency is far less consistent than that for bank failures (via the FDIC).[62] While there are occasional legislative considerations of a federal regulatory structure,[63] this approach has been rejected so far. (As the following section will show, the state systems have various and inconsistent approaches to privacy regulation.)

The final stakeholder unit consists of a symbiotic linkage between employers, insured individuals, and insurance agents. It is through this linkage that policies are sold and, to some degree, serviced. Insurance companies usually employ agents, whose compensation consists primarily of commissions on their sales, to serve as the primary interface with the customers. Agents can work exclusively for one insurance company—the case with most of the larger firms—or as independent agents handling many different insurers' products. When insurance (either life or health) is sold on a group basis, the primary sales interactions are with the employer, which makes the purchase decision. Sometimes an agent would be involved in this decision, although some negotiations—particularly for larger corporate customers—are held directly with the insurer.

For nongroup life insurance, almost all the interactions are with the agent, who fills in the application and handles some of the early underwriting duties. LifeIns's procedures are typical for the industry in this regard: in this underwriting process, LifeIns gathered health information from an applicant directly and, usually, from his or her physician as well. As many as eight release forms—mandated by state laws and varying substantially by state—were required from each applicant. The agent[64] was responsible for securing the application and release forms from the applicant. Using an age/amount list distributed by LifeIns,[65] the agent ordered blood tests and/or medical examinations—usually performed by paramedic firms—for the applicant. Examination results were returned to the agent's "General Agency Office," where some nonmedical information was entered into the computer. The medical information was *not* entered,[66] but it was forwarded to the home office for handling. The home office computer checked the age/amount authorizations, interrogated MIB, and also looked at LifeIns's own index files for other policies.

The computer then routed the application to one of the underwriting teams, where it was assigned to a particular underwriter. The underwriter used medical reference books and, in some cases, consulted with staff doctors to analyze the medical history. More information, such as an additional medical exam, requestioning of the agent, or an investigative inspection by a commercial investigative firm could be requested at this time. The underwriter then made a decision to approve, decline, or rate (charge a higher premium for) the policy. Underwriting files were maintained in hard-copy form in the underwriting area in large cabinets. LifeIns processed several hundred applications per day. The average file contained approximately ten pages of information, but some files became quite lengthy and could hold a hundred pages or more.

Nongroup health insurance applications could be entered through an agent or through other means, such as written forms mailed directly to the insurer. The underwriting process was similar to that for life insurance, although typically much less intensive. HealthIns A and B were much less likely to order a medical exam or other investigation for a health insurance application. The greatest concern in health underwriting was the determination of preexisting conditions, for which benefits would be denied for some period of time after the policy was written. In some states, insurers could deny such benefits even after the policy was written, thus limiting their liability and reducing their incentive to perform strict underwriting for health policies. One observer explained that this difference was "related to the degree of exposure for the insurer. . . . [I]f you write a bad life insurance policy, you're stuck forever, but with a bad health insurance policy, it may only be for a limited period of time."

The claims process operated in virtually the same manner for both group and nongroup claimants, with great involvement from the insured parties but little from the agents. For life insurance policies, the deceased's survivors would submit proof of death to the insurer, who would routinely pay the claim unless some suspicious circumstances indicated the need for an investigation. For health claims, claimants usually submitted their charges directly to the insurer, or providers of health services performed this task on their behalf. In rare instances, employers "precertified" charges before sending them to the insurer for payment; in this case, the claims were submitted to the employer first. Claim information, including both services rendered and diagnoses, was stored on-line. In general, a computer algorithm determined whether a particular claim would be paid or not. However, the computer often referred exceptions to claims specialists for special handling. Ordinarily, agents were not involved in claim processing, although customers sometimes asked them to intervene if there appeared to be a problem in securing payment.

Privacy Regulation

With this many interlocking parties in the stakeholder map, and with the sensitivity of the information being passed between them, one might expect a great amount of federal privacy regulation in this domain. However, there is actually very little. Insurance privacy concerns are addressed at a federal level only to the extent that insurance issues become interconnected with financial ones (leading to some coverage under the FCRA), that drug and alcohol abuse records are involved, or that insurance underwriting actions are viewed as being discriminatory based on race or other socially objectionable criteria. Beyond these boundaries, insurance privacy regulation is left primarily to the states, which—with guidance from the National Association of Insurance Commissioners (NAIC)—have enacted a largely piecemeal patchwork of laws with varying levels of privacy protection.

With respect to federal legislation, one of the permissible uses for a credit report under the FCRA is an insurance underwriting decision. When credit reports are used in this way, insurers become responsible for the duties of a report user under the FCRA, just as a bank or financial institution would. In addition, following a 1983 examination of MIB by the FTC, MIB entered into a voluntary consent agreement under which it agreed to conform many of its practices to the FCRA guidelines,[67] thus making an MIB report somewhat equivalent to a credit report under the federal law. Records of drug and alcohol abuse receive special protection under federal statutes (the "Federal Drug and Alcohol Abuse Statutes"):

> Records pertaining to the identity, diagnosis, prognosis or treatment of patients that are maintained in connection with the performance of any drug abuse prevention function, or the performance of any program or activity relating to alcoholism or alcohol abuse, education, training, treatment, rehabilitation or research, which is conducted, regulated or directly or indirectly assisted by any department or agency of the United States, must be kept in a confidential manner. Disclosures of patient records involving such drug and alcohol abuse programs are permitted only with the prior written consent of the patient [or for medical emergencies, anonymous studies, or under court order].[68]

As one industry observer noted, the practical implications for this statute are that *all* drug and alcohol abuse records are covered, since virtually every U.S. treatment facility falls under the umbrella of the statutes. Finally, to the extent that underwriting decisions violate federal discrimination laws by using, for example, race as an inappropriate criterion in underwriting, these federal laws can become relevant for insurers. However, such underwriting decisions are also regulated by many states (some of which are now considering proposals to eliminate gender-based discrimination in underwriting), so insurers must deal with both federal and state guidelines in this regard.

In almost all other areas of insurance privacy regulation, the burden of the legislation and enforcement is carried by the states. The driving infrastructure for such legislation has been the Model Privacy Act, crafted by the NAIC in 1979 and recommended for adoption by each state. As we discussed in chapter 1, the PPSC had, in 1977, made a number of recommendations for change in several industries, including insurance.

> In October 1977, the NAIC established a Privacy Protection Task Force . . . to review the insurance recommendations made by the PPSC. . . . To assist the task force in developing model legislation to implement the PPSC's insurance recommendations, an Advisory Committee was appointed that included representatives from the major insurance company trade associations, Blue Cross/Blue Shield, selected insurance companies, and an insurance support organization. Suggestions, input, and comments from consumer advocates were also received. After extensive work and hearings throughout 1978 and 1979, the [NAIC Model Privacy Act] was unanimously approved by the entire NAIC membership on December 2, 1979.[69]

The Model Privacy Act provides a number of protections for consumers. For example, "pretext interviews," under which investigators pose in a fictitious role to gain information, are generally prohibited. A "notice of information practices" is required to be delivered to all applicants and policyholders. Disclosure authorization forms must contain clear language with limited, dated periods of authorization (a major bone of contention in the PPSC study). Individuals must be given access to files containing information about them and provided with a summary of the procedures for correction. In the event of an adverse underwriting decision, the applicant is to be told specific reasons for the decision and informed of his or her rights. The act also contains a lengthy list of limitations on disclosure of personal information, including data from applications, claims, and investigations; in general, in most insurance relationships, disclosure is prohibited without approval of an applicant or policyholder, although there are a number of exceptions (e.g., an insurer who hires a third party to process its claims).[70] While some have criticized the act as having several holes,[71] it does provide substantial consumer protection in many areas.

The Model Privacy Act has been enacted, as of this writing, in thirteen U.S. states. Seven other states have adopted some of the provisions but have not embraced the act in full. In addition, some states have "health record confidentiality laws," which regulate the manner in which a health care provider releases records. However, those laws usually do not address the manner in which the recipient of the records (usually the insurer) handles them. Even in states where the Model Privacy Act has become law, one area remains basically unregulated: health insurers who provide administrative services to self-insured employers are not prohibited from releasing information to those employers, because the relationship is not deemed one of insurance but rather one of administrative procedure. When employers self-insure their employees for health care—a growing trend—the disclosure protections provided by state law under the Model Privacy Act become moot, since the act no longer applies. Instead, the employers' actions fall under the federal Employee Retirement Income Security Act (ERISA) of 1974, which

> established uniform standards that employee benefit plans must follow to obtain and maintain their tax-favored status. . . . [While ERISA] supersedes or preempts all state law otherwise applicable to pension and welfare plans covered by ERISA[,] it does not apply to state law regulating insurance. . . . While ERISA contains extensive requirements for private retirement plans, it provides very little guidance on welfare plans, such as health insurance,

group life insurance. . . . Recent court decisions have affirmed ERISA's preemption of state laws governing self-funded group insurance plans.[72]

Thus, under self-insured health care plans, most individuals have very little legal
control—at either the state or federal level—over the employers' access to their
medical records or the release of those records to others. In practice, many insurers require employers to indemnify them against any adverse actions that result
from their sharing medical information with the employers. To the extent that employers could be shown to have used the information to discriminate against individuals who had been ill, they could be liable under the growing number of federal laws against such discrimination.[73] An industry observer notes that "insurers
who divulge information to employers, even under self-insurance arrangements,
that is ultimately used in a discriminatory fashion could find themselves as co-
defendants in lawsuits. Indemnification doesn't solve all the problems." This area
seems ripe for great contention in the near future; as we will see in chapters 3 and
4, HealthIns A and B were grappling with these concerns.

In general, then, the state-dominated approach to insurance privacy regulation
offers very variable levels of protection for individuals. At one extreme, individuals who live in the thirteen states that have adopted the Model Privacy Act and
who participate in traditional indemnified health care insurance plans are reasonably well protected against disclosures of their personal information and have a
fairly good set of "due process" provisions. On the other hand, individuals in self-
insured plans and/or those in states with weaker laws have much less protection.
There are obviously areas in which some insurance actions fall through the regulatory cracks.

Technology

Insurance companies have made a massive investment in information technology
resources. A 1991 study explained:

> Historically, life insurers focused their computer resources on the automa-
> tion of transaction-driven functions: policy underwriting, policy mainte-
> nance, billing and collection, claims and benefits transactions, personnel
> records management, and accounting. . . . Since the late 1970s, horizontally
> integrated systems—cross-function systems—are integrating fragmented
> tasks to create more new jobs while they eliminate old ones. Increasingly,
> cross-functional systems are giving firms innovative ways to organize their
> business processes and changing the rules of competition in the industry.[74]

Like banks, insurance companies have an enormous number of transactions to process, but their information processing picture is further complicated by the addition of the agents, who have their own record-keeping systems but who also need some amount of access to corporate information. And, just like banks, insurance companies have traditionally dedicated most of their computing resources to addressing the transactions rather than assisting in judgmental processes. However, with new technologies that enable new applications at both the corporate and agent level, some changes are being noted.

Foremost of these changes is the beginning of a shift in technology investments from the home office to the field, which many insurers hope will bring better customer service. In a recent survey, about half the insurance companies noted that they planned a shift in workload from the home office to agents and agency offices. The offices would then have the ability to do some "basic" or "nonmedical" underwriting and to issue policies.[75] Not far behind, according to some industry observers, will be the addition of query capabilities that will allow agents to check the status of claims filed by their customers. Equipping agents with better computer applications and access to customer information operates as a two-edged sword for many insurers: along with the potential for improved customer service comes the danger of "out-brokering," under which technology gives an agent better access to customer information, which he or she then uses to the company's disadvantage after moving to a new job.[76] Also, independent agents who are already selling for an insurer's competitors could use the information to peddle a competitor's products. Because of such dangers, some companies are treading lightly in providing extensive capabilities to their agents. However, many companies have argued that assisting their agents can only improve their own financial results, and they are improving their agents' "client management systems," which help them to keep track of their customers' short- and long-term needs.[77] In addition, many independent agents are investing some of their own funds in additional computer capabilities.

Another area in which insurance companies are investing additional computing resources is the paperwork jungle surrounding health care claims. With growing utilization review processes, the need to gather information from various health care providers is increasing, and the data handling requirements are great: for computerized information at HealthIns B, approximately 83,000 characters of data were stored for each insured individual. While insurers must grapple with storage and data handling problems, most providers must deal with dozens of different insurance companies' forms, each of which carry different formats and specifications. Although only in its infancy, a technology that had previously been used more often with banking and credit card processes is beginning to be embraced by some large insurance companies (e.g., Prudential Insurance, Travelers Insurance) and doctors. A magnetic card is provided for each insured individual. When the individual visits a physician, the card is "swiped" through a magnetic reader in the doctor's office. The claim is then entered via an on-line terminal, and covered claims are approved automatically. Its proponents claim that this system, called Health Link, cuts claims processing costs by up to 50 percent and processing time by two-thirds.[78] Although it has had only a limited introduction (neither HealthIns A or B was using it at the time of the study, although HealthIns A was evaluating it), such a system may eventually be duplicated on a national level. Chapter 6 examines this prospect and its privacy implications in greater detail.

Finally, just as in banking, expert systems are being adopted by insurance companies for various tasks. For the most part, these have revolved around health claims handling procedures, since a large percentage—65 to 70 percent, according to one industry observer—are relatively routine and require only minimal levels of judgment. (HealthIns A was embracing a few expert systems applications for claims at the time of the study; HealthIns B was resisting them.) Expert systems are also finding a home in some underwriting processes; one LifeIns interviewee described a forthcoming application that would use an expert system to evaluate life insurance applications to determine whether any special examinations or other data should be gathered for a decision. Like the banking industry, the insurance industry is making increasing use of expert systems, but these systems are not widely accepted yet.

Credit Cards

One can argue about the specific date when credit cards became a part of the U.S. economy: was it in 1914, when Western Union issued cards for its customers to use in sending telegrams? Or was it in 1924, when General Petroleum of California created a gasoline credit card? Or perhaps credit cards' genesis should be placed in the late 1930s, when Wanamaker's, a Philadelphia department store, offered the first revolving-credit terms. Or it may be that the real beginning of the credit card explosion came in 1950, when a New York businessman who found himself without funds after a luncheon started the "Diners Club" card to protect others from similar embarrassment.[79]

Regardless of the specifics of their humble beginnings, credit cards have assumed a place of enormous importance in American life in the 1990s. Over 80 percent of American households have at least one card, and Americans as a group are now charging more than $200 billion a year;[80] in fact, one out of every ten dollars spent by U.S. consumers is now charged on one of the almost 300 million cards in circulation.[81] Much of the growth in credit card penetration and usage came in the 1980s, when the number of cards increased from 129 million, in 1980, to the current level; the level of charging increased, growing by greater than 15 percent per year—twice as fast as disposable income grew; and Americans' willingness to incur debt increased (the average balance owed on credit cards grew from $395 in 1980 to $2,350 in 1990).[82] But the story of the 1990s is one of saturation and leveling: with almost all qualifying households already holding at least one card—the average family has 4.6 different accounts, and those in upper income brackets ($75,000- plus annually) hold over seven credit card accounts each[83]—there are few new households left to penetrate. What is left, then, are battles between existing card issuers, and encroachment into the industry by an ever-increasing number of new issuers, all of whom are fighting for a slice of a fairly static pie. Credit card issuers must now work toward 1) avoiding "attrition," which in this case means cardholders' canceling their accounts in favor of a competitors'; 2) increasing purchase totals on the cards; 3) wooing new customers away from other issuers; 4) increasing revenue from finance charges; and 5) increasing revenue from auxiliary services and marketing of related products.

These methods are all tied to the basic structure of credit cards, which give their issuers a few different methods of making money: 1) charging annual fees to cardholders; 2) charging merchants a "discount" fee (a commission) for processing the charges incurred in their establishments; 3) charging interest on cardholders' purchases if they are rolled over from month to month;[84] and, in a few instances, 4) selling cardholders auxiliary services or products, such as credit card insurance policies. Various issuers of cards have stressed different components of this structure. The industry has two different types of cards and associated issuers, with various subgroups: special-purpose plastic and general-purpose plastic. Special-purpose plastic includes cards issued by stores, oil companies, etc., used for purchases from their own establishments. Usually, such cards are issued without fee; their issuers make money from increased sales and from interest charges. General-purpose plastic includes Visa and MasterCard, Sears's Discover card, AT&T's Universal card, and travel-related cards (called Travel and Entertainment, or "T&E") like Diners Club and American Express.

This latter category is experiencing the most radical change. Visa and MasterCard have been issued since the 1960s, traditionally by banks (about six thousand institutions, primarily banks, are in the market today)[85] but also, now, by a small but growing number of nonbank issuers: AT&T (with its Universal card), Ford, General Electric, Prudential, and so on.[86] A given credit card is associated with a particular issuer, and each merchant who accepts cards is similarly aligned. Tied together through extensive Visa and MasterCard interissuer processing networks, each issuer processes the transactions generated by its own cardholders and merchants, usually by sharing the transactions over the network with other issuers. (A small fee is exchanged for these transactions between issuers. Some small issuers, usually banks, pay a larger institution to perform the processing activity.) Visa and MasterCard issuers make most of their money from annual fees, the merchant commissions, interest on cardholder charges, and some sales of auxiliary products (credit card insurance, some merchandise tailored to cardholders, etc.). Sears's Discover card is not a Visa or MasterCard but a new creation that charges a relatively high interest rate but has no annual fee and gives a small rebate on purchases. The T&E cards are somewhat different from the other cards in that they expect their cardholders to pay off their purchases monthly; consequently, they reap no revenue from interest. (However, American Express has recently offered some cardholders an "Optima" card, which does charge interest.)

The banks see a great threat from the nonbank issuers of credit cards, since they often have great resources and some other services to offer cardholders; they are also spared some of the regulatory requirements with which banks must deal (e.g., prudential capital ratios).[87] In fact, half of the twenty largest issuers are now nonbanks.[88] AT&T has had remarkable success with its Universal card, which ties together a Visa or MasterCard with a telephone calling card. AT&T offered the card with a guaranteed "no fee for life" option during its first year and became one of the nation's largest issuers almost overnight.[89] Airlines are increasingly tying their frequent flyer plans into credit cards issued by large banks (American, for example, is linked with Citibank), making them "co-issuers." In addition, increasing numbers of "affinity cards," which carry a particular organization's or cause's logo and typically provide a small rebate to the organization for purchases charged, provide an easy marketing opportunity for issuers. As these interorganizational relationships are established, of course, an information path between the organizations and the issuer is established. Thus, more personal information can be exchanged (e.g., the credit card issuers report the total monthly purchases to the airlines, which then credit the frequent flyer accounts).

One Achilles heel of the industry, with the exception of the T&E card issuers, involves the high interest rates being charged on credit card balances. Credit cards have been one of the few bright spots in profitability for the financial industry (especially banks) during the late 1980s and early 1990s, and the primary source of this profitability is interest, which accounts for 80 percent of credit card revenues.[90] Consequently, even though interest rates in general have fallen over the last few years, issuers have been very reluctant to lower the credit card rates,[91] and customers have, by and large, proven insensitive enough to the charges that economic pressures have not forced a retreat. Thus, a certain amount of "stickiness" has been noted in credit card interest rates.[92] While there is enough competitive pressure that astute shoppers can find quite a bit of variance in rates, there has not been a wholesale reduction consistent with the overall cost of funds in the market. This fact has not escaped the attention of the government: President Bush mentioned the matter in a 1991 speech, and within the next month the U.S. Senate passed a bill—after only a few hours of consideration—that would cap interest rates on credit cards.[93] After fierce lobbying by the industry, Congress backed down. In the meantime, AT&T heeded the president's call and lowered the rate on its Universal card.[94] Although many issuers have since offered some lower rates (particularly for good credit risks), some issuers are still open to charges of "usurious" interest rates, which are increasingly leveled by consumer advocates. But issuers have also realized that there are many other marketing levers that are equally important in attracting customers. For example, while rates stayed high, there was a general increase in the number of services offered, such as automatic protection for rental cars charged with the card and doubling of warranties for products purchased with the card.[95]

Compared to other industries, the credit card industry is relatively unconcentrated, especially for Visa and MasterCards, with the top ten issuers controlling about 40 percent of the market and the next ten about 10 percent.[96] See Table 2.3 for representatives of the largest credit card issuers. Of course, many smaller issuers—for example, small banks—also exist.

CredCard was a general-purpose plastic issuer. To protect its identity, this study does not reveal whether CredCard was 1) a bank that issued Visa and/or MasterCards, 2) a nonbank issuer of such cards, 3) a nonbank issuer of its own brand of cards, or 4) a T&E issuer. CredCard was a profitable enterprise, although it was feeling the same pressures as other credit card issuers with respect to market saturation and customer attrition.[97]

Stakeholder Map

The employees are important stakeholders, of course, because their livelihood depends on the success of the company. For stand-alone issuers of credit cards, the

Table 2.3. Representative Credit Card Issuers

Issuer	Rank	Active accounts[1]
American Express (Centurion Bank)	1	25,900,000
Greenwood Trust Co. (Sears)/Discover Card	2	25,715,000
Citicorp	3	22,000,000
Chase Manhattan Bank USA	4	9,959,000
First Chicago Corp.	5	6,650,581
Bank of America	6	6,203,880
AT&T Universal Card Services Corp.	7	4,800,000
First National Bank of Omaha	18	2,000,000
First Union Corp.	41	842,624
Navy Federal Credit Union	67	323,000
First Hawaiian Inc.	83	235,150
Simmons First National Bank	100	154,653

Source: Representative data taken from Kurt Peters, publ., *Card Industry Directory* (New York: Faulkner and Gray, 1992): 67.

1. A single account can represent one or more cards.

shareholders are an important stakeholder unit; for credit card units—like Sears's Discover unit—owned by banks or other organizations, the parent organization becomes an equally important stakeholder. The cardholders, who pay the annual fees and interest and charge their purchases, as well as the merchants who accept the cards and pay the issuer a commission for processing the charges, form a combined stakeholder unit of great importance. Since credit card issuers often package their credit card receivables for sale in the capital markets, that structure is also a stakeholder in their actions. When credit card issuers operate under the auspices of a bank, they are subject to the same regulatory infrastructure discussed above. Numerous state laws pertaining to interest rate caps, annual fee limits, etc., are on the books, and they apply to all issuers. A current question in the courts is which laws should apply to a credit card: those of the state where the card is issued, or those of the state where the cardholder lives.[98]

As credit card issuers look for new sources of revenue, they are increasingly embracing marketing thrusts that utilize their database of cardholder information. These may entail offerings for credit card insurance or even general merchandise in a special catalog. Very often, these offerings are made in conjunction with a separate marketing unit, sometimes associated with the parent organization and sometimes with an outside firm. This marketing unit also serves as a stakeholder.

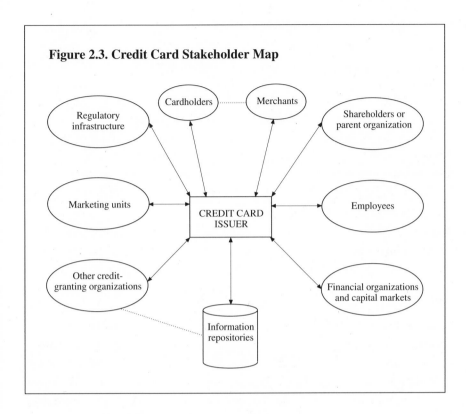

Figure 2.3. Credit Card Stakeholder Map

Finally, as credit card issuers perform their assessments of applications for new cards or for credit limit increases, they normally turn to one of the information repositories for a credit report. Usually, this process will entail an on-line request to one of the Big Three credit bureaus (or, in some cases, to one of the smaller bureaus, which are usually affiliated with one of the Big Three). In addition, the issuer will submit to the credit bureau an electronic record (usually a magnetic tape delivered on a monthly basis) of cardholders' payment records. Through this mechanism, other credit grantors will be able to take advantage of this payment history information in making their own judgments about the creditworthiness of a particular customer.

Privacy Regulation

As with any other extension of credit, the issuance of credit cards falls under the FCRA and the Equal Credit Opportunity Act. There is also one additional protection for credit card holders: under the Fair Credit Billing Act, cardholders have significant rights in disputes over credit card charges. Card issuers cannot require a cardholder to pay any portion of a disputed amount, report the cardholder to a credit bureau, or close the account until the dispute is resolved. Cardholders need only notify the issuer in writing within sixty days of the bill's postmark. The issuer must resolve the dispute within thirty days or inform the cardholder that it is still investigating. (Note one curious provision in the law: if the disputed amount is greater than $50, the merchant must be within one hundred miles of the cardholder's mailing address for the act to apply. Some state laws exempt mail and phone orders.[99])

Another area of the credit card business that has received extensive regulatory attention is the practice of "preapproving" credit card applications based on one's past payment history. Credit card issuers have purchased lists of "good credit risks" from the large credit bureaus and sent preapproved offers of credit to individuals on the lists. The practice has fallen into a somewhat gray area as a "permissible purpose" of credit report usage under the FCRA; as of this writing, the last of the three major credit bureaus still offering such lists (Trans Union) has lost a court case and must discontinue the practice, unless the decision is reversed on appeal. Some regulations regarding the practice have been clear for some time: 1) under Public Law 91–508, signed in October 1970 by President Nixon, credit card companies can send only *offers* of credit cards to individuals who have not requested them, not the cards themselves;[100] and 2) the FTC has ruled, in a 1991 interpretation of the FCRA, that a preapproved offer must be a firm offer— it cannot be contingent on another credit check.[101]

One aspect of consumer information that is *not* protected is the transaction history created whenever a cardholder makes a purchase with the credit card. By scrutinizing these transactions, issuers can create a very good profile of one's purchasing patterns and life-style characteristics; this profile can then be used in targeted marketing activities. The privacy law has focused much more closely on the credit side of the card-consumer relationship, with very little attention to the transaction side. Thus, under current law, cardholders who assume that their transaction histories are protected from disclosure are mistaken. This topic will be discussed in much greater detail in chapters 3 through 6.

Technology

Information technology is used for two basic purposes in the credit card industry: to manage 1) the credit process and 2) the transactions that occur when cardholders use their cards.[102] The process followed at CredCard is quite representative of the industry's data storage and processing.

When an individual applied for a credit card, he or she submitted an application containing rudimentary financial information. The information on this application was keyed into a computer. The computer then requested a credit report from one or more of the three large credit bureaus and checked to see whether the applicant had an existing account history with CredCard. Using this information set and a number of scoring algorithms, the computer made one of three decisions: approve (in which case cards were mailed), decline (in which case a letter was sent to the applicant), or "refer to analyst." In the latter case, the analyst would verify information, check on incomplete data, handle individuals who had moved recently and had little credit history, etc. Some cards were issued through preapproval programs. In such cases, the level of scrutiny was lower. However, the social security number, name, and address were still checked for consistency with the offering.

As the individual built a history with CredCard by charging purchases and paying for them, this information was captured in a large database. Subsequently, this information was used in assessing the cardholder's creditworthiness for purchases or additional credit. CredCard had a credit policy group with responsibility for developing complex statistical models for such credit decisions. Increasingly, CredCard was considering additional information in making credit decisions; for example, many algorithms were considering the type of establishment in which a customer was attempting to use the card.

As a cardholder's purchases were processed, a transaction record was created in the CredCard computer files. Of course, this record included identifying information for the merchant as well as the date and amount of the charge. In addition, a four-digit code was associated with each CredCard transaction. This code provided computerized information about the type of establishment in which the cardholder used the card. This information was quite useful for creating profiles of cardholders.

Trends in the industry include, as with banking and insurance, a thrust toward the automation of more judgmental processes through expert systems. (CredCard was embracing some of these systems in both application processing and transaction approvals.) The length of time taken to approve a transaction is also being reduced by many issuers and merchants through the use of a "VeriFone" system, which operates via a terminal with a magnetic stripe reader in the merchant's place of business. Merchants swipe the cards through the unit, which compares the card number to a prestored list of stolen and lost cards. A new list of invalid cards is downloaded daily to the VeriFone unit over the television airwaves, using the dead space between frames of a television signal.[103] A similar technology is being installed at self-serve pumps at many gas stations: customers swipe their own cards, the system verifies the charge and prints a receipt, and no clerk is ever involved. Another new technology, which is being adopted much faster in Europe than the U.S., is the "smart card."[104] The card is enhanced with microcomputers and digital memories and, in some cases, a small keyboard. Developed in France as part of a plan to revolutionize the phone system, and recently introduced in New York City—one can now use a smart card instead of change at some public phones—this improved intelligence allows a credit card to keep track of its own available credit. Futuristic applications might include the combining of the credit function with a "frequent shopper club" function, so that one could earn points as the card tracked one's purchases. As of this writing, the only such shopping application in the U.S. is at the Parris Island (South Carolina) Marine Corps Recruit Depot's PX, where 6,500 cards are in use. But other tests are under way:

> Visa . . . is currently testing about 3,000 "Supersmart Cards" in Japan. . . . Supersmart cards are essentially encryption devices with three-year batteries. A keypad on the card enables its use whether or not a merchant has a computer terminal. The user simply authorizes a transaction via the card's keypad; the card itself verifies that the amount is available, producing an authorization number that the merchant can use to receive payment, much as he would with a handwritten check.[105]

Is this technology for technology's sake? Not if it can improve the transaction processing that is the bane of every credit card issuer's computer infrastructure. Time will tell, but the potential is clear.

Across the Industries

In looking across the industries in this study, one is struck by some consistent themes: 1) the need for personal information in the industry's business processes; 2) the potential for new technologies to change the processes; 3) the manner in which new technologies enable new business applications; 4) the effects of those applications on a broad number of stakeholders; and 5) the difficulty of keeping a regulatory infrastructure synchronized with the ever-changing information environment.

These trends are providing a milieu in which information privacy policies and practices are becoming real, not merely abstract, concerns. In chapters 3 through 7, these concerns will be examined in much greater depth. Before turning to those study results, however, it will be instructive to examine one final phenomenon: the corporate response to a study of information privacy.

A Study That Almost Wasn't

A good measure of the currency of this study is the amount of corporate concern that it has caused. Based on the experience of this study, the topic must involve volatile tensions within society.

The study began with contacts to three credit bureaus, four credit card issuers, three banks, and five insurance organizations, asking for their cooperation. The results were enlightening. All three credit bureaus, three of the credit card issuers, and two of the insurance organizations declined the study. Based on feedback received from many of these prospective sites, it was clear that the sensitivity of the investigation caused great discomfort to many corporate players.

This set of responses was all the more disturbing because of three factors: 1) the study was to be totally anonymous, with the identity of all participants well protected; 2) the requests had been made at quite senior levels; and 3) many of the senior executives were in favor of the study, but other groups in their organizations (especially their lawyers and subordinates) would not comply.

In letters to and conversations with the prospective sites, I stressed that the study was to be totally anonymous. No corporate or individual identities were ever to be divulged. On several occasions I offered to sign nondisclosure agreements. However, these offers were not convincing to some of the organizations.

It should also be noted that the research was to be carried out under the auspices of a leading business school, and this connection was clearly evident to all the companies I approached. The school has a long tradition of performing sound and practical business research with a high level of integrity and protection for the studied companies. This tradition was well known to most of the companies that were contacted, making their refusals even more surprising.

The study was proposed at the highest levels of the organizations: to presidents, executive/senior vice presidents, and vice presidents. In many cases, the contact process made use of working relationships between the corporate officers and faculty members at the school. Thus, in only a few situations was the request a "cold contact." Rather, most requests were under the umbrella of cooperation between the university and the business community, framed in light of an existing relationship. Usually, these high levels of contact, under the auspices of known relationships with faculty members, led to immediate and polite responses from the executives contacted. Almost all of these individuals indicated an interest in the study. The cold contacts were less prompt in responding to the request, but some level of interest was usually apparent. (In only one case—a request to a credit bureau—was the study immediately rejected.)

However, this interest rarely translated into an approved study. The organizations were uncomfortable with bringing their own policies and practices under the scrutiny the study would entail. The path from executive sponsorship—which was gained on numerous occasions—to an approved study was a tenuous one. Often, the sponsoring executives could not overcome resistance within their own organizations.

Repeatedly, the same scene was played out: a high-ranking executive approved the study in concept only to have this approval undercut by either lawyers or subordinates. At two different sites (a credit card issuer and an insurance company), an initial contact was made with a senior executive under the umbrella of an existing faculty relationship. The initial response from the executive, in both cases, was prompt and polite. Both indicated that the study would be an interesting one with benefits for their organization. Only one hurdle remained, they said: the corporate lawyers should be consulted for their approval.

This step proved to be a stumbling block of enormous proportions. Despite offers of complete anonymity, the lawyers were unswayed. The executive's assistant at the credit card issuer said, "If it were almost anything else, we would say yes. The policies you're talking about, though, cut at the heart of our business. I know the level of detail you'll need for your study, and it just won't be possible, given what I'm hearing from our attorneys and corporate policy people." When I suggested that some negotiations regarding anonymity might resolve the problem, the executive's assistant responded, "I really doubt it, given the positions that they're taking." Profuse apologies were extended both to me and to the faculty member who had assisted in the contact.

In another case, one of the top executives at an insurance company—who had a long relationship with the school and a sponsoring faculty member—gave strong support to the study but wanted to consult the corporate attorney before giving full approval. The attorney—called "very conservative" by another member of the organization—stopped the study before it began, noting that the topic was "extremely sensitive." The attorney claimed that the company relied on "complex procedures that were constantly being updated and approved . . . often

Table 2.4. Study Refusals

Company type	Level of initial contact	Reason for refusal
Credit bureau	President[a]	Sensitivity; how others who read the study might use it
Credit bureau	President	"The management time it would take"
Credit bureau	Marketing President	Sensitivity in light of congressional studies
Credit card issuer	President	"Policy considerations within our organization"
Credit card issuer	Executive Vice President[a]	Policy issues "at the heart" of the corporation
Credit card issuer	President	(No response despite repeated phone calls)
Insurance company	Senior Vice President[a] and Division President[a]	"Extremely sensitive"
Insurance company	Vice President[a]	"Not particularly interested at this time"

Note: [a] indicates that a personal contact was utilized.

using proprietary systems that cannot be discussed."[106] Interviews that had previously been scheduled were canceled, and the study was scrapped. Again, my arguments regarding anonymity were ignored.

On another occasion, the chief executive of the organization initially approved the study, but his subordinates eventually stopped it. In this case, a credit bureau's president—to whom a letter had been written—approved the study. One of the vice presidents was assigned as the study's sponsor, and an interview schedule was being constructed. As this process unfolded, various members of the organization were informed of the study. At this point, concern began to grow. As the vice president said, "A lot of people are quite concerned, since there are people out there who could take things in your study out of context and use them against us and our industry. This is true even if your conclusions paint us in a positive light. I personally think we need a good academic study on this topic, but a lot of people around here are unconvinced." As a result of this concern, the study was canceled at this company. Even with the chief executive's strong support, the study could not take place.

The Refusals

The companies that refused the study, and their stated reasons, are detailed in Table 2.4.

In light of other evidence uncovered in the study, these refusals are not very surprising. Many individuals are uncomfortable with their own organizations' approaches to information privacy. Many executives are quite aware of the potential problems in having their policies and practices come under external scrutiny, even if they are not subjecting them to such scrutiny themselves. While such external scrutiny would receive a response if imposed upon the firm, many corporate players are reluctant to accept it voluntarily.

But despite these problems in gaining access to research sites, encouraging responses were received from three banks, three insurance organizations, and a credit card issuer. As organizations handling extensive amounts of sensitive personal information—medical information in the insurance organizations, credit and transaction information at the credit card issuer, financial information at the banks—they served well as study sites. Senior executives at all seven of these sites admitted to some trepidation in exposing their operations to intense scrutiny. Upon approving the study, one executive at a health insurer said:

> I feel somewhat like we are standing nude before you. I honestly don't know what you are going to find in the course of the study. It will probably be a healthy experience for us to see ourselves through the eyes of an outsider, but I imagine it will ultimately be painful. Something tells me that you will find things that I wouldn't find if I were to ask my own people these questions. . . . If we are really serious about wanting to be strong in [information privacy], we should be willing to have an outsider look at us.

Another, at a bank, said, "I suspect that this study is going to be quite revealing, because privacy is, quite frankly, not the number one item on our priority list. I really do want to know what is going on down in the depths of the company. I'm glad the bank's name is going to be kept out of this, though, because you probably will find some stuff that we'd just as soon not publicly admit to!" To all of these organizations and their courageous executives, I offer my thanks.

What is happening inside these organizations? How are they handling issues of information privacy? Through its results, which are described in the following chapters, this study answers these questions.

Chapter 3

The Policy-Making Process

With issues of information privacy making front-page news, with the U.S. public indicating very high levels of concern, and with legislators debating new and more restrictive laws on data flow, corporations are increasingly occupying the "hot seat" regarding their privacy management processes. It is important that both corporate executives and members of the privacy coalition understand how corporations approach privacy issues in their own management processes. To the extent that executives wish, of their own accord, to correct any deficiencies and make their privacy approaches more acceptable, they need a careful understanding of the existing approaches. To the extent that the privacy coalition wishes to *motivate* executives to take a different approach, the existing process must be considered as input in the crafting of a new incentive system.

Therefore, we now consider a fundamental question: how are policies and practices regarding the use of personal information developing within organizations? A naive view might suggest that the process would be an overtly rational and proactive one, in which executives of the organizations meet regularly to consider the salient privacy issues in their organizations, debate alternative proposals for addressing the issues, choose the most appropriate one, and then communicate the policy downward into the organization, where it is translated into effective practices. It turns out, however, that such a view is more wishful thinking than reality, if the seven organizations in this study are any indication. Despite their differences in some areas, all seven organizations exhibited a remarkably similar approach: the policy-making process, which occurred over time, was a wandering and reactive one. Because of these characteristics, the process lent itself to an environment of confusion and emotional disruption within the organization, to a milieu in which many policies were poorly formed and improperly implemented, and to a state of conflict with observers outside the organization.

A Wandering Cycle

Because information privacy is not an area with clear-cut boundaries on appropriate and inappropriate behavior, organizations are often left to plot their own course through a thicket of differing opinions. The path chosen by each organization reflects its own management's priorities, its own organizational values, and its own culture. Even so, the *process* through which the organizations passed was remarkably similar, and troubling to those who expect forceful, voluntary leadership on information privacy issues. Such top-down leadership was only evident when an external threat forced executives to confront information privacy issues, and even then, such leadership was of a reactive nature.

The cycle was a consistent one: the organization for a time experienced a period of "drift" in its information privacy policies, in which executives abdicated responsibilities to mid-level managers, who crafted their own sets of practices based on their localized interpretations. During this period, pragmatic approaches were taken; if something did not work, it was changed. Even though the issues were value-laden, they were usually not viewed as such. Instead, they were perceived as operational or economic in nature. Then, a perceived external threat of some form—usually negative publicity or legislative scrutiny—struck.[1] This threat was followed by an immediate and forceful reaction from top executives, who then focused attention on the process.[2] At this time, the various practices were considered in a "batch" process, and codification was attempted. However, differences in opinions within the organization could then become a stumbling block, as employees were not always amenable to altering the previously determined practices, by then somewhat ingrained in the organizational infrastructure. Depending on the industry and other environmental factors, the time frame for this cycle could be as short as several months—in the case of LifeIns's and MIB's approach to AIDS test data—or of a length that is still undetermined: at the time of the study, the banks had yet to experience their external threat, so they had not entered their period of reactive policy-making and were still drifting.

Since its response was most pronounced, the life insurance industry's experience with AIDS test information—reflected by both LifeIns and MIB's cycles—

will be examined first. Next, the study will recount the experiences of HealthIns B, which was struggling with changing societal norms as well as extreme cost reduction pressures, and CredCard's evolving uses of cardholder information, which were being buffeted by increasing media and legislative scrutiny. Finally, a discussion of Bank A's experience will demonstrate that industry's more leisurely period of policy drift. The experiences of HealthIns A, Bank B, and Bank C were similar to those of the profiled sites and are not considered in detail here, except where salient differences are noted. However, they are summarized in a table at the end of the section.

LifeIns and MIB: The AIDS Policies

Drift. For AIDS policies in the life insurance industry, the period of drift was a short one. In the 1985–86 time frame, as the AIDS virus became an increasingly large health problem in America, the life insurance industry began to realize that the virus could have detrimental effects on life expectancy. Their obvious response was to attempt identification of those individuals who were most likely to die from this new threat. However, to acquire that information it was necessary that applicants' blood be tested for HIV (the AIDS antibody) and that the results of those tests be used in the underwriting process. With that use came requirements for storing and managing the test result data—arguably one of the most sensitive types of data that could ever be gathered.

The director of underwriting at LifeIns remarked:

> AIDS has moved the privacy/confidentiality [debate] to a different plane, since there are so many issues involved. Of course, we need information about applicants' health conditions—AIDS being just one example—to determine the risks. Economically, we can't ignore this. Today, about 1.5 percent of claims are AIDS-related; but, assuming no cure, that number will rise to 10 percent by the year 2000. . . . But what about privacy of test results? What kinds of disclosures need to be made ahead of time? How do you store the information, and to what extent do you release it? What kind of counseling do you need to do for people who test positive?

Reflecting the economic consequences, many insurers began to use AIDS blood tests in their underwriting procedures in the mid-1980s. The results of these blood tests were usually stored in the insurer's computer databases. In addition, insurers began to exchange the test results through MIB's shared industry database. "Nobody was claiming that this was the *right* thing to do," a LifeIns executive said, "but lots of companies thought they had to do *something*. The easiest thing was to use some tests, which at the time were not always very accurate." LifeIns was initially hesitant to embrace the AIDS testing and to store the results in its database, even though many competitors had adopted the procedure. However, the issue was not viewed as a moral one; rather, it was perceived as a financial matter. The early decisions apparently gave little consideration to potential societal reactions to the testing and data collection procedures. The director of underwriting explained: "We [the LifeIns company with respect to the industry] were late coming on board with this one. We didn't start HIV testing when a lot of other companies did. Nothing noble about that position; we just weren't sure it made economic sense . . . we were thinking in terms of the costs of tests versus the potential savings. . . . [O]nly later did the legal and [advocates'] arguments come into play."

LifeIns did not start its AIDS testing until 1987, but many other insurance companies started much earlier, and they wanted to exchange their results in the industry's medical database. Thus, in late 1985 the MIB Steering Committee approved a code list that contained four codes that may relate to AIDS and related conditions and tests. The first code's exact definition encompassed "AIDS-related complex or condition (ARC) or acquired immune deficiency syndrome (AIDS)." The second code involved "unexplained history of thrush, other opportunistic infections, weight loss, generalized chronic swelling of lymph nodes, persistent fever, or diarrhea." The third code referred to an "abnormal T-cell study." The fourth referenced an "abnormal blood test for which there is no specific code." While the first code referred to an explicit diagnosis of AIDS, none of these codes indicated a positive blood test without a subsequent diagnosis— the most common situation. Thus, in March 1986 a fifth code was added. That code meant "two or more different types of antibody tests indicating exposure to the HTLV-III (AIDS) virus." When this code was used, MIB and other insurance companies knew that an applicant had tested positive for AIDS virus antibodies.

Later, a life insurance industry observer reflected on the nature of this "drift" period:

Looking back, I realize that the industry didn't know what it was doing *at all* during that time. Insurers saw a problem and jumped to a very quick conclusion: test it! But they didn't think about how those tests were going to impact the applicants, and I saw very few companies taking extra precautions in their [data management]. . . . I even know a couple that were testing blood without telling the applicants, and one of those had left the decision up to a lab manager. . . . [T]heir senior management hadn't even been involved in the review of [the testing process].

It was very common during that period to see companies change their testing processes from one week to the next. [Interviewer: Why was that?] For one thing, the tests were not all that reliable, and there were several competing [tests] that could be run, so there was some sorting out of those [technical questions]. Then, there were the decisions about how the results would actually be used in the underwriting process itself. Most companies just saw a positive and said "end of underwriting process, denied," but some others wanted to dig deeper.

Another industry observer, who at the time had been an executive in another life insurance company—one that embraced AIDS testing much earlier than LifeIns—noted the operational focus of the early efforts:

When I'd go to [industry] meetings on AIDS back then [mid-1980s], I'd remark that it was like the "Keystone Cops." I'd see these rooms full of [middle-level managers] who would all be arguing about different ways of testing and using the [test results]. None of them really knew what they were talking about, though—including my own people! The discussion was all "mortality"-based and very rational. [Interviewer: Did you also hear them talk about policies for handling the information or for protecting applicants?] Not nearly as much at that point, but you've got to remember that these usually weren't executives, they were lower down [in the hierarchy], and they didn't think that way. Also, at that time, we hadn't gotten quite as many protests as we saw later. If you had the same kind of meeting two years later, you'd have higher level people and all sorts of concerned looks.

External Threat. The reaction of privacy and gay rights activists was swift and forceful. Because of the stigma of AIDS, many took strong exception to the testing and reporting of such information. Protests became common. The media began to focus on the concern being expressed publicly by the protesters. One activist remembered the time:

I thought it was criminal that these insurance companies were blacklisting [gay people] because of these inaccurate tests. Plus, they'd put this stuff in their database and share it in that industry storehouse [MIB], and it would follow people around forever. So, I got our group to mobilize around some

big cities in the North, because I thought we'd get a more receptive response
from people up there than in the South. We'd protest outside the insurance
company headquarters, things like that, . . . to get attention. Plus, we'd go
to the media and try to get them to cover our protests. We tried to get legislators excited about the problem. . . . [W]e started with some of the
stronger gay rights supporters like [names of specific representatives at both
state and federal levels]. But, basically, we just tried to annoy the insurance
companies.

(Although this activist's claims could not be independently verified, his comments are included to show the level of concern in many quarters.) An industry
observer also remembered:

There were several events that set [the protesters] off. Of course, stories
about companies testing blood without telling applicants were a problem. I
also remember an unconfirmed report that one insurance company's nurse
had leaked some test results to a friend of an applicant. There was also a
story about a life insurance company that instructed its underwriters to take
all the applications from single males in San Francisco and sort of "lose"
them in their desk drawers, on the assumption that they were high-risk applicants. That wasn't directly a question of AIDS testing, but it fueled the
fire. When you had all these things happening and then added in the enormous anxiety surrounding AIDS in the gay community, it became an emotional and explosive situation. [Life] insurance companies had to deal with
that.

In response to many of the protests, state legislatures began to pass a bewildering array of laws that required different disclosure statements in different
states. In addition, the process for informing applicants of positive test results
varied by state. Some states, such as Maine, required that the life insurer pay for
counseling for anyone who tested positive. Some required that the applicant's
doctor be informed of any positive results. Others allowed the information to be
transmitted directly to the applicant.

Reaction. As the advocates began to complain, and as the state legislatures
began to impose controls on AIDS testing, a number of industry task forces confronted the issues of testing, storage and disclosure of results, and counseling.
The sensitivity and social stigma of the AIDS information caused many insurers
to establish new policies within their organizations.

But the task forces and insurance companies did not always read the public sentiment correctly. The underwriting director at LifeIns, who was familiar with the work of the task forces, said:

Early on, the stigma of AIDS was very large. People were being fired because they had AIDS. We were attacked on the right to do testing, to use the results in the underwriting process, and to share positive results in the MIB database. We made a mistake in our early responses. We said, "We have handled confidential information for over a hundred years, and inappropriate disclosure has never been a problem. Why are you making such a fuss now?" This was thrown back at us with the challenge, "If you say AIDS is like any other disease, you don't understand AIDS." Eventually, we agreed that added safeguards would be appropriate.

The president of MIB described the process through which the AIDS decisions had been made in his organization:

We took the same approach with AIDS that we have with other issues; we made some *voluntary* changes after individuals brought serious concerns to us that were persistently stated. Some organizations, when faced with the same types of situations, choose to simply defend their existing practices. Eventually, this results in unilateral legislation. It is not a good idea to get legislators mad at you; they may come up with a system that is more draconian than you'd like!

Our new AIDS policy [implemented in May 1987] was formed during an industry task force on HIV testing. The task force had several insurance people as well as some noninsurance people . . . including two spokespersons from the gay community. Among many other items decided during those meetings, the new MIB coding scheme was proposed. At the same time, several state insurance commissioners were also indicating concern about the reporting of test results. Although we sometimes take issues such as this one to all the 750 members of MIB, we chose not to do that in this case. The logic was irrefutable, and we could not have listened to naysayers. The MIB managers and the board of directors made the decision, and the new procedure was communicated to the members in published form.

If we had stonewalled, saying "we don't need changes," a legislative committee would have provided a statutory formula that we couldn't live with or be comfortable with. We think it is better to solve problems so that we are responsible to the issues but are also responsible to MIB members and organizations.

The result of these task forces was a change in MIB policy. The fifth code ("two or more different types of antibody tests indicating exposure to the [AIDS] virus") was discontinued in May 1987. Since then, the fourth code has been used when insurers receive a triple positive antibody test result from their lab. Because the fourth code is general rather than specific, MIB and other insurers never know that an insurance applicant has tested positive for AIDS virus antibodies. MIB's documentation noted, "MIB deleted this specific code so that the insurer's need for MIB information to protect against fraud can be balanced against the applicant's right to confidentiality."

At life insurance companies themselves, the reaction primarily involved a tightening of practices surrounding AIDS test data. Notifications to applicants, describing the testing to be done, became common. The AIDS test data were also handled with special care once collected. The director of underwriting at LifeIns described the evolution to their new environment:

> We were quite lucky, in that we didn't really start doing much AIDS testing until the industry's task forces were complete. Now, we follow the policies that most of our competitors do: [Although most of the usual] blood test results are reported via computer phone lines[,] . . . that's not true for the AIDS tests. They are hand-delivered to one of our doctors who handles all the AIDS cases. It may be an overreaction, but we keep all the AIDS cases in a special locked file. . . . Of course, when a file is pulled from a regular underwriter and sent to the "AIDS doctor," the underwriter knows pretty well what's going on. Other than that, though, the transaction is kept very quiet. We never put anything about the AIDS tests in our computer (but, for that matter, we don't put the other medical information in there either, at present). It's all kept in written form. From what I understand, these policies are consistent with most other insurers'.

The director then described the notification process for positive test results:

> In almost all cases, the applicant doesn't know that he or she has the problem. This is usually their first indication, and it requires great sensitivity on our part. When a positive test is received, our doctor writes a strong letter to the applicant. It says something like, "We found an abnormality in your blood. We think it is in your best interest to follow up. We would like to send

the test results to your doctor." The letter is sent by registered mail. If we have not heard within ten days, we send another registered letter. We have never had a case where the person did not respond to the second letter. I don't know what we'd do if that happened.

Special circumstances sometimes make the process a troubling one:

Normally, we do everything in writing and refuse to discuss these items over the phone. One time, however, a pregnant woman received our letter. Her doctor called us and wanted to know what the abnormality was; apparently the woman was in his office and was quite upset. Our problem was that we did not know who was on the other end of the phone: was it really her doctor? We bent our own rule by having her "fax" us a release form; then we disclosed the information verbally.

In general, we try to be very sensitive to the people involved. We don't have that many of these unusual situations—in fact, there aren't that many positive results to begin with—but we feel like we are walking on eggshells with some of them.

One industry observer confirmed that LifeIns's current policies were fairly representative of the industry as a whole. However, after hearing of LifeIns's experiences in formulating their policies, he remarked:

They were indeed fortunate to have delayed their use of [AIDS] testing. Some of the earlier companies that did it earlier—and whose actions were publicized—bore the brunt of the negativism. Also, the company you've described [LifeIns] did not have to confront a set of existing policies, which needed to be changed, once the industry figured out what it was doing. I've seen some life insurance companies that, early on, were letting their underwriters deal with the test results and were taking no precautions at all. Of course, they've tightened that up now, but it's much easier if you just start off doing it right.

Another industry observer, who had been involved in privacy issues for over two decades, reflected on the AIDS testing experience:

As an industry, we learned a lot from this episode. I think the main thing we learned was . . . [to] wait for the technology and approval of it before you start testing. Don't use tests that might turn out to be bad. . . . Make sure it's the best test available before you do anything. AIDS has given the life insurance industry a new moral: go slower! We weren't accustomed to being put on the defensive at that point, but AIDS showed us how uncomfortable that can be.

In the life insurance industry, an attempt to confront the issues surrounding AIDS testing had included only a short drift period and an industry-wide response after a double-tiered external threat—from protesters as well as state legislation. The industry involved many relevant stakeholders in its decisions, which led to changes at several levels: at MIB, the entire reporting procedure for AIDS test results was changed, with modifications to the coding scheme; at LifeIns, the company's fortuitous decision to delay its introduction of AIDS testing meant that it was able to adopt policies *after* the industry as a whole had already grappled with the issues.

HealthIns B

Background. Of all the sites in the study, HealthIns B had devoted the most effort to creating what many interviewees called a "culture of confidentiality." Unlike those at many of the other sites, HealthIns B interviewees often came into the interviews with a full cognizance of the issues and a rich appreciation for what one interviewee called the "sacred trust" of handling sensitive personal information. While there were still disputes between organizational units and individuals with respect to the appropriate methods for handling the information, as well as many lapses in the formulation and implementation of policies, on the whole HealthIns B's management exhibited a real interest in privacy issues and a true desire to improve the organizational approach.

As significant evidence of this desire, HealthIns B was the only site in the study to exhibit an overt, official campaign to make its own employees aware of privacy issues and cognizant of their own duties in managing them. Although the campaign, called "Mum's the Word," had occurred several years before this study (apparently between 1979 and 1982), some vestiges were still evident. The details of the campaign were, by the time of this study, fuzzy components of the organizational memory. However, one executive with long tenure recalled:

In the late 1970s, we were having a lot of talk about privacy at a national level, and there had been a federal study about different industries [probably a reference to the 1977 PPSC study] that said things maybe weren't right, and we were concerned. I was only a [middle-level manager] then, but I remember that the president asked one of his sidekicks to set up a work group or task force, and I was assigned to it. We did a study of each department and decided that things were in reasonably good shape, except that people just sometimes *forgot* about the sensitivity of the information they were working with. As we reviewed the results, we realized two things: first, we needed a much better written policy on confidentiality and, second, we needed to get people to rally around the idea.

So, we were thinking about how to accomplish these two things. For the written policy, a work group split off, debated forever, and finally got something we could all agree on a couple of years later [actually, 1983]. To get people's attention, we started thinking: how do you do that? How do you make sure people care? Somebody said, "What we really want them to do is keep the information to themselves and not spread it about." Then [a junior executive, now retired] said, "Just keep mum!" And we all said, "That's it! 'Mum's the word!' " So, we proposed a campaign that had several components: a kickoff meeting, a bunch of posters, stickers for phones and file cabinets, and a film (maybe it was a videotape, I don't remember) that was shown in department meetings. Then, each manager was supposed to talk to [his or her] people about the importance of confidentiality. . . . [W]e gave them a semi-script for that talk.

We distributed stickers for a few months and left the posters up for a year or so, but then they started to come down. I see a few of the stickers around now and then, but I haven't heard anybody say much about the campaign for quite a while.

Although the "Mum's the Word" campaign[3] had long since faded, HealthIns B as a whole was still devoting a moderate amount of effort to maintaining its culture of confidentiality. These efforts were observed in several areas.

First, new employees were exposed to the issue of confidentiality during their first few days of employment, usually by the personnel department. A corporate confidentiality videotape—a successor to the one used in the "Mum's the Word" campaign—was used in this process. New employees were also encouraged to discuss confidentiality issues with their supervisors.

Second, the need to observe confidentiality in all matters was continually reinforced in several official ways. Regular meetings, usually at a departmental level, encouraged awareness. In addition, some functional areas placed wall plaques in various locations to remind employees of their duties. And although this practice was not uniformly implemented across HealthIns B, some executives occasionally wrote to their employees to remind them of the confidentiality policies. One paragraph from a sample HealthIns B letter read: "*All* members of the . . . staff are required to maintain the confidentiality rule of this [organization]. *No* case information and/or proprietary information will be shared with anyone outside this [organization]. If you have any questions regarding this policy, discuss your concern with your immediate supervisor. In addition, please review the corporate policy. . . . Breach of confidentiality is cause for immediate dismissal."

Finally, many executives referred to the need for "setting a good example at the top." Thus, in their regular day-to-day affairs, they attempted to provide visible leadership in how information should be handled. According to one executive, this effort included "not talking about medical information in elevators, etc." Another executive said, "I don't care how many times I show films or give speeches, if they see me talking loosely about [medical files], leaving them where I shouldn't, or things of that nature, my credibility is shot. [Interviewer: What would be the impact on privacy and confidentiality?] Well, it certainly would have done nothing to improve it."

One might wonder how well these efforts were reflected in the actual operating policies and practices of the organization. Was the culture of confidentiality a reality, or was it all mere verbiage? The best source of insight may be comments from the employees themselves. A lawyer said, "I once worked for the attorney general's office, and we regularly made jokes about the cases that came across our desks. That doesn't happen here, though. It's taken quite seriously." A write-in survey comment read as follows: "My contact with [these issues] is only from overhearing a few discussions on the topic. People here seem serious about the issue, and I have not heard any cases of people doing anything unethical." Another survey respondent wrote, "I think there is a lot of inappropriate discussion among employees but I do not believe much is discussed with nonemployees. I think most employees recognize and respect the confidentiality of the information we handle." A claims manager said: "To the extent that we do discuss cases, it's usually in the context of 'the account' or 'the claim.' It doesn't involve individuals' names. Occasionally, we do joke about some of the claims; I remember one for a 'penile implant' that caused a number of chuckles."[4] The personnel director noted:

> The culture of confidentiality is so strong that it has caused some problems from my perspective. When I first got this job, I noticed that we did not have home addresses for our employees. The other executives—being very sensitive to issues of confidentiality—opposed gathering and storing that information. The culture developed around medical information, but it bled over

into other areas. I had to convince them that we needed this basic information in our files.

While these positions were not unanimous (one respondent wrote that "[the] attitude of most employees is unprofessional and immature regarding sensitive information"), most HealthIns B employees spoke positively about their organization's privacy culture. In addition, one of the most telling commentaries on the
company's commitment to privacy related to this study: after a HealthIns B executive read an earlier version of this study's report, he wrote a note offering his
thanks and announcing that he was convening a task force to consider the issues
unearthed in the report.

As chapter 4 will show, however, HealthIns B's focus on privacy did not always result in perfectly crafted policies and, of even more concern to some employees, it did not ensure that the actual operational practices in the organization
would always be appropriate. In addition, despite its culture, HealthIns B was
not immune to the "ebbs and flows" of the privacy domain. A senior executive
explained:

> It's hard to keep up with the changing environment and to make sure that we
> keep our policies in sync with what's going on. When we did the "Mum's
> the Word" campaign and wrote our last policy, we were operating at an
> amazingly manual level. Since then, we've computerized everything. We've
> started to gather much more information. We're analyzing things we've
> never analyzed before. We have information overload. But we've never gone
> back and made that policy consistent with how we now operate. So, while a
> lot of our people think we're doing the right thing (or at least have the right
> attitude), that doesn't mean everything is working right. We've been lazy on
> the privacy [issues] for several years now, because we haven't had anybody
> beating us over the head about them. We didn't do a whole lot about privacy
> in the mid- and late 1980s, at least not officially. It's time to get moving
> again.

Drift. As this executive noted, despite its efforts to create a culture of confidentiality, HealthIns B underwent a dramatic period of drift, from 1983 to 1989,
before undertaking an overt policy-making effort. The omnibus policy statement
from 1983 was still in effect, but the organization had "outgrown it," in the words
of one executive. This growth had not taken place in an overnight, gigantic leap.
Instead, it occurred in small, evolutionary steps, as various organizational units
addressed specific policy items with their own procedures.

For example, the customer service unit, which fielded phone inquiries from subscribers, had considered a trend in society—the disintegration of the nuclear family unit—and had become much more cognizant of remarriages, combined families, etc., in its procedures regarding the sharing of medical information with callers. The director of the unit now took issue with the official policy statement that permitted disclosure of information to a "member or any other person covered under the same family subscription certificate." She viewed that policy as a dangerous one in light of the societal trends. Although not formally documented, procedures within the customer service unit had evolved to a much more conservative position, in which queries for information were given more scrutiny in many cases. Information that would have been released under the official policy was sometimes refused. The director discussed the evolution in one area:

> Twice in the last few years, the same situation has caused us to reevaluate our sensitivity to pregnancy information. A wife received an "Explanation of Benefits" form describing a payment for pregnancy. She called for more information, and it turned out that she hadn't been pregnant! Apparently, the husband had gotten someone else pregnant and had filed claims as though she were his wife. Our sensitivity towards revealing information about pregnancies has been heightened by situations like this. It affects our procedures.

At the same time, the utilization review process—in which providers of health care were asked for more information to determine the validity of claims—had evolved from a limited process, started in 1985, to an integrated operation affecting over half the company's claims. None of the procedures used in the utilization review process (the letters to providers, etc.) were addressed by the 1983 policy, of course; in fact, utilization review was not even mentioned in that document. Since that time, middle management in the utilization review organization had effectively drawn "invisible information walls" around the organization, and little information was released to other organizations. Their computer system could only be accessed by members of their own group. The marketing organization often requested information about particular subscriber situations. A director in the utilization review group said:

> I'm often known as the "wicked witch" because of my approach to this situation. We're seen as not accommodating or as restrictive, because we do not share the information with the rest of the company. (We only share upon the written request of the subscriber.) The marketing people often say, "But we

all work for the same company, and we need to know what's going on with a member so we can manage the relationship with the account." That is not a convincing argument, though, because *respect* for the *member* is the key. I will go to my grave before I will give information out. I will quit if I am told that I have to. I don't feel strongly about a lot of things, but this is one of them.

The director noted that only on rare occasions had she had problems with subordinates in this context: "Once or twice, one of our people got trapped in a discussion with the marketing group and gave out some information they shouldn't have. It was close to detrimental but not quite so. We called the marketing person and told them that, in the future, they should speak to me directly with any requests. That put a stop to it." The drift period provided ample ground for organizational disputes over privacy. Despite HealthIns B's culture of confidentiality, different organizational units took differing approaches. Personnel outside the marketing unit reported that marketing representatives tended to take the most liberal view. The utilization review group was probably the most conservative, perhaps because they tended to gather the most in-depth medical information. The claims processing group, which handled the initial input of claims and processed routine forms, had access to a smaller amount of data for each claim and were, according to an interviewee outside the group, "a little loose-lipped." Even a member of the claims processing group admitted to talking about certain claims, such as the one for a "penile implant." Because of these inconsistent approaches across organizational units, some disputes inevitably arose. One interviewee reported being told by a marketing manager, for example, "If you don't give me the information, I'll just go over and get it from [another group]. They don't have a [expletive deleted] confidentiality hang-up like you do."

In yet another example of drift, middle managers in the underwriting organization—which evaluated the few applications HealthIns B received for individual insurance coverage—had been confronted during the 1980s by increasing information regarding AIDS applicants and, late in the decade, had created their own set of procedures for handling such applications. One underwriting manager described this process: "It was early in 1987 when we got our first AIDS case. It was such a sensitive area that we didn't know what to do with it. We wanted to make sure that nothing so sensitive ever left our unit, so we [two middle managers] made a decision to put some new procedures in place. We would have changed those procedures if they hadn't worked, but that's never been necessary."

But all of those examples of drift paled in comparison to the greatest complication faced by health insurers: a trend toward more competitive marketing of health insurance and an increasing focus on reducing health care costs. The combination of these two forces led to pressures from employers—who served as HealthIns B's primary customers—to learn more about their employees' medical claims, because their success in reducing their employees' medical costs would ultimately be reflected in lower insurance premiums. HealthIns B and its competitors were trying to woo the employers in an increasingly competitive environment, so there was an incentive to respond positively to the employers' requests for information about their employees' medical conditions and treatments. However, the boundaries on such releases of information were immediately unclear. The story of the 1980s had been one of progressive liberalization—from a policy of *no* release of medical information to one in which, with certain boundaries, some employee medical information was exchanged in summarized format. HealthIns B had maintained a more conservative posture than HealthIns A, refusing, for example, to reveal employees' medical diagnoses under any conditions. (With some self-insured accounts, HealthIns A exchanged information rather freely.) The path through the 1980s had not been a smooth one. At HealthIns B, in a spirit of "improving our responsiveness to [accounts'] concerns," according to one executive, a number of reports were being provided to employers on a monthly basis. But the reports had undergone several iterations of changes based on their sensitive content; one interviewee, who was close to the process, said:

> We have changed the content of these reports so many times that I cannot always remember what is in them. First, we were only going to tell employers the total charges for their companies. Then, we decided it was okay to do it by division, but we would never put any [sensitive medical information] on the reports. But now we're giving out totals in small categories that sometimes only include a few claims, so employers can figure out which employees had which charges, even if we don't explicitly tell them. So, we say we don't give out diagnoses, but I think it could sometimes be figured out. It's been a confusing experience, and I'll be glad when we finally get it all straightened out.

HealthIns B executives reported losing "a small number" of clients because the company had refused to release detailed claim information regarding the clients' employees.

Pressures from employers for additional claim information were common across the industry. One industry observer—an executive of a midwestern health insurer (not HealthIns A or B)— told of a pointed request from a southern employer: "He said, 'I want you to pull me a list of all the people working for me who've filed anything for AIDS. I'm going to fire every one of those sons-of-bitches.' We told him no, so he canceled his account."

At HealthIns A, the wandering nature of the drift stage had led to repeated friction between the marketing organization and some other groups over the same issue: access to individuals' health records. One marketing project entailed a new computerized application to be made available to selected accounts so that they could more closely manage their employees' medical expenditures. The marketing executive in charge of the project wanted to make explicit medical information available in the database, but managers in the health claims and legal departments were fighting the application. The marketing executive said, "We keep going around and around on this. They [the other managers] approved an earlier prototype that had almost this same information in it, but now they're rejecting this version." In a later interview, one of the health claims managers said, "[The marketing executive] told us that he would have no more information in the computer database than is on the present printed reports, so we agreed with his earlier system. Now, it turns out that he is going to put *everything* in there, including employee names and detailed [medical information]. That's *not* on the printed reports." Because the legal department had agreed with the claims managers, the marketing executive had temporarily been stopped from distributing some medical information in the database. However, he said in an interview, "It will continue to be discussed."

The growing tension with respect to employer access to employee medical claims was not a problem unique to HealthIns A and B; it was being felt across the industry. Other studies have also documented this concern. In his 1989 book *Privacy in America*, for example, David Linowes detailed one example described by a union representative: " 'I have had complaints where someone, a secretary in an office, will say "Gee, Jane Doe really had a great time on that cruise three months ago because I have a claim form for an abortion here." You get that because someone in that personnel department is given the responsibility of going over claim forms.' "[5] Linowes' study showed that 50 percent of the companies in his sample used medical records about personnel in making employment-related decisions, and, of those companies, 19 percent did not inform the employee of such use.[6] While not all this medical information comes from insurance claims— companies often have their own medical staffs to perform physicals and monitor employees' health—the link between health insurers and employers is certainly one source of such information.

The chief financial officer of a mid-sized regional company ($40 million in annual sales) said:

> We're pretty much self-insured now, since we couldn't afford to pay the insurer to bear our risk anymore, but we do have a stop-gap provision. Our insurer processes our employees' claims and pays routine claims out of our own trust fund; the insurer covers amounts above our "catastrophic limit."
> . . . Right now, they give us reports that tell us how much they spent on each employee on our behalf, and they also give us a report with totals by expenditure category, like "total surgical benefits." They *don't* tell us why they spent a certain amount on a certain person. Of course we want more information from our [health] insurer. As it is now, we have to do a lot of investigating ourselves. If we see that somebody has a huge expenditure, we have to call them and say "What's wrong? what can we do to help?"
>
> We've never had a situation where we wanted to get rid of somebody because they were costing us too much for health care or because of the things they were being treated for. We try to be a humane company in that regard. There's no question, though, that a company could use information about individuals' health claims to keep tabs on them or, if they appeared to be driving the health costs up, to manage them on out of the company. We haven't done it (and we won't ever do it, as long as I have any say in it), but I'm sure it's tempting to some others to do it.

It appears that the relationship between employers and health insurers is fertile ground for extensive privacy concerns. But it also appears that it is an issue that has not been extensively considered by either the industry, the employers, or legislators. A health industry observer said:

> This is an area that has not gotten the focus that it should. In the old days (say, twenty years ago), all the health insurance risk was borne by the insurer, and the employer was viewed as having no right to confidential medical claim information. Over time, because of health cost trends and so on, there's been a tendency for employers to do a lot more self-insuring with, perhaps, some stop-gap coverage by the health insurers. As employers bear more of the risk themselves, they press the insurers to tell them more about the claims. There's no specific law dictating what [the insurers] can and cannot say, and there's certainly no consistency across the industry. There is one factor that sometimes will limit the insurer's revelation of information, though: if they tell the employer something that leads to action against an

employee, and if the employee sues under, say, the equal opportunity laws, the insurer could be named as a co-defendant. That threat would probably deter some insurers from revealing some information. [Interviewer: Isn't that sort of an indirect prohibition?] Yes, it's *very* indirect, and it's in no way a specific prohibition on the insurers. This is an area that needs a lot of study, and I can't tell that *anybody* is looking at it.

External Threat and Reaction. Although HealthIns B's senior management was aware that procedures in various units were evolving, the company had not focused on an overall reevaluation of the omnibus policy until an external threat struck. In late 1989, a state law regarding the handling of AIDS information in the health insurance industry went into effect in one of the states served by HealthIns B. An executive remarked:

> We knew then that we would have to reconsider the overall policy in light of the new law. However, it also reminded us that there were several organizational units that had developed procedures—for AIDS but also for other items—that were not addressed by our overall policy. We needed to get in a room together and consider where we were all going. The policy needed attention. In fact, it probably needed it several years earlier, but we didn't focus on it until the law was passed!

Also, within the same time frame, I made the results of this study available to senior management. Many executives were troubled by the findings. Consequently, at first as a result of legislation but then reinforced by this study, a task force of high-ranking executives had been formed to rewrite the 1983 policy. All of the various organizational procedures that had evolved over the past seven years were to be considered, and both the new laws and the study results were to be addressed. A senior executive said:

> I knew that we had different [organizational units] approaching privacy issues over the last few years, but I hadn't really focused on how they were doing it. I can now see that we need to study this a bit, to figure out how the new law[s] will affect us, and to see what we're actually doing inside the [company]. I always cringe when somebody says "task force," because I don't always see them as productive. I don't see any other way to approach this problem, though, so I'm going along with this.

One member of the task force commented on some difficulties that he expected:

Each of these organizational units has created its own way of looking at the world. The utilization review people have their procedures, and the underwriting group has theirs. Customer service hasn't really written theirs up, but they have their own way of doing things now. All of these groups have moved to positions that are more conservative than the 1983 policy. Of course, in this same [period since 1983], the marketing group has been getting more aggressive in trying to solicit business, as our industry has become more competitive. They have come to see . . . confidentiality as inhibiting their ability to sell, since what they perceive as service to [employers], like telling them about claims their [employees] have filed, the other groups see as a violation of [privacy]. Now, we're trying to get all these groups to agree on a new policy for the whole corporation. That's going to be a fight.

What's even worse, though, is that somebody is bound to lose during the fight. That means that one or more of these groups is going to have to go back and revise the procedures they've been using. I suspect that they will kick and scream about that and tell us [about all the] resources it's going to take them to change their procedures.

HealthIns B had devoted much effort—particularly in the late 1970s and early 1980s—to developing a culture of confidentiality. While it had achieved this goal to a great degree, it was still subject to the societal trends of the decade—changes in family units, shifting health care agendas, etc.—and its practices, like those of HealthIns A, drifted during this period. By the late 1980s, the AIDS scare was affecting health insurers as well as life insurers, and new laws were being passed at the state level. These legislative reactions, buttressed by the reaction of HealthIns B's executives to the results of this study, were forcing a response in the form of a task force that was to revisit the policy statement of the early 1980s. To the best of my knowledge, HealthIns A's executives were not as troubled by this study's findings, but they did react to the new law in a manner similar to HealthIns B. Thus, the cycle of drift–external threat–reaction observed in the life insurance industry was also evident among health insurers.

CredCard

Background. If HealthIns B's goal was to create a culture of confidentiality, one could probably say that CredCard's was to craft a symbiotic embrace between itself and its cardholders. This embrace (or "lock-in," as one executive described it) would allow CredCard to offer additional products and services to its cardholders. In particular, insurance products (such as credit card loss prevention plans) and general merchandise (such as luggage) seemed ideal tie-ins for card-holder marketing. CredCard executives generally acknowledged the importance of privacy in establishing the embrace with their customers, because they knew that the relationship depended on trust. Yet they often seemed quite unsure of where the lines on privacy should be drawn, as they were also well aware of the revenues to be gained from their greatest strategic asset: information about their cardholders. Their database, which held not only cardholder financial informa-tion but also data about millions of cardholder transactions, could be "milled" to create quite narrow lists for targeting the cardholders in marketing campaigns.

CredCard had made a massive investment in information technology, and this technology was in use in several different areas of its cardholder services: pro-cessing of new applications, handling of transaction approvals (i.e., when a card-holder tried to use a card, CredCard's computers would approve or decline the charge), billing processes, credit line evaluations, and collection processes. In one sense, of all the sites in the study, CredCard was the most dependent on tech-nology in its strategic business plan. While the other sites tended to use informa-tion technology only as *support* for their regular operations, CredCard had taken this one step further, weaving the technology directly into its *strategic* plans.[7] While this use of technology provided great strategic advantage, it was also the driver for most of CredCard's privacy issues. In particular, as CredCard attempt-ed to use this technology in furthering its symbiotic embrace with cardholders, the drift–external threat–reaction cycle became evident.

Drift. CredCard's approaches to marketing to its current and prospective card-holders had evolved over time. At the time of the study, CredCard was using information about cardholders' purchases to place them in various psychograph-ic categories (see Figure 3.1 for a discussion of psychographic profiling). These were used, in turn, to target cardholders for various product offerings, either via mail (sometimes utilizing varied inserts in customers' bills and sometimes through direct mailings) or through telemarketing campaigns.

The creation of information-handling procedures for such efforts—including questions regarding the appropriate and inappropriate uses of cardholder transac-tion information—had occurred on a case-by-case basis, but there had been a shift over time. A CredCard executive explained:

A few years ago, we were very short-term oriented. If we could think of a way to market something to the cardholders, we did it. We began to hear negative things from them, though . . . concerns about uses of their names and telephone numbers, and so on. Plus, the mere quantity of the messages

Figure 3.1. Psychographics

"Psychographics" is a marketing tool defined as "the study of consumer values, attitudes, and lifestyles."[1] Marketers have for many years used demographics to segment the marketplace (for example, men between the ages of twenty-five and thirty-four were expected to respond in a certain way), but psychographics takes that process to a deeper dimension by examining individuals' feelings:

> [Psychographics allows one to] find out what consumers are thinking and feeling, get inside their heads. . . . Demographics is about facts—age, sex, race, income, household type, and so on. Psychographics is about feelings. Both determine what we buy. Psychographics is what's left after demographic factors are held constant. Men with identical demographic characteristics, for example, will drive different kinds of cars, eat different brands of cereal, and go to different movies. Those differences are the psychographic cut. . . . Demographic segments are easy to define because they are based on facts. . . . In contrast to demographics, psychographic segments are based on feelings rather than facts, which makes them more difficult to define.[2]

Psychographics allows one to view a population as segments of individuals with similar feelings and tendencies. Marketers can then make more efficient use of mass media advertising as well as targeted offers.[3] Typically, these segments have been identified through a survey instrument of one sort or another. These instruments are used in identifying factors that affect consumer buying behavior, called "activities, interests, and opinions" (AIOs). Specialists believe that AIOs reveal insights about shopping habits.[4]

To determine the segments, researchers have developed alternative schema. The List of Values (LOV) system was developed at the University of Michigan Survey Research Center, and the Values and Life Styles (VALS) system came from SRI International.[5] The surveys include a number of different questions, from the mundane to the esoteric (e.g., "Could you skin a dead animal?" or "Would you vote for a Communist to be mayor of your city?").[6] VALS, the most widely used survey, then used individuals' responses to map them into nine segments, with names like "Survivors" or "Emulators." A newer version of VALS, called VALS2, was unveiled in 1989; it has eight segments.[7]

Once a marketer determines the appropriate segments for a particular product, the task becomes one of finding the right individuals in the segment and delivering the message. Recent years have witnessed both success and failure in such endeavors: General Foods was wildly successful in repositioning its Sanka product through psychographics, while Anheuser-Busch failed with Natural Light beer.[8]

CredCard used some value assessment schema to determine general groupings of consumers and also relied on its own psychographic profiling: it used the transaction records to place the cardholders in various categories based on their purchases. For example, a cardholder might be placed in a category called "Travel." The psychographic properties of that category were determined by a value assessment; CredCard could thus assume that individuals in the Travel category shared certain similar characteristics in terms of consumption patterns.

1. Rebecca Piirto, "Measuring Minds in the 1990s," *American Demographics* (December 1990): 30–35.

2. Cheryl Russell, "How to Get Invited," *American Demographics* (September 1989): 2.

3. Emanuel H. Demby, "Psychographics Revisited: The Birth of a Technique," *Marketing News* (January 2, 1989): 21.

4. Seymour H. Fine, "Buyer and Seller Psychographics in Industrial Purchase Decisions," *Journal of Business and Industry Marketing* (Winter/Spring 1991): 49.

5. Thomas P. Novak and Bruce MacEvoy, "On Comparing Alternative Segmentation Schemes: The List of Values (LOV) and Values and Life Styles (VALS)," *Journal of Consumer Research* (June 1990): 105–9.

6. Rebecca Piirto, "VALS the Second Time," *American Demographics* (July 1991): 6.

7. Martha Farnsworth Riche, "Psychographics for the 1990s," *American Demographics* (July 1989): 24–31, 53–54.

8. Bickley Townsend, "Psychographic Glitter and Gold," *American Demographics* (November 1985): 22–29.

was excessive. Over time, we've moved to much more of a long-term customer service perspective—building relationships—and away from the short-term viewpoint. We still stuff things in envelopes (in fact, we may do more of that than we used to), but we've cut back drastically on the telemarketing. It was all based on responses to customer concerns. . . . We often didn't know what was the "right" answer, but we just kept responding to what we heard.

One thing we've learned through these years: the law [has been] much more lenient than customers are. Legally, the guidelines on what we can do with our customers are not the tightest in the world. We've decided, though, that what's really important is what the customers would disapprove of. Those are the things we want to avoid.

In fact, as discussed in chapter 2, the law seemed to offer few boundaries on these uses of customer information. Although CredCard's credit-granting activities were governed by laws such as the Fair Credit Reporting Act, information about customers' purchases did not fall under that—or any other—federal law.[8] Thus, CredCard was somewhat free, from a legal perspective, to use its cardholder database for its own marketing purposes or even to sell lists to outsiders. While this situation provided great legal latitude for CredCard, it also allowed for trouble.

In combination with existing product offerings— sometimes internally and sometimes through selected third parties—the CredCard customer base was quickly becoming a source of strategic advantage. Increasingly, CredCard was using the transaction information to create psychographic profiles of its cardholders for targeted marketing efforts. A four-digit code was associated with each purchase transaction, and CredCard computers had been programmed—often using expert system techniques—to sort those codes into purchase groupings. Several dozen general purchase groupings had been created, and these had been further reduced—through multivariate statistical techniques—to a limited set of behavioral categories, such as entertainment; travel; family/home/auto purchases; and personal retail purchases. Offerings to these categories might vary; for example, some of the "best customers" in entertainment/travel categories were being offered increased credit privileges. Products were occasionally offered for sale to the cardholders, and the ability to target certain cardholder segments was quite useful in this regard. For example, in one recent mailing, three different mixes of products had been offered to three different customer sets based on their behavioral patterns. In addition, the behavioral patterns had been helpful in a quite successful campaign against card attrition, since CredCard had been able to determine which cardholders would be most likely to cancel and to offer the most appropriate incentives to avoid such attrition. The objective was to determine, in advance, why a particular cardholder might cancel the card and to take a proactive step to force the cardholder, in the words of one executive, "to cut up one of our competitor's cards instead of ours."

The strategic value of the database was quite apparent to CredCard executives. However, from past experience, they had also become well aware of consumers' concerns about some marketing practices. In response to some customer complaints, CredCard had instituted a policy through which cardholders could opt out of certain marketing practices. However, CredCard continued to utilize customer transaction information for psychographic profiling and did not inform the cardholders of this practice. No cohesive statement regarding information privacy had been formulated or debated—that is, until the external threat was perceived.

External Threat. In 1989, media attention to targeted marketing began to increase, and U.S. House subcommittee hearings on the Fair Credit Reporting Act focused on various uses of customer information. Several new bills that would have regulated the credit-reporting and marketing industries were introduced into Congress. And, as mentioned in chapter 1, some credit card issuers began to exploit the privacy issue in competitive marketing tactics: another credit card issuer began a televised advertising campaign for its cards' "privacy protection plan," under which it promised, "We'll never give your name and number to one of those telemarketing firms." In the television advertisement, this phrase was followed by the image of an individual yelling "No!" into a phone before slamming it down.

Reaction. By late 1989, CredCard had assigned a vice president the responsibility for creating a privacy policy for the organization. At the time of the study, the vice president was struggling with this assignment. Unlike the process utilized at the insurance companies, in which task forces were convened, CredCard's approach was to have the vice president draft a policy statement, circulate it to other executives for their comments, then revise the statement and repeat the process. The vice president's early drafts, in which he detailed a "utopian" view of privacy, were rejected by many of his colleagues. He said, "Some of the other executives pointed out that some of our current practices were not consistent with some of the things I had written in the draft. The question became: should you publish a policy statement as something to aim for, or as something that describes what you're currently doing? We decided that we should not publish something that we weren't living up to." As the statement was refined through a number of iterations, some practices were changed and then codified in their new form. In particular, CredCard once again reduced its telemarketing and targeted mailing activities, and it discontinued some sharing of customer names and addresses with outside parties. CredCard also increased the visibility of its opt-out campaign: a notice was included in monthly statements explaining some marketing practices and telling customers how to opt out of them.

CredCard drifted for several years in its use of customer transaction and credit data in its targeted marketing efforts. When customers complained, usually about excessive intrusion from mailed or phoned offers, CredCard scaled them back. The complaining was dampened somewhat, however, by the fact that many of the uses of customer information (e.g., credit reports, psychographic profiling from transactions) were hidden from the customers. Thus, practices drifted even more than they might have under more public scrutiny. Once CredCard experienced an external threat on legislative, media, and competitive fronts, it reacted with a quest for an official, cohesive policy. Like the insurance companies, CredCard was observed in all the periods of the drift–external threat–reaction cycle.

Banks

Background. In stark contrast to the culture of confidentiality at HealthIns B stood the banks in this study. Particularly at Bank B, where little attention had been paid to creating a corporate culture of information privacy ("not one of our high-priority items," according to one senior executive), many employees could only pay lip service to information privacy issues. "We joke about it all the time," noted one employee assigned to handle high-income accounts, "because we officially say that we don't reveal information and we treat it with the utmost respect. What a crock. I hear people laughing in the elevator about credit reports they've pulled!" Another Bank B employee said, "I was at a party the other night, and I heard some [Bank B] employees talking about customer accounts and mentioning names. I thought, 'How unprofessional!' But I guess, to be honest, I may have done the same thing at some time in the past. I'm sure our executives would all say we shouldn't do that, but I bet they do it, too." When asked what sort of investment had been made in creating a culture of information privacy at Bank B, one executive said, "A lot smaller one than has been made in company picnics, I can assure you."

Bank A and Bank C interviewees did describe an environment that was slightly more sensitive to privacy discussions than the one at Bank B, but neither bank's executives placed privacy issues high on their agenda. In fact, a high-ranking executive at each of these banks indicated, at one point or another in the interview process, that I would probably not learn much about privacy from their organizations. At the same time, however, at Banks A and C I did not encounter the overtly cynical view toward privacy that was evident at Bank B.

Drift. Unlike the insurance companies and CredCard, the banks had not yet entered a period of privacy policy-making, because an external threat—such as the AIDS test backlash at LifeIns and MIB, the new law and study results at HealthIns B, and the media and legal scrutiny plus competitive pressures at CredCard— had not yet been encountered. Even so, a period of drift had been under way for some time, as middle managers created procedures to handle questions of information privacy. This process was especially visible with respect to the sharing of customer names, addresses, and telephone numbers outside the organization. All of the banks were trying to increase their targeted marketing efforts by choosing small sectors of current or prospective customers for particular offers of products or services. Some early telemarketing efforts at Bank A, which utilized an outside vendor, had resulted in a large number of privacy complaints from customers, and new practices had been embraced. Creative uses of existing customer information and purchases of additional demographic information on existing customers were also under way at Bank A. Under the latter plan, Bank A would submit a computer tape of its customers' names and addresses to an outside vendor. The vendor would append additional data elements of demographic information regarding those customers, such as estimated income, dwelling size, propensity to use credit, etc.

Managers were not sure whether modifications to the practices would be appropriate in the future. One executive stated, "We will certainly change anything that customers have problems with. We're still learning at this point, but we need to take the first steps to see where things go." Another referred to being "in the garage and ready to roll the car out, to see how things run." A marketing manager noted that the organization was becoming more sensitized to privacy concerns because of its past experiences:

> We have become more aware of customers' feelings over time, and we have come to realize that they feel their relationship with the bank is sacred. . . . Early on, we did not realize this, but it is becoming more apparent. . . . [It] was driven home during an unintentional experiment a few months back.
>
> We hired an outside telemarketing firm to call some of our customers with questions about a new bank offering. They began the conversation by saying "This is [name] from [marketing company] calling on behalf of [Bank A],

where I understand you have an account." They then asked a set of questions. A lot of customers were incensed, and they called the bank to complain: "How dare you tell another company I have an account with you!"

So, we tried a different approach: we had our *own* telemarketing people call and ask the same questions, but they started by saying "I'm calling from [Bank A] . . ." We did not have a single complaint. That raised our awareness of customers' feelings on this topic.

Another marketing manager said that sensitivity in mailing offerings to holders of loans had increased since "a guy's wife opened a mailing, and she didn't know he had taken out the loan. He was trying to keep it a secret." But procedures for buying customer information and for using existing information in new ways were being crafted largely on an ad hoc basis at Bank A. Middle managers were sometimes "pushing the limits to see how far we can go," in the words of one interviewee. Another mid-level interviewee said, "The top executives rarely ask for [privacy] policy implications of these new uses of information. If anybody worries about that, it's my [mid-level] colleagues and myself. And we don't usually know the right answer, we just try something."

Another matter creating some confusion at Bank A was the level of access to customer data that should be granted to various employees. New computer applications were providing tellers and customer service representatives with information that previously had been available only to specialized bank employees such as loan officers. In other cases, employees of some departments were being given access to files that were arguably outside the bounds of their responsibilities. A manager said, "Quite frankly, in most cases, a supervisor's saying that an employee needs access is all that is required." Another said:

> We are not really consistent on how we manage this. . . . In general, I can say that we do not control access at the level we perhaps could or should. For example, if someone from a certain department (say, loan) says they need to see the checking account information for their customers, they probably wind up with access to *all* the checking account data for *all* customers. They don't really need that much information, but we don't control their access to customers who aren't their own. . . . There definitely are some privacy implications here.

No attempts to create new, cohesive policies for either targeted marketing or access were evident, as the banking industry—and Bank A, in particular—was receiving little media or legislative attention regarding privacy at the time of the study. Thus, the drift period was continuing without interruption.

The Policy-Making Cycle

As Table 3.1 illustrates, some portion of the drift–external threat–reaction cycle was observed at all of the sites.

Implications of the Cycle

The cycle of drift, external threat, and reaction, which was observed repeatedly in the study, has a number of implications for both corporations and society in their approaches to information privacy.

The period of drift is especially dangerous for corporations. During this period, information privacy procedures are being determined at a middle-management level with little involvement and leadership from senior management. This approach suffers from several shortcomings:

• During a period of policy drift, the organization is operating somewhat without a rudder. This lack of central direction can often be embarrassing, as employees are unable to produce an official policy to support their actions in various situations. Instead, they can simply tell those who ask that "this is the way our department does it." They are usually unable to supply a justification that has the support of the larger organization.

• Until the organization gives the issue policy attention at a high level, middle managers tend to treat the decisions as routine when, in fact, they may be deserving of senior management involvement. At the least, senior management may wish to be apprised of the various practices that are being implemented. If a number of decisions of the same type are being confronted by various organizational units, executives might be prompted to evaluate the consistency of the various responses. However, if middle managers assume that the decisions are routine, the information never moves upward, and such a comparison is never possible.

• Allowing each unit's middle managers to set their own procedures can lead to conflicting resolutions. At one insurance company, as we have seen, one manager berated another for not releasing medical information and argued

Table 3.1. The Policy-Making Cycle

Site	Areas of drift	External threat	Reaction

HealthIns A	Disclosure to employers
	Collection of claim
	  information
		Legislative	Task force to create
			  new omnibus policy

HealthIns B	Disclosure to employers
	Collection of claim
	  information
	Customer service unit
	  procedures
		Legislative
		Results of this
		  study
			Task force to create
			  new omnibus policy

LifeIns	AIDS test results	Media Legislative	Industry task forces New internal, official policies

MIB	Database codes for
	  handling AIDS test
	  results
		Legislative	Task forces
			Deleted database code
			Official policies
			  for insurance
			  companies

CredCard	Customer data used for
	  marketing, credit
	  decisions
	Customer data shared
	  with other firms
		Media
		Legislative
		Competitive
			Policy statement
			  circulated for
			  consensus
			Changes in data use

Bank A	Customer data used in
	  targeted marketing
	Purchasing data about
	  customers
	Access to customer data
		None	None

Bank B	Customer data used in
	  targeted marketing
	Purchasing data about
	  customers
	Access to customer data
		None	None

Bank C	Customer data used in targeted marketing Access to customer data	None	None

Note: Although it was not one of the official sites in the study, MIB is included here for the sake of completeness.

that another group in the same company *did* release the information. Such conflicts cannot be avoided during a period in which policy-making responsibility is abdicated to small organizational units without any coordination between the units.

Attention to Short-Term Goals

During the drift period, managerial attention is often focused only on items that benefit the corporation in the short term: small matters of organizational efficiency and effectiveness. Since information privacy guidelines would be more likely to reap organizational benefits in the long term, they do not receive as much attention as, say, a cost-reduction program. To be sure, some managerial actions can still affect the company's privacy position even in the drift period, but abstract concern for privacy issues will not usually be the *motivation* for the actions. Without an external threat, managerial actions will be focused on items that directly, in the short term, improve the corporate bottom line.

As an example, consider the banks in the study. Since they were mired in an extended period of drift, their approaches to information privacy can give us great insight into managerial focus during such a period. Specifically, their controls on data errors, where such controls existed, often seemed to stem more from a concern for the company's profitability than from a concern for individuals' privacy. To some extent, of course, the two often overlapped. A security professional at one bank said:

> It's a sad fact that the bank worries a lot about the integrity of the business data [for example, correct rates on a Certificate of Deposit] but much less about the confidentiality of customers' data. After all, if a customer's information is revealed inappropriately, who really knows about it? There's a good likelihood of a lawsuit if the integrity is bad, but with confidentiality breaches, who can really tell?

This approach on the bank management's part is understandable, yet shortsighted. The banks devote extensive effort to ensuring that funds are not embezzled and that day-end totals match—items that directly affect short-term profitability. Yet only rarely does one find a bank paying the same attention to information privacy issues, since the effects of such efforts come largely in the long term.

Such a phenomenon is not unique to issues of financial information privacy. While studying police information systems, Kenneth Laudon observed similar reactions on the part of police management. Information regarding police informants, the protection of whose identity is critical to police investigations, was carefully guarded in most police computer systems. Yet arrest and conviction records of most citizens were treated in quite a cavalier manner.[9]

Emotional Dissonance

Because the corporations drifted until they perceived an external threat, employees often had to endure an extensive period in which explicit policies were either nonexistent or inconsistent with present practices. Especially during this period, many employees reported experiencing value conflicts regarding their corporation's information-handling approaches. Psychologists often refer to the "cognitive dissonance" that individuals experience when trying to reconcile two competing ideas in their mind. Employees in this study often experienced a sort of "emotional dissonance" as they struggled to reconcile two competing *values*.

This sort of emotional dissonance is not unique to privacy issues, of course; it occurs when we are faced with issues about which we "feel very strongly both ways," in the words of one wag. For some people, for example, the abortion issue falls in this category: on one hand, they feel strongly about the value of a woman's personal choice, but on the other hand, they feel strongly about the value of the unborn child's life. In some but not all cases, emotional dissonance originates in a role conflict, in which one individual has to act differently depending on which "hat" he or she is wearing. A person might feel one way in the role of a corporate employee, another way in the role of a spouse, and yet a third way in the role of a parent. Many times, though, individuals feel emotional dissonance without role conflict: even in a single role—say, as a teacher—one grapples with the competing values of teaching hard facts, which might be achieved by crafting a high-pressure classroom environment and testing the students' memorization skills, and communicating more subtle "lessons of life," which would require a more intuitive teaching style with greater latitude.

Many managers—especially those in the I/S ranks—experienced emotional dissonance as they struggled to reconcile their personal concerns with the organizational value system; they resolved these dilemmas by subjugating their personal beliefs to the morality of the organization.[10] The corporation's managers are not merely individuals; rather, they are operating within the corporate environment, with its own ethos regarding information use and protection. In this light, individuals within the companies revealed varying degrees of comfort with their own corporations' information-handling activities, and some amount of role conflict. Some, especially those at the banks and CredCard, applied their own definition of privacy and expressed a disbelief that anyone could object to personal information being used to "offer people products and services that may be of interest." But on many other occasions, within the same corporations, interviewees indicated great discomfort with their own companies' policies and practices. One marketing executive, for example, spoke of wearing "two different hats" in thinking about uses of personal information:

> If you ask me, as a consumer, what I think of these uses of personal information [in our company], I will tell you I don't like it. As a consumer, I don't see why a company thinks it can look at information about me and use it to sell me things. It seems like an intrusion.
>
> But as a marketer, I think this is the greatest thing in the world. We are becoming much better at targeting messages to individual people. How? By using personal information about them. Sure, I have my own concerns about some of the information uses, but I have to keep them to myself. As a marketer, I know this is something we must do.

When confronted with their own emotional dissonance, many employees went to great lengths in their attempts to soothe their discomfort. They often did this by resorting to a somewhat suspicious rationalization process—"kidding themselves," as one interviewee put it in a moment of great honesty. They devoted great emotional energy to convincing themselves that their company's actions were really not so bad. But their rationalizations, clouded by their own contorted feelings and emotional turmoil, were sometimes questionable ones.

For example, one CredCard executive, while admitting that he was uncomfortable with some of his firm's uses of personal information for marketing purposes, nevertheless contended that those uses were innocuous. What is questionable is the *logic* he applies in his argument:

> I don't think that our uses of personal information are really a problem. . . . When we use transaction information to create psychographic categories . . . the process is *not very individualized* [emphasis added]. Only broad categories are used. . . . We don't have categories like "purchaser of sexy underwear." . . . And, after all, it's not like we're examining your transactions ourselves[;] . . . *only the computer sees it. It's not like people are looking at your purchases* [emphasis added].

The executive did not consider two important points: 1) that the level of individualization in the process could be viewed as irrelevant, since the fact that the transactions were being utilized *at all* was really the point of contention; and

2) that the evaluation of cardholders' purchase transactions, whether performed manually or by a computer, might constitute the use of information for an unapproved purpose. He satisfied himself by ignoring two major issues. While this rationalization made him feel better and, at least at a superficial level, reduced his own emotional dissonance, it did not reflect a true consideration of all the underlying issues.

In another situation, a marketer at a bank defined privacy in an unusual way:

> We do not violate people's privacy, even when we gather information about them that they may not know we have. We are careful in how we word our letters to them. . . . [We don't] say "Dear prospective customer, we know you make $120,000 a year, buy pantyhose, and live in a blue house, because we bought a file on you, so we are writing to offer you a fantastic opportunity." Instead, we'll just say "We are writing to you because we believe you would be interested . . ." So, *we don't really violate their privacy. We don't say how we found out about them* [emphasis added].

Two other interviewees, while wondering openly about the ethical implications of "invading people's little spheres," nevertheless argued that consumers' ignorance of information use validated it. One bank executive said, "I hate to say 'what they don't know won't hurt them,' but that's really how I see it. If we buy personal information from an outside vendor, or even if we pull some from another database [internally], there's never any way the customers will know about it, is there? They won't ever be able to figure out how we found them [smiling]. So, how can they complain?" There is much room to debate whether or not buying files on prospective customers or pulling information from an internal database is really a violation of privacy, and later chapters will entertain those arguments to some degree. What is important here, however, is that these interviewees ignore those questions and instead include a qualifier in their definition of privacy: if individuals are not *aware* of a use of information, it could not *possibly* be a privacy violation. Yet it is reasonably clear that most objective observers would disagree with this definition, since a privacy violation can occur whether or not the individual is aware of it. These interviewees have soothed their own consciences by redefining privacy, but their definition does not withstand even casual scrutiny. However, their new definitions do reduce their own level of emotional dissonance.

While concerns about their own company's use of personal information were raised by individuals in all functional areas, nowhere were these concerns more pronounced than in discussions with I/S professionals. Many members of the I/S community expressed concerns about their companies' policies and practices, yet they felt it was not their role to recommend changes. The following comment, made by an I/S executive at one of the banks, was typical:

> If you ask a lot of the executives here at the bank if we are violating customers' privacy, they will probably say no. But some of the things that are done with customers' information would make them angry, I believe, if they knew about it. . . . Even though I have these concerns, it is not our role in the I/S community to beat the business people over the head about this. It is our role to take their requirements and to implement them[,] . . . not to bring our personal views in. They are the owners of the information, and they make the decisions as to how it is used.
>
> Our job is to ensure the integrity of the data. *Use* of the data is *not* our job! We should keep our eyes open for stupid things, I suppose, but that's as far as it goes.

Another I/S executive, at a different bank, said that "we make decisions, not policies." A CredCard I/S executive, in referring to the release of customer information to third parties, said, "We're enforcers[,] . . . vehicles for controlling the release of information from a technical standpoint. We have no control over *what* is actually released. That comes from outside our [I/S] organization."

Repeatedly, interviewees reported emotional dissonance between their own feelings regarding information handling and their actions inside the organization. Yet only on rare occasions did they speak out, and their protests were usually muffled by organizational indifference. "I told a group of the marketing executives . . . that I thought they should think twice about using customer loan applications to get information for marketing purposes," remarked a mid-level mortgage manager at one bank, "but they just laughed and said, 'People will tell you anything when they want to borrow money, that's the best time to ask them,' and they made some derogatory comments to [my superior], so I dropped it. The marketing people are very powerful around here. I'll never mention something like that again."

Particularly at the banks and at CredCard, emotional dissonance drained the resources of employees and diverted some of their attention from their tasks. They expended a fair amount of energy in resolving their own concerns in their minds, and they sometimes felt real conflict in wanting to speak out about privacy concerns but being afraid to do so in their corporate environment. A derivative of the reactive drift–external threat–reaction cycle, emotional dissonance caused problems at both the individual and the organizational levels. But while emotional dissonance could be overlooked as an internal problem that affected only single organizations, the drift–external threat–reaction cycle had a more troubling derivative in its creation of a leadership vacuum across the industries.

Followers, Not Leaders

Most executives in a recent survey[11] said they wanted to adopt privacy policies only after there was a clear consensus in their industry. This was also true of most executives in the study's sample. Of all the interviewees, only three at HealthIns B indicated a desire, in the future, to have their company be viewed as a leader in privacy issues. One said:

> I have come to think that it might be to our advantage to have better controls on [medical] information than our competitors and to be seen that way by people who are purchasing health insurance. I know that this runs counter to this notion of "tell the [employers] everything they want to know so that they will be more likely to offer [our policies] to their employees." We are already more conservative than most other health insurance companies in this regard [privacy], anyway, so why not get out in front of them and tell people we are doing it? [Interviewer: Do you want the other health insurers to follow your lead?] That might be flattering, but I can see that it might be to our advantage if they do *not* follow us. If we can convince people that we are doing a better privacy job, and if people who are buying insurance care about that, I'd just as soon have that as our [competitive] advantage.

Far more common, however, was a desire to avoid leadership in privacy issues. One bank executive stated pointedly:

> Why be a leader in privacy? You will only lose money in the short run, unless you can turn it into a selling point, and I haven't figured out how to do that. If someone wants to say, legally, that "nobody in the banking industry can use customers' information [for marketing] in this way," we'll certainly abide by it. But if other people can do it, we will, too. If everybody in the industry wants to agree that we won't let tellers see any customer information except for account balances, we'll go along with that. I'm not going to be the first one to implement it, though.

An interviewee at one of the sites said, "Let's face it, you can't tell in this industry what you should and should not do with this [information]. What seems right today will seem wrong next week. I am not about to take this company out on a limb by limiting the ways that my people can be creative in their jobs, and that includes what some might call 'creative uses of personal data.' When others define for me what is 'ethical,' I will be ethical. Until then, I will make money."

In an earlier study, Robert Jackall[12] found that most managers determined their moral positions by checking the reactions of others in their organization before taking any action. His finding also held true, in this study's sample, for the information privacy policies at a corporate level. Most executives are comfortable in having their companies follow the lead of others, but few want their companies to be at the forefront. When the organizations' employees were surveyed regarding the best way to solve privacy problems in our society, the concept of organizations setting their own policies without outside guidance was the least favored approach among those offered. Table 3.2 shows how respondents answered when they were given three options for improving privacy protection:

• The best way to protect personal privacy would be through stronger laws.

• The best way to protect personal privacy would be through technological safeguards (for example, password protection on computer databases).

• The best way to protect personal privacy would be through corporate policies developed by the corporations themselves.

They were asked to agree or disagree with each statement on a scale of 1 to 7, where 1 equated to "strongly disagree" and 7 to "strongly agree."[13] In general, preferences could be ranked as follows: 1) technology, 2) laws, and 3) corporate policy set by the corporations themselves.

The most interesting finding is that laws are generally preferred to corporate policies, if companies are left to set the policies themselves. Surprisingly, respondents preferred legal mandates over this ambiguous scenario. There are two possible explanations for this finding: 1) the respondents do not trust their own corporations to make policies; or 2) the respondents feel that the government's legal boundaries would be a welcome addition to what, in many cases, are areas of great ambiguity. The evidence from the study offers some support for both of these conjectures. In many cases, corporate employees did indicate some distrust of their own corporation's activities. However, there were also three interviewees who, although they used different words, generally agreed that "it would be okay if these uses of information were outlawed for all companies, but if anybody can do it, we should be able to." More likely, corporate employees would prefer to receive guidance from others in their industry rather than the government. In a 1990 opinion poll by Equifax, the majority of executives agreed that "we want to adopt

Table 3.2. Ways to Protect Privacy

Site	Mean: Law	Mean: Technology	Mean: Policy	t-stat: Law vs. technology	t-stat: Policy vs. technology	t-stat: Policy vs. law
Bank A	5.071	5.381	4.191	−2.38[b]	−8.53[b]	−5.82[b]
CredCard	5.026	5.362	4.444	−1.95[a]	−4.56[b]	−2.77[b]
HealthIns	5.254	5.512	4.209	−2.31[b]	−11.6[b]	−7.87[b]
LifeIns	5.323	5.419	4.307	−.44	−4.51[b]	−3.58[b]

Note: In this book's tables, t-tests represent tests of research propositions for paired comparisons of responses to the noted survey items. One-tailed tests correspond to propositions that test "greater than" or "lesser than" relationships. For example, in this table, "law vs. technology" tests a proposition that respondents will have a significantly greater preference for technological solutions than for legal ones. For the t-tests above, [a] denotes a greater preference significant at the .025 level; [b], at the .01 level.

new privacy policies when a consensus is developed in our industry about what is right to do."[14]

While one could criticize executives and employees for taking this stance, one should also remember that today's economic and legal environment offers companies little incentive to lead in these matters. Furthermore, it does not offer executives clear direction for making their decisions regarding information privacy. It is easier to "[change policies] later rather than sort out in advance" the various implications of particular uses of information, according to one interviewee. And, in the American free enterprise system, why should executives introduce information privacy policies that undercut their own firms' profitability, when competitors continue to operate in a fashion that yields higher profits? Unless there is some long-term economic advantage to be gained from taking a first-mover position on information privacy issues, executives may rightfully argue that it is their fiduciary responsibility to the shareholders to forego such an approach.

Yet evidence is mounting that the opposite condition may hold in the coming years. There may be great danger in moving early into new uses of personal information without first crafting strong information privacy policies.[15] As Lotus Development Corporation, Equifax, and Blockbuster Video learned early in 1991, new and creative uses of information technology, when embraced by the first movers in the marketplace, can yield negative societal reactions at great corporate expense. Thus, waiting for others to lead in information privacy may be a reasonable executive path only if one also waits for others to lead in strategic uses of information. However, this latter approach can also have dire economic consequences, as it puts a corporation in a perpetual "catch-up" role.[16]

Consequently, because they do not wish to lead in information privacy issues, most executives wait until an external threat forces them to consider their privacy policies. This approach yields negative consequences during the period before the threat, as discussed above. It also exacerbates the difficulties when the policy-making effort is eventually confronted. Because the approach is reactive, the organization is placed under intense pressure during the policy-making stage. To answer the external perturbation quickly, the organization is forced to consider a multitude of complex practices and pressures at once—usually under immense time pressure. There is often some external entity that the organization wishes to mollify, and this circumstance places the organization in a defensive position during the process.

After the policy is codified, the various organizational units must then reconsider their own practices in light of the new policy. This process will necessitate disruptive changes. Had the policy been considered in an earlier time frame, many of these changes could have been avoided. In addition, the creation of policies earlier in the cycle may actually reduce the number of external perturbations with which the organization must deal. To the extent that the perturbations (such as legislative inquiries) are also reactive, a forceful policy-making effort may in fact preempt some of the crises.

But probably the most troubling problem with the existing, reactive policy-making cycle is that it leaves large holes in privacy policies and leads to numerous gaps between these policies and actual organizational practices. Chapter 4 considers these problems in further detail.

Chapter 4

Policies and Practices

Executives and members of the privacy coalition should all be interested in this important question: how well are current corporate policies and practices meeting societal expectations with respect to uses of personal information? In many areas, the answer appears to be "not very well." This answer should not be surprising, though, given the wandering process through which the policies and practices evolved. The reactive nature of the process provided for drift periods of varying lengths, during which changes in the environment were seldom reflected in new, codified policies. And even when policies were ultimately crafted, they were usually formed in reaction to a particular external threat. Consequently, unless the external threat pointed out a danger in a particular area, there was no guarantee that this area would receive attention even during the reaction period. Furthermore, in the absence of continual vigilance on the part of executives and an infrastructure stronger than any observed at the sites in this study, a "policy/practice gap" can be expected, in which the actual organizational practices are at variance with the official policies.

This chapter evaluates the policies and practices in light of apparent societal expectations for handling personal information. The adequacy of the policies themselves is presented in light of the societal expectations, and differences between policy and practice are described in each situation. To determine the societal expectations, I assessed privacy advocates' writings, the U.S. federal law, and professional codes; I also considered insights gleaned from the interviews with privacy and consumer advocates, executives and managers at the sites, and industry observers, and from the consumer interviews and focus groups (see chapter 2 and the Appendix). This research revealed several areas in which society apparently harbors some expectations regarding corporate policies and practices—areas in which advocates, lawmakers, and consumers agree that a "reasonable" level of policy attention from corporations is appropriate. Yet because of the wandering policy-making cycle in the organizations, these areas are not always receiving the attention that the advocates, lawmakers, and consumers intend. As Figure 4.1 illustrates, there are three societal issues that directly affect information privacy: collection, new use, and sharing. Threats from errors, reduced judgment, the fact that "the sum is greater than the parts," and improper access are forces that both affect information privacy directly and exacerbate the three issues. A problem with disjointed policies affects all of the other areas, so it is shown at the outside of the diagram. The next section will consider each of these areas of societal concern. In each case, some real-world examples will be used to illustrate the concept, and the concept will then be applied to the policies at the sites.

For the purposes of this study, the unit of analysis is a policy, observed within the organization, in each of the areas mentioned above. In drawing conclusions regarding the various corporate approaches to privacy, it is helpful to distinguish between explicit policies, implicit policies, and practices. Explicit policies provide an official focal point for the entire organization and, subject to the communication of the policies, a valid reference for decision making. Thus, explicit policies will generally be codified in a written form and will have been approved by a senior executive. Implicit policies, less formal than explicit ones, serve a useful purpose in moving the organization toward a particular goal; however, they may not be as easily communicated, and they can be more difficult to enforce. An employee can always claim ignorance of an implicit policy, but it is much more difficult to do so with a well-communicated explicit policy. In this study, a policy is considered to be implicit if it has not achieved the level of internal codification but, nevertheless, can be repeatedly quoted by numerous interviewees in a consistent fashion. In some situations, neither explicit nor implicit policies exist; in those cases, though, practices still are evident.

Note also that, for the purposes of this study, a policy's existence or nonexistence is documented irrespective of the reason for which the policy exists. In some cases, the policies apparently exist not as a reaction to privacy concerns but, rather, for other corporate reasons (e.g., protection against fraud). Thus, in those circumstances, a privacy policy exists as a by-product of some other corporate desire and not simply to protect privacy per se. In other cases, some practices— or even implicit policies—are affected by federal or state law. In these situations, the existence of a law does not automatically translate into an explicit policy within the organization. A state or federal law outside the organization can still be

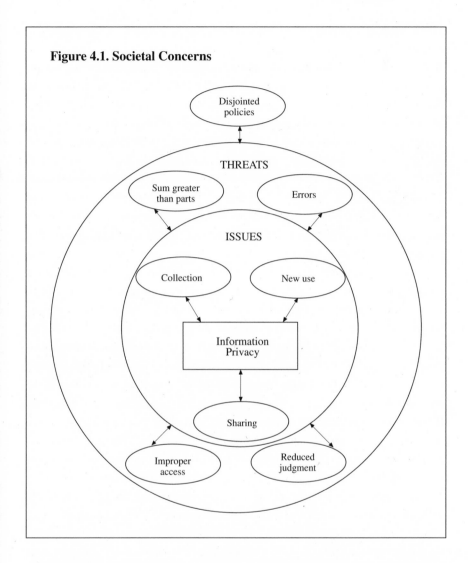

Figure 4.1. Societal Concerns

observed as an informal policy inside the organization; this study is concerned with the latter.

A "snapshot" of the approaches taken by the various corporations is presented in Table 4.1. The table considers only the *existence* of policies; as noted in chapter 3, some, like the health insurers', are outdated and are being reconsidered. Also, as we will see shortly, there is often a mismatch between the policies in the table and the actual practices in the organizations. It should not be surprising that many of the areas of concern in the drift periods are also areas in which policies and practices are at variance with societal expectations.

Improper Information Collection

The Association for Computing Machinery (ACM), a major association of information processing professionals, has a phrase in its Code of Professional Conduct dictating that members shall "always consider the principle of the individual's privacy and seek . . . to minimize the data collected." This area of concern refers to the *collection* of information. However, information about an individual held by one entity—a corporation, a government agency, etc.—and used for the purpose for which it was originally collected does not pose a problem. All parties would agree that such use was reasonable. For example, when a person applies for a loan and gives information to a loan officer, the person is not harmed in any way if the information is used for evaluating the loan application and *only* for that purpose.

Consider, though, the case of extremely sensitive data: some might claim that such data should not be collected at all—that *any* use in a particular organization—or, sometimes, in society in general—would be "unreasonable." Some argue that one's religious preference falls into this category and that it should not ever be collected or used in any decision process except within religious institutions themselves (for example, Catholic churches can require their priests to be Catholics). During the debates over life insurance blood testing, privacy advocates often argued that the results of AIDS screening procedures were too sensitive to be collected and stored. (In fact, some state laws now restrict the writing of such test results on a patient's chart or any other storage of such information.) Psychological tests used in screening new employees have come under attack in this regard for asking questions about religion and sexual orientation/practices.[1]

Furthermore, even if the information itself is viewed as appropriate for collection, the manner in which the information is collected could be challenged. Deception in data collection certainly fits into this category. Such deception can include practices such as "sugging"—the use of a fictitious survey to collect data to be used for marketing purposes—or the clever packaging of information collection processes as a "contest" in which few, if any, prizes are actually awarded. Investigative services, especially in the insurance industry, have long been known to utilize a practice known as "pretext interviews," in which an investigator poses in some other role to gather records. The 1977 PPSC report, for example, detailed numerous instances in which investigators were able to gain access to sensitive medical records in hospitals through this technique, which often involved little more than wearing a white coat and identifying oneself as a doctor.[2] A recent videotape entitled "Do You Know Who You're Dating?," sold through mail order,

Table 4.1. Sites' Policies

Area of interest	Banks' policies			Insurance industry's policies				CredCard's policies
	Bank A	Bank B	Bank C	Life-Ins	Health-Ins A	Health-Ins B	MIB[1]	
Collection	N	N	N	I	I	I	E*	N
New use	N	N	N	I	I	I	E*	N
Sharing	I	I	I	E*	E	E*	E*	E*
Deliberate errors	E*	E*	E*	E*	E*	E*	E*	E*
Accidental errors	I	I	I	I	I	I	E*	I
Reduced judgment	N	N	N	N	N	N	N/A	N
Sum greater than parts	N	N	N	N	N	N	N/A	N
Improper access (computerized)	E*	E*	E	E	E	E*	E*	E
Improper access (hard-copy and oral)	E* (minor)	I	I	I	I	E* (minor)	E*	N/A
Extensive omnibus policy	N	N	N	E*	E	E*	E*	UC

Note: N = none; I = implicit; E = explicit; N/A = not available; UC = under consideration; * = written documentation of the policy was made available to the researcher.
   1. Although it was not an official site in the study, MIB is included here for the sake of completeness.

describes pretext interview techniques for discovering various life-style facts about a subject from sources such as banks. Or consider a car dealership that allows customers entering its showroom to enter information about their personalities into a computer terminal. The terminal is attached to a small printer, which then prints for the customer a "recommended car profile" that purports to match an automobile with the prospective buyer's personality. Most customers are amused by this computer system's recommendation and accept the use of the computer as "fun." But what the customers are not told is that, in a back room at the car dealership, another printer is operating. It is printing a copy of the personality profile along with a "suggested sales strategy" based on that profile—for example, a "hard sale tactic" for certain customers, a "friendly approach" for others. But there is little doubt that the data collection smacks of deception, since few people would willingly provide such data to give the salesperson a certain advantage in the bargaining process.

Secrecy in data collection—prohibited by one of the 1973 Fair Information Practices[3]—would also fit into this category. According to the 1973 guideline, information collection should always be visible and organizations should not have files that are hidden from the subjects. The targeted marketing industry, as of this writing, has many files that might reasonably be labeled "secret," at least from the perspective of most consumers. Publications such as *DM News* ("DM" stands for "direct marketing"), which are distributed to insiders in the industry, advertise lists that are likely, from the standpoint of those on the lists, to be perceived as "secret." For example:

- A list of 106,378 names of individuals who have been rejected for bank cards.

- A list of 57,153 active subscribers to "Private Lives," a "monthly adult-oriented newsletter," and a list of 40,000 subscribers to "various 'swinger' publications" who "also purchased adult merchandise."

- A list of donors to the Canadian evangelist Ken Campbell, recommended for "charitable, conservative, evangelical, pro-family, and pro-life appeals."

- A list of 28,768 callers to "a 900-number national dating service that allows men and women [to] meet. They are primarily middle- to upper-middle class and between the ages of 25 and 50." Phone numbers, presumably captured by Automatic Number Identification technology, are available.

At the Sites

The policies at the study sites were remarkably silent on the issue of improper data collection. Only at MIB were explicit policies with respect to information collection observed—and, as will be seen in chapter 5, many advocates dispute whether consumers are aware of the MIB database and its use.[4] The insurance companies had implicit policies, but banks and CredCard did not.

Information collection at the insurance companies (both life and health) was governed by a set of implicit policies. In general, explicit policy statements that said "We do not collect this type of information" were not evident. Rather, guidelines on what information was and was not collected were embedded in the organization's standard operating procedures. An overarching theme was that personnel collected sufficient information for making an informed underwriting or claim payment decision; there was no indication that the companies collected any information beyond that needed for those purposes.[5] Consequently, information collection fell into the following categories:

• Health insurance underwriting: health conditions within the last three years;

• Health insurance claims: diagnosis and treatment information;

• Life insurance underwriting: health conditions affecting mortality; some life-style activities (e.g., skydiving) that might also affect mortality.

Of particular interest was the life insurance underwriting process, in which some pieces of information that could be considered relevant were not, as a matter of implicit policy, collected or used. A LifeIns executive described the situation:

> The policy is not documented in our manual in an official manner, but the gist is this: we will collect and consider any information that has a direct and definable impact on a person's health and longevity *unless*, for societal reasons, it should not be considered a factor in the decision. In this category we place things like sexual preference, race, and blindness (unless it is caused by some disease that is relevant). Those items are not on our application, and we do not gather information about them. That's not to say that you can't show a statistically significant relationship to longevity from them, because you can: members of different races, for example, *do* have different life spans. It is neither legal nor appropriate to differentiate on [certain] criteria, however, and we do not gather that information.

The policies were codified in four ways: 1) in contracts with their accounts; 2) in forms used for data collection; 3) in procedures—some documented and some simply used by particular work groups within the organization; and 4) in training materials given to new employees in the work groups. In addition to these procedures and training materials, some information collection protocol was imparted through "mentoring," in which senior staff members assisted more junior employees. "In those situations," explained an executive, "a senior person might say 'This one needs a physician's statement' or 'We don't usually ask about this type of treatment.' A lot of it is judgment."

As noted in chapter 2, an increasing number of health insurance account contracts were specifying utilization review rights before subscribers received certain treatments. This new practice contrasted with the policy of a decade earlier, when claims were paid without such a review. The utilization review departments seemed to have a number of internal procedures for their operations, including sample letters to be used in asking for information. However, the only explicit policy statement on confidentiality encountered was in the HealthIns B utilization review literature prepared for external parties. That document stated, "During a review, [we] may require clinical records to determine if payment is warranted. We are not interested in the intimate details of a patient's record, only in diagnosis and treatment. Even so, we have strict internal policies to protect the privacy of all patients and providers."

Information collection policies were much more explicit at MIB than at the insurance companies in the study. Since MIB's files were, by design, available to over 750 different companies, consistency in information collection was required. Consequently, MIB used an explicit set of codes and communicated these codes to the subscribing organizations. Information beyond these codes was not accepted into the MIB system.

No explicit policies with respect to collection of information (for example, codified statements such as "only the information needed to service an account shall be collected") were observed at the banks. In addition, there did not seem to be any implicit policies about such information collection.[6] Interestingly, trends in banking indicate that information collection is increasing.

As at the banks, no policies relating to information collection were encountered at CredCard. No interviewee comments with respect to restricting such collection were noted, either.

Banks A and B both had plans to collect even more information about their customers in a computerized format. This information was to be gathered from 1) expanded forms used when customers opened accounts and 2) new automation systems, in which bank employees entered personal customer information (such as number of children, whether home was rented or owned, household income) gathered during casual conversations with customers. One bank's marketing executive said the objective was to "get any information you can *from* people and *about* people." The banks had no policy statements regarding the privacy implications of this additional collection of information.

Survey respondents' interest in database contents mirrored the corporate attention being paid to the information collection issue: a relatively small number of respondents indicated a strong concern regarding the kinds of information being collected in their company's databases. Respondents could indicate the areas in which they believed that actual practices deviated from policies in their organizations. Only 9.0 percent of the respondents from Bank A, 13.6 percent from LifeIns, 15.6 percent from HealthIns B, and 20.3 percent from CredCard indicated concerns about the "kinds of information in databases." (Survey results for this area and others are shown in Table 4.2.) In comparison with some other policy/practice areas in the survey, this area indicated fairly lukewarm concern on the part of respondents.

Using Information in New Ways

One of the 1973 Fair Information Practices stated that "there must be a way for a person to prevent information about the person that was obtained for one purpose from being used or made available for other purposes without the person's consent."[7] This area of societal concern, then, revolves around those situations in which a corporation gathers information for one purpose and then uses it for another. There need not be any intentional deception at the time of data collection for this concern to arise later. An organization often gains access to much information during its normal business processes for very valid purposes, and it does not deceive individuals in any way in gathering that information: for example, a telephone company must keep a file of an individual's long distance phone calls for billing purposes. There is certainly no deception in this action, and very few individuals will dispute the company's maintaining such a file. However, if the same phone company then begins to use the list for marketing purposes—especially by calling a customer's acquaintances and referring to the apparent connection between them and the customer—many would be quite offended. Information collected for one valid purpose—billing—would then have been used for an invalid and unapproved purpose—marketing. The actions of the consumer goods companies, which have created databases using information from contest and rebate forms to create a targeted marketing database have been alleged to constitute a "new use" violation. Consumers submit rebate forms, redeem coupons, etc., believing that the information they supply is to be used solely for the purposes of receiving a rebate or entering a contest. While that is certainly the primary purpose of the information, the secondary uses—for which the individuals' permission is usually not garnered—are said to violate the individuals' privacy.

At the Sites

Neither the insurance organizations, the banks, nor the credit card issuer had an explicit policy addressing this issue. In the insurance industry, this finding can be

Table 4.2. Policy/Practice Gap

Potential mismatch	CredCard	Bank A	HealthIns B	LifeIns
Kinds of information in databases[b]	20.3%	9.0%	15.6%	13.6%
Who can access the databases[b]	34.7%	31.6%	44.4%	31.8%
Error detection and correction	40.7%	33.0%	38.6%	39.4%
How decisions about [clients] are made[c]	31.4%	9.4%	23.1%	31.8%
How people handle information in the office[a]	46.6%	45.8%	56.9%	50.0%
How information is shared with others[c]	35.6%	30.7%	45.4%	50.0%

Note: These items answered the question "In what areas do these mismatches between official policies and actual practices/operations occur?" The percentages of respondents noting each of the mismatches are listed in the table. The chi-square likelihood ratio, indicated by [a], [b], and [c], reflects the result of testing the research proposition that there are significant differences in response patterns between the sites. Significant differences at the .10 level are denoted by [a]; at the .05 level, by [b]; at the .01 level, by [c].

explained by the implicit policies regarding the uses of information. As chapter 3 explained, the insurance companies had a number of boundaries between their own functional units. These boundaries often worked as proxies for official policies against new uses of the information.

Neither the banks nor CredCard had created an overt policy regarding this issue. CredCard was in the process of formulating a privacy policy, but this was not true at the banks. However, the banks and CredCard were actively using existing information in new ways.

For the last three years, Bank A had been increasing its use of customer information for targeted marketing purposes. This process had been frustrated somewhat by the consolidation of several computer systems. At the time of the study, because of technological constraints, some pieces of information collected from customers (e.g., income and home ownership information on loan applications) were not being entered into computer databases. However, there was a movement under way to capture increasing amounts of such information in digital computer form. A marketing executive said, "We must find ways to use the information we already have about our customers to our best advantage in our marketing efforts." Another referred to banks as being "in their infancy" in terms of using their customer information to its best advantage.

Several marketing campaigns had used the customer information (such as account information) to target certain customer sets for mailings and telemarketing, and other such activities were planned for the near future. A blueprint for customer segmentation had been created, with the customer demographics for each segment clearly defined. The blueprint was in the form of a pyramid, with customers from different income sets, different demographic sets (mid-twenties versus elderly, etc.), and different life-styles (e.g., "accumulator") categorized and labeled according to their presumed banking needs. Each of the dozen or so wedges of the pyramid had its own sources of data for targeting appropriate individuals. Almost all referred to income,[8] but some also utilized data on existing checking account balances, while others looked at credit card usage or at certificates of deposit and other savings vehicles. Once an individual was placed in one of the categories based on these characteristics, he or she was destined to receive a number of mailings and/or telemarketing offers for additional banking products.

Bank B had a similar (and probably more aggressive) program in the works. It was trying to create an expert system that would correctly profile individuals based on the total pool of information that the bank had about their background, financial status, and activities. It was estimated that the system, once properly implemented, would allow Bank B to segment its existing customer set into several dozen categories—many more than at Bank A. And Bank B's system was to have an added feature that Bank A's lacked: the ability to infer some missing details based on other pieces of information in an individual's file. For example, if an individual's file did not contain any information about marital status, the expert system would scan all the entries for joint accounts or other information that would indicate the existence of a spouse. If none were found, the system would surmise that the individual was not married but would note that this answer was only a guess; it would also assign a probability of correctness for this guess. This factor, coupled with other information about the person, would allow the system to make a "best guess" placement of the individual into one of the quite tiny segments. Then, offers for additional banking products could be tailored specifically to the individuals.

New uses of customer information were troubling to at least one Bank A employee. In answer to the question "In what areas do . . . mismatches between official policies and actual practices/operations occur?," the employee noted, "[The] company sometimes uses information gathered for a specific purpose for other reasons."

As noted in chapter 3, CredCard was using the transaction information to create behavioral profiles of its cardholders for targeted marketing efforts. Such uses of information seemed to be well outside those intended when the information was collected—processing the transactions for payment—and also represented a second problem: the CredCard cardholders were never notified that the transaction histories were to be utilized in this manner.

As part of this study, a colleague of mine applied for and received a CredCard credit card. There was no consumer notification—either on the application form, in the materials mailed with the card, or in the monthly statement—that transaction information would be used for marketing purposes. However, references to telemarketing efforts, and instructions on how to opt out of those practices, were prominently noted.

It is interesting to note that MIB had an explicit and forceful policy prohibiting the use of its data for inappropriate purposes. For example, member companies were not allowed to deny an application solely because of the MIB report. In addition, uses other than insurance underwriting were strictly prohibited under the MIB policy.

Sharing Information

Another societal concern, mentioned quite often in articles in the *Privacy Journal* (a leading monthly publication for privacy advocates), is the sharing of information between corporate entities without permission from the involved individuals. All the problems of the new use issue are still present. But these concerns do not stop with unintended uses of information in one organization; the problems can be compounded by the diffused responsibilities that result from sharing information. In such situations, all parties have some measure of responsibility for outcomes—a "co-responsibility"—because processes, whether implemented through computers or structured bureaucracies, act as intermediaries between human agents and ultimate outcomes.[9] Due to this diffused co-responsibility as well as the consumer's perception of a loss of control, such sharing of information is quite likely to be labeled "unreasonable."

For example, consider once again the actions of the several large credit bureaus mentioned in chapter 1. They have used pieces of information from their credit files in new databases. From these new databases, they created mailing lists that were sold or rented for targeted marketing purposes. This practice was attacked because it allowed the use of information collected for one purpose—credit checking—for another purpose—marketing; and this concern was exacerbated because the information use was not confined to one entity. Rather, the information was shared between the credit bureau and the marketer who purchased the list.

The sale or rental of more general mailing and telemarketing lists in the targeted marketing industry often causes problems because of the sharing issue. When one subscribes to a particular magazine, for example, one's name and address are often sold to other organizations on a targeted marketing list. Concerns about this sharing activity were crucial in the strong public objections to Blockbuster Video's reported plan to sell names of its customers sorted by their rental propensities. Sharing between the public and private sectors is increasing in frequency, too: the post office shares its lists of new movers, contained in the National Change of Address (NCOA) system, with targeted marketers, and some new lists gleaned from driver's license records (e.g., "individuals over 6'0" who wear corrective lenses") hit the market in 1992.

At the Sites

At all of the sites, the act of sharing information with other organizations had received much policy attention. In some cases—at CredCard and the insurance companies, for example—this set of policies was codified in a written statement. At the banks, policies against such sharing were widely understood but were not codified in such an official manner.

Of course, CredCard shared information with credit bureaus on a regular basis. In addition, on a very limited basis, CredCard shared customer name/address/ telephone information with selected third-party companies that, in a collaborative arrangement with CredCard, offered certain products to CredCard's customers. For example, credit insurance products might be sold in this manner. CredCard did *not* sell mailing lists, per se, to unaffiliated outside parties. Under strict contract, an affiliated merchant might be able to buy either a list of customers who had charged items in his or her establishment or a list of customers who had patronized merchants in the same shopping center.

When such sharing of information with third parties occurred, it was tightly controlled. The products to be offered were scrutinized for quality; the third-party organization was carefully screened for its timeliness in filling orders; the third-party organization signed a contractual agreement prohibiting any re-use of the cardholder information; and an audit of the third-party organization was subsequently conducted. Approval of the agreement occurred at a senior executive level. As a computer tape of cardholder information was prepared and released to the third-party organization, CredCard adhered to a single-spaced, eleven-page set of written policies. Eight different forms—including the third-party nondisclosure agreements—were required for the sharing of such information.

The sharing of customer information—as well as CredCard's own mailings to customers—were receiving much scrutiny in the CredCard executive suite. One executive noted that CredCard "has been cutting back the number of marketing contacts with our customers—both from our own offerings and from third-party ones—recently" due to feedback received from the customers. Also, CredCard was making an effort to allow customers to opt out of telemarketing arrangements.

The insurance companies typically had written policy statements that addressed the release of information about applicants and policyholders. At LifeIns and HealthIns A, those policy statements had their genesis in the NAIC Model Privacy Act discussed in chapter 2. Although most states had not passed the legislation, the model act was viewed as a guideline. LifeIns had adopted the act for all its operations, even in states where it was not legally required to do so, since that action was both "administratively easier and the right thing to do." However, in some cases, LifeIns did not comply with certain notification procedures in states where they were not required. HealthIns A had also used the NAIC model for its guidelines. MIB's guidelines also expressly prohibited unauthorized sharing of its data.

HealthIns B had its own set of policies, which had been developed and distributed in 1983. (At the time of the study, the policies were being reexamined, and a task force was about to consider rewriting them.) Similar in concept to HealthIns B's, HealthIns A's policy dated back to 1980. As noted in chapter 3, an increasing area of tension at both of these companies related to the amount of medical claim information that was shared with employers. The official policies addressed these issues, but they were becoming less useful over time due to the changing pressures in the health care industry. In fact, information was freely exchanged with the employer under self-insured arrangements at HealthIns A, although this exchange was not technically allowable under their official policy. Only sensitive categories of charges (e.g., mental health, AIDS) were protected. For other group policies, employers were typically told of an employee's total medical charges. In addition, the aggregate charges for particular procedures or treatments were reported for the entire group. However, specific payments for specific individuals were not detailed.

At HealthIns B, information regarding diagnoses was never exchanged—even with the self-insured accounts. "I think we are somewhat unique among insurers in this regard," noted one marketing executive. Over the past five years, a number of additional reports—detailing mostly aggregate claims data but also giving totals in certain categories that sometimes included only small numbers of claims—had been made available to larger accounts. To some degree, these new reports stretched the limits of the 1983 policy. An employee in the account reporting area said:

> When I first started working on these reports, it really worried me that companies could figure out which employees were making which claims. I was afraid that they'd see a category in which there was only one employee or dependent (say, "long-term psychiatric hospitalization") and could figure out who it was. That was particularly true if they combined these new reports with the detailed listings. Over time, I've become less concerned because I don't see the benefits directors at the companies using the reports that way. The opportunity to figure things out is still there, though, even though we don't, on the surface, give them the identities.

Another HealthIns B claim manager noted, "You have to be careful, because employers can put the information together to identify specific employees." A survey respondent wrote, "[I have a] concern as to how information is shared with accounts. Although names are not given, it is possible through account reporting that assumptions can be made about matching type of illness to an employee." The dangers of such actions were apparent to many industry executives, who often referred to the problems associated with employers knowing about their employees' sensitive health conditions. ("A lot of them will try to fire them," according to one interviewee.) Consequently, the health insurers were quite reluctant to release any AIDS-related information to employers. At HealthIns A, such a situation had led to the cancellation of a large account's contract, according to one manager: "A large account wanted AIDS claim information, and we said no. They canceled their contract, and we lost their business." An executive at HealthIns B also reported "losing some accounts because we wouldn't tell them what they wanted to know about their employees' claims."

Why were the health insurers so concerned about releasing such information to employers? For the most part, they appeared to be concerned about the possibility that employers might use the information to make job-related decisions about employees. Although the interviewees at HealthIns A or B did not explicitly mention this point, one industry observer recently noted that if an employee experienced an adverse personnel action (e.g., firing or demotion) based on such a release of health information to an employer, the health insurer might be named as a co-defendant with the employer in a lawsuit filed on the employee's behalf. Certainly this potential threat existed, but it was to some degree reduced by the policy of indemnification practiced quite often by HealthIns A: before they would release much of the sensitive claim information to an employer, they required that the employer indemnify them against any claims that might result from the use of the information. Thus, HealthIns A would not be expressly liable for any damage that might result. Even with these protections, though, the executives were uncomfortable with the release of the claim information. "There's no telling what might be done with it," remarked one interviewee. "It scares me when I think about some of these [employers] seeing this stuff," said another.

One insurance executive noted that the problems were compounded by the fact that the sensitivity of the items could be less than obvious:

> A woman had a pregnancy test, and the charges were reported on a summary report to the employer. Only the name of the laboratory and the charge appeared, however; the nature of the charges was not reported. However, it turned out that the laboratory in question only performed a limited number of tests, and most of them were for pregnancy. Since the woman was trying to keep her possible pregnancy a secret at work, she was upset. She claimed that she was passed over for a promotion because of this.

Employer access to claims data was not the only area of concern to health insurers. Another unit in which the official policies had become outdated was the customer service department. This unit, which took phone inquiries from subscribers, had become much more conservative over time about releasing information to callers. In most cases, the unit's practices were now at variance with the official corporate policy from 1983; moreover, the practices were not even consistent across all the workers in the unit. Depending on which of the unit's telephone representatives happened to answer one's call, one might or might not be given information one requested. As part of this study, the director of customer service prepared a set of hypothetical situations in which callers might request medical information from a customer service representative. This list of situations was then presented to a random sample of customer service representatives. The list included situations in which a husband was asking for information about his wife, a teenage daughter for information about a parent's claim, etc. The director's suggested responses were more restrictive than the official policy would indicate. For the most part, the representatives' answers agreed with the director's. However, especially in the situation of a child asking for claim information about her parent, the representatives were more liberal in their responses than the director. After seeing the results of this survey, the director remarked, "Looks like we need some reeducation in a few areas."

Although they did not have to worry about employee health claims or calls requesting information about them, life insurers had yet another problem in the sharing domain: dealing with their agents. How much should agents be told about the results of the underwriting process for the applications they submitted? The official policy at LifeIns held that "as a general rule, information beyond usual underwriting notice will not be given to the agency or agent, and all communication should be in writing." In practice, though, this posture was not always maintained. The director of underwriting said:

> We do not always take a hard line on this, although we do lean in that direction. Sometimes, you have an agent on the phone yelling "Why did you reject this application?" They threaten to take their business away if we don't tell them the medical details. Usually, we don't tell them, and it could lose us business. So it goes.
>
> My feeling, though, is that if it's clear the applicant knows of the medical condition (for example, they *know* they have a heart condition or high blood pressure), and if the agent is someone we can trust, we might give them some details. You have to look at who you're dealing with. If there's any doubt, though, I say "Don't tell the agent."

The gray area in this practice was apparently troubling to at least one underwriter, who wrote the following on a survey: "Too much information is given out to unauthorized people. We should protect our applicants by not releasing *any* information we develop in underwriting. I will not divulge any information to *anyone* but later find out that this information is given [to agents, etc.] 'because they can be trusted'? No one knows how far this information has gone—or how it could harm an applicant down the line."

The explicit sharing policies at CredCard and at the insurance companies corresponded to implicit policies at the banks, all of which exhibited a refusal to share information with any outside entities except for courts, when under specific legal orders to do so, and for credit bureaus.[10] However, the banks had not codified their policies and had them approved by senior executives in an official format, as had CredCard and the insurance companies. Almost all bank interviewees were able to describe the policy verbally, but none could produce any official evidence to support it. Bankers were quick to note their responsibilities to their customers, as in this comment by one Bank A executive: "Customers often feel they have a semi-fiduciary relationship with their bank, sort of like a doctor-patient relationship. They believe that telling anyone that they even have a relationship with us is a violation of that trust." Another interchange also illustrates this point:

> Some of it is ethical—we shouldn't violate their trust. But, to be honest, the better part of it is that we don't want to deal with the fallout. [Interviewer: What do you mean?] It could come back to kill us. If we violate the customers' privacy by [for example] giving their names and information to somebody else, well . . . you can only do that once! There won't be a second time. [Interviewer: You mean you'll lose customers?] Worse. We'll lose customers, plus get a bad reputation and not be able to get new customers.

For this reason among others, the banks—while increasingly using the information for targeted marketing activities of their own—were quite reluctant to allow the information to be used outside their own organizations. In addition to concerns about consumer reactions to such sharing, the banks did not wish to dilute the value of their own strategic asset—their list of customers—by allowing others access. "We could make some money in the short run by selling lists," noted one executive, "but I think it would hurt us in the long run. Customers would get mad, and we would have leveraged one of our most important assets." In fact, there was sometimes tension between a bank's own subsidiaries, as noted by one marketing executive: "I don't really trust some of our subsidiaries with our customer lists. I don't know what they will do with the information, and I try to discourage sharing anything with them. I feel like it is out of our control once they get hold of it."

But it is interesting to note that the banks had apparently not issued policy statements on this matter in written form. One marketing executive said, "I don't know that we would *never* share customer information with another firm for a promotion, but it would really be tightly controlled. We're afraid of it. Still, we have not, to my knowledge, stated that officially. Everybody just knows it."

While the banks were reluctant to share their own customer information with others, they were becoming *more* inclined to buy additional information about their customers from outside vendors. At Banks A and B, the purchase of demographic information from an outside vendor was either under way or about to be embraced. (See Figure 4.2 for details of one such offering.) According to a marketing vice president, the system was expected to work this way: the bank would submit a tape of customer names and addresses to a vendor. The vendor would return that tape and would supply an additional tape that contained income, ages, and other information on the customers. (Bank A expected an 80 percent "hit rate.") The bank would then append the new information to its existing customer files.

When it came to sharing information, a gap between policy and practice was apparent at all the surveyed sites, according to the anonymous respondents to the written survey. The survey asked respondents to indicate the specific areas in which information privacy practices did not match the policies in their companies. The item "how information is shared with others" was checked by 30.7 percent of the respondents from Bank A; 35.6 percent from CredCard; 45.4 percent from HealthIns B; and 50.0 percent from LifeIns (see Table 4.2). This response serves as ample evidence of a troubling policy/practice gap.

In contrast to their disregard of the collection and new use issues, then, all sites did focus on either explicit or implicit policies to control sharing activities, even if the policy/practice gap was a large one. However, it should be noted that the motivation for the banks' and CredCard's actions was not always to protect privacy per se. Rather, they seemed equally or more concerned with the strategic value of the customer database than with improper divulgence of sensitive information. Seven different interviewees explained the information-sharing policies by referring to such a loss of strategic value.

Errors

The issues of collection, new use, and sharing of information cause enough societal concern in their own right. But their impacts are magnified when we consider several other threats to information privacy that are often raised by advocates, consumers, and executives and that are often revealed in the literature. Certainly one major threat to privacy, which exacerbates any other issue under discussion, is erroneous data in the files. The 1973 Fair Information Practices addressed this threat by proclaiming, "There must be a way for a person to correct or amend a record of identifiable information about the person."[11] Publications such as *Privacy Journal* or "War Stories," a compendium of privacy-related anecdotes,[12] include numerous references to erroneous information and the problems it creates for individuals. Several situations in which erroneous data have been observed, and the problems created by those errors, were detailed in the PPSC report (which considered, among others, credit card authorization services)[13] and by Linowes (who discussed check authorization services and other organizations).[14]

Although the literature does not always make it clear, there are actually two

Figure 4.2. Information Offered to Banks

The following list summarizes the package of information on individual customers that one vendor had offered to Bank A:

Purchasing Power Data

1. Buyability index: Available spending power indexed to a national mean.

2. Credit card activity index: How actively the customer uses revolving credit accounts.

3. Fixed payment index: Degree to which the customer is willing to commit to fixed payment obligations.

4. Open installment accounts index: The number of fixed monthly payments a customer was able to handle, on an indexed scale.

5. Type of credit used: A segmentation of payment types—bank credit cards, retail card, travel and entertainment, oil and auto credit cards.

6. Estimated household income code: An estimate of household income.

Purchasing Activity Data

7. Active bank card index: A measure of a person's propensity to use bank cards.

kinds of errors that imperil data: deliberate and accidental errors.[15] Deliberate errors—such as the intentional misreporting of information—are usually small in number, and they are subject to audit controls. Many of the security precautions in existing computer systems are tailored to catch deliberate errors: a person without access who enters a database, for example. Of course, an approved but unscrupulous operator has opportunities to inappropriately alter records, and it is precisely this type of error that often becomes a focal point for audit and control processes. But as systems increase in complexity (and, especially, in intercon-

8–10. Same as 7 but regarding retail cards, travel cards, oil and auto cards.

11. Total accounts held index: Total number of active revolving accounts a customer has, indexed to a national mean.

Consumer Shopping Data

12. Shopping psychographics: Segmentation based on the consumer's shopping preferences; one of nine distinct behavioral characteristics (cash shopper, prestige shopper, value shopper, price shopper, etc.).

Demographic Data

13. Date of birth: Derived from public records and other sources.

14. Marital status: Inferred from joint account status.

15. Dwelling unit type: Developed from U.S. Postal Services Zip+4 file, which identifies types of dwelling unit for each address in the United States.

16. Gender: Inferred based on first name.

17. Market segment codes: One of sixty-four consumer cluster groups based on financial and geodemographic data.

---

nections across enterprises), such deliberate errors become harder to spot and contain.

While deliberate errors are relatively small in number and, on the whole, easier to control for, accidental errors present a different set of problems. Because audit procedures are often unprepared for them, and because information technology resources make them so stubborn, accidental errors often go undetected and uncorrected. At their simplest, these errors can be data entry mistakes. However, they can also exist as mistaken identities or as improper clustering of information. Statistics regarding the frequency of accidental errors in databases are elusive and subject to dispute because of the ways in which they are reported. For example, one recent study held that 48 percent of consumer credit reports contain errors.[16] However, a spokesperson for the credit-reporting industry claimed that, of the reports challenged by consumers, only one-half of 1 percent would actually have resulted in an adverse credit decision.[17] Depending on one's perspective and interpretation, one can represent the level of erroneous information quite differently. However, all parties agree that accidental errors are unfortunate and to be avoided.

The accidental errors are not the result of any evil intent; they are an unfortunate by-product of information handling. This does not excuse their existence, however, since safeguards could have been included in the system design. Many executives tend to attribute errors to individuals using systems rather than to the systems in which the errors occur,[18] because this move makes for an easier defense. It is easier to blame a clerk who entered an item incorrectly, for example, than to admit that the entire data-entry procedure in a particular system is poorly designed and thus increases the probability of such errors. In reality, the system's designers—not the users—are often the real culprits, as one key decision made during systems design processes is the reasonable threshold for error protection. Such key human decisions in creating information systems[19] are an important area in which the value choices of the system designers become obvious.[20]

Since it is the category of *accidental* errors that causes the most problems in today's information technology environment, we will look at a few examples. The same problems apply to the few deliberate errors that occur—their correction is still difficult. The impact of the errors increases as they occur in concert with new use and sharing issues. When information is contained in one organization and used for its original purposes, errors are harmful but can often be easily contained. As information is used for other purposes, the impact of errors increases; when information is shared across entities, the errors snowball until they are almost impossible to contain.

Basic errors that occur when information is used for its original purpose by the collecting organization are sometimes easily resolved. They might include, for example, a misstated bank balance; while an annoyance, this error could be easily corrected if it had affected nothing other than the customer's own bank records. But these basic errors are not always of a trivial nature, and the consequences can be severe. A local police computer might contain an erroneous warrant, and an innocent person could be arrested based on the false information, with consequential damage to reputation. Even so, correction of the error would be easier in one system than in a diffused one.

Once a piece of information is used for a new purpose, errors present greater difficulties because the information is subject to interpretation. An error in the original information can easily be magnified when it is interpreted. Consider the erroneous bank balance discussed earlier. If it is used by another bank department to change credit limits (a use the customer did not intend or approve of), and if the customer's credit is then changed based on the erroneous balance, a "double error" has occurred. Even worse, the bank will likely correct the balance when the customer brings it to their attention, but the fact that the same information was used in making a credit decision may by then be forgotten.

When information is shared across organizational boundaries, errors become even more problematic. The snowballing effect of erroneous information is a diffused one, since many databases and links are involved. A pointed example centers on the National Crime Information Center (NCIC), a nationwide computer system linked to many state criminal justice information systems. Outstanding warrants, parole violations, etc., are often entered into local systems and later uploaded to the national system. Law enforcement agencies then query the NCIC system to see if individuals are wanted in other areas.[21] However, problems with inaccurate data and mistaken identities abound. Improper arrests and incarcerations have led to numerous lawsuits and a reevaluation of the system.[22]

At the Sites

Because of the significance of errors in maintaining the integrity of a database, one might expect official policy statements addressing them. In fact, at most of the sites in the study, official policies covered only deliberate errors. MIB was the only organization that had devoted policy attention to accidental errors and their prevention.

At all sites, a great amount of effort had been devoted to protecting the computer databases in a technical manner against unauthorized entry, thus protecting the security of the data. The organizations typically had installed a file protection system (for example, RACF or ACF2 on an IBM mainframe) and created a set of policies to accompany that system. (See Figure 4.3 for an overview of a representative policy.) Almost all interviewees who were acquainted with them agreed that such systems had tightened up the computerized environment to a great degree as compared to, say, the environment of a decade earlier.

Figure 4.3. Access Policy Excerpts

Access policies typically devoted several paragraphs to defining the roles and responsibilities of various parties. The following excerpt is typical.

I. *Roles and Responsibilities*

A. Information Security Function

The Information Security Function ensures the security of the information assets owned by or in the custody of the [corporation]. As such they:

 1. Develop overall policies, goals, and objectives for securing the information assets.
 2. Develop and ensure implementation of standards, procedures, and guidelines, which are necessary to secure the information assets.
 3. Develop methods and techniques to secure the information assets.
 4. Evaluate the effectiveness of information security systems.
 5. Provide direction and advice to information owners, custodians, and users in regard to securing information.
 6. Communicate information security requirements to information owners, custodians, and users.
 7. Monitor information security compliance and investigate related security threats.

B. Administrative Information Security Function

[section similar to that under A]

C. Information Owner

The information assets of the [corporation] are not legally owned by any of its employees. However, for the purposes of this policy, "information owners" are those who are recognized as having direct responsibility for the integrity and authorized use of information under their control. [A list of five specific duties followed.]

D. Information Custodian

[section similar to that under C]

E. Information User

[section similar to that under C]

II. *Management's Responsibilities*

Managers assume various responsibilities when authorizing users to access computer systems. The most significant of these is that the manager is accountable for the protection of information.

Specifically, the manager's responsibilities include the following:

—Requesting user access

1. Ensuring that access is granted on a need-to-know basis.

2. Ensuring proper completion of the Access Request forms.

—Transfers and terminations

It is mandatory that management notify Information Security immediately of any transfers or terminations.

III. *Signature Approval*

Each request form submitted to Information Security requires an authorized signature. The level of authorization depends on the type of access requested. [A list that followed specified which management levels were needed to authorize certain requests; the policy then continued with a set of instructions for filling in the various authorization forms, which varied for each system.]

In addition to policies regarding deliberate errors in computers, the sites had some procedures for isolating a number of deliberate errors in noncomputerized processes. Banks had extensive audit procedures that used control totals, and the insurance industry conducted some self-audits to ensure compliance with certain practices. For example, MIB conducted annual audits to ensure that its members used the medical information appropriately.

But, in spite of the explicit policies at the sites, one survey respondent noted that employees *could* inappropriately manipulate data if they wanted to do so; no specific examples of such violations were cited, however. The write-in comment, from a HealthIns B employee, read, "Employees have [the] ability to manipulate relatives/friends' data and claims." Although the companies had all invested considerable sums in computer access control facilities, the case of "people giving their access code to others" was cited as a concern by a bank employee. Obviously, such sharing of codes renders control facilities impotent; the extent of such sharing was not determined by this study.

More commonly cited, particularly by banking security executives, were instances of embezzlement and other manipulations of funds for personal benefit. However, such violations—while they could conceivably harm an individual customer—are rarely privacy violations per se. The policies seem to be grounded more in the protection of corporate assets than in the protection of personal privacy.

The attention that was given to deliberate errors—which usually included some written procedures as well as technical controls—was more muted with respect to accidental errors. Certainly, some audit controls were present, especially in the banking industry: for example, daily closings in branches ensured that totals matched the expected records. Debit and credit checks were included in all systems, according to an I/S executive. In addition, at an industry level, certain provisions for inspection of individuals' files were provided as one check against accidental errors. MIB allowed individuals to examine their medical records,[23] and credit bureau files—containing bank information as well as other credit data—could be accessed and challenged under the Fair Credit Reporting Act of 1970. In general, however, the sites seemed to view accidental errors as unfortunate by-products of human information handling, to be corrected as they became visible. There were apparently no explicit policies for dealing with the "trickle factor" of errors that may permeate other databases as information flows between them. In interviews, I/S professionals repeatedly referred to "standard data edits"[24] and described the involvement of security professionals during the systems design process. They did not, however, indicate that any additional consideration was being given to accidental errors in information processing. Except at MIB—which provided inspection/correction processes for its files—there were no official policies addressing these items.

Exactly how accurate was the information stored in the companies' databases? Although the databases were not audited in this study, survey respondents' perceptions can be telling, as the policy/practice gap appears to be a large one for error-handling. As Table 4.2 shows, from 33 percent (Bank A) to 40.7 percent (CredCard) of the respondents checked "error detection and correction" as an area in which policies and practices were at variance in their company. A survey respondent at Bank A noted that "neglect [and] carelessness" were common. Another respondent wrote: "I find that errors that are noticed go unresolved. Why?" An executive at Bank B noted that the error level had become embarrassing on one occasion: "We had some information on customers' ages in our files, and we checked some for correctness. It turned out that 35 percent of them were in error. It's embarrassing—especially if you use that information for something that the customer sees."

Reduced Judgment

An additional threat to information privacy could stem from the problem of reduced judgment. When the flow of information becomes large, most organizations' response is to contain the flow by becoming more formulaic and rules-oriented. Thus, decisions that were formerly based on judgment and human factors are instead often decided according to prescribed formulas.[25] In today's world, this response is often characterized by reliance on a rigid, unyielding process in which computerized information is given great weight. Facts that actually require substantial evaluation could instead be reduced to discrete entries in preassigned categories.

Adding to the problem is an unconscious and widespread assumption that computer records are more accurate than paper ones. "A computer record can . . . appear more accurate than it really is and can be used for decisions about you without any human intervention."[26] The characteristic of these responses is a perceived replacement of judgment by rigid reliance on an unyielding computerized process. However, one should not conclude that computerized processes always result in a reduction in judgment. For example, depending on their design, some artificial intelligence applications (expert systems, self-learning systems, etc.) can exhibit a reliance on a computerized process, yet human judgment has been incorporated into the process itself. At issue are processes in which judgment—in either computerized or human form—is altogether lacking.

The use of automated versus customized handling in a process denotes yet another important value choice on the part of the process's designers.[27] How a system is designed reflects the biases of the organizers and influences the ideas of users.[28] As human beings, we are responsible for not giving a computer control over information that it is unequipped to handle and for providing some way to revert to manual methods when things go wrong.[29] In theory, of course, organizations could handle *all* situations as customized processes that required human involvement. They could avoid automation altogether, although this would obviously be a poor economic approach. On the other hand, organizations could automate all processes and consider none of the situations as exceptions for human handling. The line drawn between these two options indicates a judgment on the part of the designers, and it is around this line that disputes over "reasonableness" often rotate.

The rise of expert systems in decision-making processes increases the visibility of the threat of reduced judgment, as processes that were once regarded as the domain of human experts are increasingly being implemented through rule bases. Depending on how they are implemented, however, expert systems can actually *reduce* the concerns by providing a thoughtful consideration of individuals' circumstances on a more consistent basis. The thoroughness with which the rule base is created, the manner in which the system's decision rationale is communicated to the individuals in question, and a provision for human intervention in exceptional situations are key criteria in alleviating public concerns.

Some examples of this threat revolve around the excessive reliance on a computer to the point where an absurd situation results. For example, in 1974 a man named Richard Nolan died. For fourteen years, American Express continued to mail offers of credit cards to his address, despite the fact that his widow had written "deceased" on several and returned them. Finally, in 1988, she decided to seek revenge. She actually filled in one of the applications and returned it. For his Social Security number, she entered 000-00-0000. For employer, she wrote "God." For "date of birth," she wrote "date of death." Rather than refuse the application, however, American Express's automated system processed it and returned it to Mrs. Nolan because it *had not been signed*. So she rolled the application into the typewriter and, on the line labeled "signature," typed "no pens in heaven." Two weeks later, American Express's automated process worked to perfection: Richard Nolan, dead fourteen years, received a Gold Card in the mail.[30]

In another well-publicized case, Citibank made an assumption about college students that was codified into its processing, causing an embarrassing situation. Because Citibank believed that their employment prospects were so poor that they would not be able to repay their debts, college students majoring in English, history, and art were routinely denied credit cards. The assumption came to light when a Citibank credit card holder—a student who had initially majored in math—changed his major to rhetoric and then applied for a second card, which Citibank denied. The incident was reported in the press along with the fact that Citibank's own chief executive had been a history major.[31]

In both of these examples, individuals were treated as numbers and facts, with little human judgment being applied to their situations. Assumptions were made, and processes were followed, but both Mrs. Nolan and the math major–turned–rhetoric major no doubt felt that some amount of requisite judgment had been traded away in favor of an unyielding computerized process. Societal concerns about this reduced judgment appear to be growing in light of increased computerization. That the computerized processes often yield more consistent judgments based on facts is seldom disputed, but individuals often wish to be treated as something more than mere facts. As corporations push the limits of the decision-making technology, one would expect that their policies would be reflective of the societal concerns about these developments. Yet this was not the case at the sites in the study.

At the Sites

At no site were policies regarding reduced judgment noted. Two interviewees (one at Bank A and one at HealthIns B) saw these items as privacy concerns, but no specific policies addressing these items had been formulated, even though substantial movement toward increased automation in decision making—especially through expert systems technology—was apparent at LifeIns, in the underwriting process; at Bank A, in the consumer lending process; and at CredCard, in the credit review process. In addition, at HealthIns B an expert systems application had been considered for use in the health claim review process; however, one responsible executive indicated that he was resisting its adoption.

The employees who responded to the anonymous survey indicated moderately high concern regarding "how decisions about [clients] are made" in their organizations (see Table 4.2). From a low of 9.4 percent at Bank A to a high of 31.8 percent at LifeIns, respondents noted that official policies and practices were often at variance in this area. Note that the respondents were not necessarily reflecting on the use of automation in decision making when they answered the question, so direct associations of this survey item with the threat of reduced judgment may be tenuous ones. Nevertheless, the survey findings indicate that many employees are not comfortable with the way in which their company is handling its information-intensive decisions about people.

Sum Is Greater Than the Parts

Also cutting across the issues is an apparent perception that the "sum is greater than the parts." This perception arises from an assumption that, even if disparate pieces of information are somewhat innocuous by themselves, they become more threatening when combined. When an individual's records are all available in one comprehensive file, they can be inspected with greater ease and depth than would otherwise have been possible. Of course, the same information would have been available before it was combined into one file, but investigators would have had to devote more time and effort to collecting the information—and some of it would likely have been missed. Technological barriers to combining and using large quantities of information are declining. In addition, technology has increased the ability to detect patterns in large volumes of data. The "sum is greater than parts" threat was noted in a different form in the 1977 PPSC report, as it detailed both the increased accumulation in records and the indirect relationships that were growing between Americans and their record-keepers.[32]

This issue has been driven home pointedly by the recent rise of entrepreneurial businesses that are often called "super-bureaus." These organizations operate somewhat like credit bureaus but with a larger domain. The super-bureaus collect information that is available in many places—from regular credit bureaus (both major and independent), driver's license and motor vehicle records, voter registration lists, Social Security number lists, birth records, court records, etc. They can combine this information and sell the reports at hefty fees.[33] Peter G. Neumann, of SRI International, sees the super-bureaus as a definite threat, according to a recent article:

> These new small businesses are making available to hundreds of users information that formerly was available only through disparate sources. . . .
> They invite abuse more than the distributed system . . . because they make it easier to access many databases. [They could spawn] a new generation of "derivative services" that will run one database against another, to generate mailing lists or even "attack lists" of individuals who meet certain criteria.[34]

Arthur Miller has referred to the overall societal impression that "there's too much damn data collection going on."[35] The "sum is greater than parts" threat mirrors this feeling at a societal level: even if one is hard-pressed to pinpoint one particular application that is offensive, one has a vague sense that something is awry and is getting out of control. Perhaps that explains why 71 percent of Americans, in a 1990 public opinion poll, agreed that "consumers have lost all control over how personal information about them is circulated and used by companies."[36] In the same poll, 90 percent of the respondents said that consumers' "being asked to provide excessively personal information" was either a "major" (57 percent) or "minor" (33 percent) problem.[37]

At the Sites

Of course, policies for the "sum is greater than parts" threat would have been of the order of "Information from various sources is not combined to create larger files" or "We do not participate in efforts to create centralized databases," etc. However, no such policies were observed at any sites, in either explicit or implicit form. An absence of such policies is not surprising, since this societal concern is a fairly subtle one and, in addition, one that a single organization is somewhat powerless to address. Though polls indicate that many members of society are concerned about this threat, individuals would face overwhelming obstacles in effecting changes in this area.

Improper Access

While the privacy literature addressed this threat only in an oblique fashion, it was clear from interviews that many corporate employees and consumers were quite concerned about the threat of improper access: unauthorized people within an organization being able to see personal information. In addition, computer professionals have codified their own obligation in this regard: the ACM Code of Ethics dictates a responsibility to "limit authorized access to . . . data."[38] The problem really has two parts: 1) are there sufficient technical controls to provide restricted access to the information? and 2) are there appropriate policies for making sure that only individuals with a "need to know" are given that access? However, the interpretation of which individuals have, and do not have, a need to know is often a cause of much controversy. An organization's clients might object to the organization's employees' having wide access to their personal information, even though the organization might claim that this widespread access was a legitimate business need. A recent discussion with a hospital records administrator, for example, revealed that over three dozen different categories of individuals in the hospital ("doctors," "nurses," etc.) were allowed access to patient records in one form or another. One of the categories listed "TV hostess," which, explained the administrator, was the "person who goes to each room each day to see if the patient wants to rent the TV in the room." A hospital's chief executive officer (and physician) stated: "Almost anyone who walks around in a white coat in a hospital can get patient records. In fact, I sometimes jokingly say that almost anybody can see the records *except* the patient!"[39] Both the records administrator and this hospital executive agreed that the system was too loose, and both were taking steps to correct it in their own hospitals. However, these observations stand as a realistic example of the threat of improper access in a real-world environment.

At the Sites

Of course, one might expect that improper access would have received some explicit policy attention at the sites. In fact, for computerized information this assumption was quite true. All of the organizations had some computer safeguards to insure that only authorized individuals could access specific records,[40] and all of the organizations referred to a need-to-know policy with respect to such access. Forms for securing computer access rights were commonplace, and procedures (sometimes called "policies") were published at each site. These procedures usually outlined the sign-off process for gaining access to a particular file or computer application.

Typically, in the banks, each information source had a designated "owner," and it was his or her responsibility to determine the need-to-know criteria for the information. In practice, most requests for access seemed to be rather routinely approved, with requesters often receiving access to more information than they really needed. A Bank C executive commented:

> I think we need to focus a lot more on controlling access to information. We are too loose on the concept of "need to know." There is a prevailing feeling that "if you work for [the bank], it's okay to see this information." I challenge that.
>
> We've spent a lot of time worrying about who can update certain pieces of information, and that has improved our control over the data. We also need to think about who can *see* the information. We have not really confronted

that as directly, but we need to. However, it's an uphill battle, since people view this as taking function away.

A Bank A executive clarified the need-to-know principle in his bank's context: "We say information is provided on a need-to-know basis, but that's perhaps an overstatement. We don't want information to be 'unreasonably withheld' (a phrase we use occasionally). So, if an employee needs information on an occasional basis, we go ahead and grant access." One comment on the written survey read as follows: "I am very concerned with the way that personal data [are] handled. I . . . don't like the idea of, or appreciate the fact that, any customer service person or data processing employee could pull up information on the accounts and see . . . financial situation[s]. . . . There is no such thing as privacy." A private banking executive at one bank said:

> The truth is that almost any officer of the bank (especially, one with lending authority) can get at any information in the computer system . . . even for our private banking customers. This bothers me, since I want to provide confidentiality. If somebody who is now a loan officer hated you in college, they could get at your file without any trouble at all. If I call and ask for a credit file, it comes in the internal mail; nobody asks any questions.
>
>   I never promise my customers total privacy, because I know I cannot deliver it. A lot of them assume they are entering into a confidential arrangement, however, and I don't tell them otherwise unless they ask. We could fix this by making our department more insular, but the bank has traded off that need for greater confidentiality against the increased administrative burden it would create.

At another bank, some of these problems had been resolved by creating numbered accounts for some private banking customers. "Even bank employees don't know who the accounts belong to," noted a private banking manager, "so the customer doesn't have to worry about someone seeing their statements."

At Banks A, B, and C, the tellers and platform personnel were given computer access to information about all a customer's accounts: checking, savings, credit cards, loans, mortgages, etc. Tellers usually shared a single computer terminal at the back of their work area; platform workers usually had their own terminals with the same information. The information included account balances, outstanding amounts owed, and, in some cases, transaction information (e.g., recent checks and credit card charges). A teller in one branch stated that customers requested information about their loans or credit cards only on an "infrequent" basis. One survey respondent at Bank A was concerned about a related item: "Customers can clearly see information [about] other customers displayed on our screens."

While the access to information was somewhat controlled through the safeguards and procedures on mainframe computers, this was not the case with personal computers at one of the banks. A manager described the environment:

> We have a number of global files that can be made available for downloading to PCs if people want them. Just about anybody at the bank who wants them can get access. You'd have to know the names of the fields in the files, and so on, but that would [not be a] major inhibitor to an unauthorized person. These global files have customer balances for checking accounts, savings accounts, CDs, credit cards, installment loans, and so forth. People can download the information and play with it on their own PCs. I suppose they could also copy it to their own diskettes if they really wanted to.
>
> Diskettes are running rampant around here; we don't have any idea what anybody has. The LAN [local area network] software walks away regularly. Then there are problems with people coming in at night and using people's PCs; all of the areas are open.

In contrast to the situations at the banks, HealthIns B exhibited tighter access controls with respect to information that their own employees could see. HealthIns B's computer security personnel rejected over 10 percent of the requests for access to computerized information, claiming the requester had no real need to know, and secondary approvals were still required for all of the remaining requests. Those approvals always came from the owner of the information—not the employee's own supervisor—so some amount of contention was evident in the system.

In some areas, as we discussed in chapter 3, functional groups seemed to have information barriers between them, and this situation often led to organizational tension. For example, the utilization review group jealously guarded the medical information it received during its investigations. Its computer system could only be accessed by members of the group. But even with the high level of awareness at HealthIns B, a few individuals had access to information that, one could argue, they had no need to know. For example, the enrollment data entry personnel saw application forms for nongroup applicants after the underwriters had completed the underwriting process. At the bottom of the forms were a number of questions relating to the applicants' health histories—information that could have been removed before the data entry process.

MIB extended this need-to-know approach into the very design of its system, which was described as being, intentionally, "very user-unfriendly": unless someone had been trained on the specific access protocol for the system, he or she would likely be unable to gain entry, even with a set of access codes. The system dialed each inquiring terminal back to deliver its reports and required a unique code from each terminal accessing the system. The MIB system kept a record of all inquiries from each terminal, and MIB regularly audited each location to determine that all access was appropriate. Restrictions on the personnel who had access at each site were clearly documented.

At both insurance companies and at one bank, concerns about the use of "live" data in software testing were raised. "We have been unsuccessful in getting a good set of test data created," said one I/S manager, "so we pull live data for test runs. Of course, that means that programmers have access to information that they arguably shouldn't see." Another manager noted, "The programmers see it all. I hope they can be trusted." At HealthIns B, one survey respondent noted a concern regarding "using actual claim data in vendor demonstrations."

At all of the official sites in the study, some special provisions for handling employee data were noted; usually, a small, special unit had been set up to handle transactions for employee accounts. Thus, a query to a bank's customer files would yield no account information for employee accounts unless the user had a special, restricted access. At the health insurance companies, any information about employee claims was available only through a special unit. These provisions were explained by an insurance executive: "We try to keep employees' personal information from others in the organization, since there is just no need for them to see it. In the regular course of business, one might occasionally see the file of a neighbor or other acquaintance. That can create a problem, but it is somewhat unavoidable. At least with the employees, who we know will work together every day, we can control the access." One survey respondent noted this disparity in a write-in comment, stating, "[The company] treats its employees with much greater confidentiality than I've seen for [customers] in general." Another noted that "it pleases me to know that if you, as an employee, [request it] . . . there can be a privacy flag put into the computer so that no other employee can access your information." Written policy statements detailing these prohibitions on access to employee data were apparently nonexistent.

Unlike the other sites, CredCard did not have special restrictions for *access* to information about employee accounts; the same controls applied as for regular customers. However, any *changes* to employee accounts (e.g., credit line increases) were given special handling. For example, although most CredCard customers could request a credit line increase in an expedited manner, this option was not allowed for employees. Their requests were subjected to a special, more lengthy review.

To effect controls on the need to know, it would appear that a consolidated data dictionary—cross-referencing different data types and the personnel with access to each type—would be a prerequisite; otherwise, it would be impossible to say exactly who could access any particular customer data element. However, it did not appear that such a dictionary existed at the banks or insurance companies.[41] Interviewer requests to "tell me the types of people who can see each type of data" usually left interviewees in a state of confusion and frustration. While access to particular applications could be ascertained through access control records in the computer, only the programmers of each application seemed to know which data elements were accessed by the applications. This problem was acknowledged by an I/S executive at Bank B, who said the matter "deserved attention, which it will get in the near future." The implication of this situation is clear: if one cannot create a list of which employees can see which data elements, one is hard-pressed to control such access.

Once the information was printed in hard-copy form or transmitted verbally, the controls became even more muddied. Access controls for hard-copy and oral information were seldom documented in any depth except at MIB. Rudimentary documentation was observed in two instances: a brief reference in an employee "Code of Ethics" at Bank A, and a reference in HealthIns B's omnibus policy.[42] There were usually some procedures within a particular work unit (such as "Keep a list of the files you remove"), but these were far less stringent than those for computerized information. The application of the procedures varied, with banks being the most lenient on access rights and HealthIns B (and MIB, of course) being the most conservative.

In general, the official sites in the study exhibited much variance between policy and practice. One problem that cut across both banks and insurance companies dealt with the security of hard-copy printouts containing sensitive customer information. While a great amount of policy attention had been given to the computerized information itself, the handling of the information once it was printed out was often overlooked. The following comment from a banker was typical:

> It's really funny that so much money and effort is spent in securing the computer systems, when printouts that have [financial] information on them are lying all over the place. In fact, we have no secure way to dispose of them.

A printout sat on my credenza for thirty days because I didn't know of a safe way to get rid of it. Finally, I put it in a wastebasket next to the coffeemaker, because I knew that people would throw used coffee grounds on it. I figured that it would be so messy that nobody would bother to pick it up.

This issue was mentioned several times as a write-in comment on the surveys in answer to the question, "In what areas do . . . mismatches between official policies and actual practices/operations occur?" Answers included "discarding of sensitive reports," "shredding information versus throwing in trash," "improper destruction of customer information after it is used," and "the handling of printed reports and hard copies." One survey respondent felt that some employees did not exercise good judgment with respect to information access: "Patient and employee medical [records] should not be used for personal reading sources."

In addition to issues of disposal, several interviewees indicated some discomfort with the fact that sensitive customer information was kept in unlocked files in areas that could be accessed by many individuals. This concern seemed to be particularly strong in insurance underwriting areas; however, one mediating factor was described as "[a] complex filing system that makes finding a particular file a challenge for people who are not familiar with the system." On the other hand, some interviewees revealed unwarranted confidence in the physical security of their work areas. One executive claimed that the work unit had "carefully controlled access." However, I was able to walk into the work area and remain there for over five minutes without being challenged or asked for any identification.

Consistent with the qualitative findings from the study, survey respondents noted their concerns about access to personal information. When asked about the areas in which policies and practices were at variance in their company, reasonably large percentages of respondents checked "who can access the databases" as a problem area: Bank A, 31.6 percent; CredCard, 34.7 percent; HealthIns B, 44.4 percent; and LifeIns, 31.8 percent (see Table 4.2). Clearly, the employees were not convinced that their companies were controlling access appropriately, even if official policies were in place.

Even more disconcerting, though, was the policy/practice gap regarding handling of information in the office, also indicated in Table 4.2. Directly related to access issues, this area caused the greatest uneasiness for the survey respondents, with over 50 percent of the respondents at some sites calling "how people handle information in the office" a policy/practice gap concern. Many concerns about access were raised by I/S interviewees. One said, "I wonder sometimes who is setting the *policies* about this information. I know that we have the data security people doing paperwork. That's fine, but who's deciding on the policies that undergird that? I have a scary feeling the answer is, 'Nobody.'"

Disjointed Policies

Finally, one might ask whether an organization has an official, cohesive, omnibus policy encompassing all the areas of privacy concern or, alternatively, whether each piece of the privacy policy is viewed as a discrete and disconnected entity. While the literature is rather silent on this requirement,[43] consumer advocates, consumers in focus groups, and some corporate employees expressed a desire for such a policy statement. These comments were common: "A company should be able to give you a document that explains all its privacy policies." "All the policies should be consistent, and you should be able to understand all of them as a unit." Thus, a final societal expectation might be that companies have a single, omnibus privacy policy covering all the territory from the other policy areas.

At the Sites

Except at MIB, no omnibus privacy policy was observed in its most pristine form. However, the insurance companies had created and distributed omnibus policies of moderate depth and comprehension. While these policies were not all-inclusive or up-to-date (e.g., HealthIns B's dated from 1983 and was in need of update), their objective was consistent with the omnibus approach.

An even more interesting facet of this issue is how all the organizations had struggled to some degree with the *communication* of their privacy policies. Since they were not very precise, banks' policy statements were quite problematic in this regard. Far from being omnibus statements, the banks' policies consisted of separate fragments tailored to specific situations. For example, Bank B had recently conducted a "file transfer task force" to determine the appropriate controls for PCs and LANs. The study resulted in a set of policies, which were being documented for distribution to users.

Omnibus policy statements, to the extent that banks used them at all, were at such a high and vague level that they did not merit the label of "official." In addition, such statements were usually included in other documents. Bank A had distributed a Code of Ethics to its employees; one section addressed "Confidential Information." Bank B had the following clause in its Business Conduct Policy Statement, which employees were to sign: "Confidential information about the bank and its customers, prospective customers and suppliers is to be used solely for the bank's purposes and is under no circumstances to be revealed to others, except as required by law. Employees must be careful not to disclose confidential information unintentionally by indiscreet conversation (for instance, on elevators or radio telephone) or careless handling of sensitive documents." Each year Bank C required its officers to sign a nondisclosure statement that included clauses relating to confidential information. Nonofficers were not required to sign such statements, but a Bank C executive noted that "it wouldn't be a bad idea to require it."

Probably because of this passive approach to overall documentation of the policies, the written surveys revealed a number of concerns regarding the communication of policies at Bank A. Employees wrote:

- "The policies are unclear. I believe there are policies, [but] I am uncertain as to how they are implemented [and] monitored."

- "Policies are not documented well."

- "Official policy is not well known."

- "Policy on handling of customer information [is] probably not well known."

In contrast to the banks, the insurance companies had written omnibus policy statements regarding the use and sharing of information. Because of these broad statements, their communication of the policies had been much smoother than at the banks, if not without some glitches. The policies were usually distributed to managers and were communicated to employees through department meetings and memoranda. During new employee orientation, employees received education regarding confidentiality; at HealthIns B, employees viewed a videotape on the subject. In addition, all of the insurance organizations had occasional updates to remind employees of the policies. The frequency varied: in some groups, bimonthly meetings were common, but others referred to having meetings "at least once a year."

The insurance companies did not require their employees to sign statements agreeing to the confidentiality policy; however, one executive noted that such a discussion was "on the table" at the time of the study. When suspected violations of policy did occur, most executives chose to handle them on an individual basis. The following comment was typical: "Very rarely (say, twice in ten years), we have had to counsel an employee about confidentiality. We have done that in private discussions, and we have warned them that breaches of the policy can result in dismissal. That should not be a surprise, however, since that is covered in all our meetings." Often, allegations of confidentiality breaches were found to be groundless. A utilization review executive said, "On a couple of occasions, doctors have alleged that some of our nurses have revealed information about patients to other doctors. Upon further investigation, we found that this really did not happen. In truth, the doctors simply resented being managed by our program, and this was their method of striking back."

At the time of the study, CredCard was in the process of creating a privacy policy. One of the issues confronting the organization was, in fact, how the policy should be communicated after it was codified. Should it be made available to cardholders, or should it be considered an internal document? The vice president in charge of the policy-making effort explained: "The question then will [eventually] become: how do you disseminate such a policy? Do you put it on the walls at headquarters, or do you insert it into the customers' statements? We haven't done that with policies in the past, but it might be something to think about."

Summary: Policies and Practices

One can conclude that, with respect to the corporations in the three industries in the study, the formality of policies varied, as seen in Figure 4.4. Positions on the scale in this figure were determined in a subjective manner by examining the mix of explicit and implicit policies at each site (see Table 4.1). In making this determination, explicit policies were considered to be more formal than implicit policies. Insurance companies, which handle medical information, had the most formal policies, and banks, which handle financial information, had the least formal.

In addition, employees at the insurance companies seemed to report more variances between policy and practice in two important areas: information handling in the office and sharing of information with others (see Table 4.2). While this response could conceivably reflect looser information-handling practices at the insurance companies, such an assessment contradicts the qualitative findings from the study. In fact, interviews, archival documents, and direct observation by the researcher all revealed that controls were tighter at the insurance companies. A better explanation for this difference seems to be a higher sensitivity regarding the type of information being handled in the corporate environment. Medical information, which is handled by the insurance companies, is apparently perceived as being of a higher sensitivity and deserving of better protection than the financial information and purchase histories handled at the other sites. Survey respon-

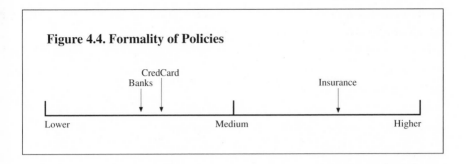

Figure 4.4. Formality of Policies

dents likely answered the questions in light of the information being handled in their own offices, and expectations for handling medical information might well have been higher than those for, say, financial information. While other factors could also be at play (for example, the banks had not yet perceived an external threat), the body of evidence on the whole suggests a relationship between information type and privacy approaches. Note, however, that the hierarchy of such information types, if it exists, has never been empirically investigated. This promising area for future research will be discussed in chapter 7. On a similar note, the formality of the policies appears to be correlated with the type of information being considered: medical information (insurance) has been addressed with more formal policies than has financial information and/or purchase information (banks, CredCard).

Furthermore, based on the findings shown in Table 4.1, one can conclude that there is a perceived hierarchy in terms of the offensiveness of certain information practices. The formality of policies was higher for the sharing issue than for the collection and new use issues. Similarly, policies regarding deliberate errors were more formal than those regarding accidental errors. This hierarchy is quite interesting, for it is consistent with the perceptions of the survey respondents, who were employees of the companies studied. At a significance level of .01, those respondents reported that their levels of concern were greater for sharing uses of information than for new use and collection. In addition, also at a significance level of .01, they reported a higher level of concern regarding deliberate errors than accidental ones (see Table 4.3.) Of course, these survey items represent only a rudimentary and exploratory attempt to capture a set of fairly complex perceptions. Even so, the consistency between corporate policies and employee concerns is comforting, for it shows that—at least in one respect—the managerial response is consistent with the mind-set of individuals in the organization.

Perhaps the most troubling finding is the persistent policy-practice gap. Cer-

Table 4.3. Employee Perceptions

Site	Mean: Collection	Mean: New use	Mean: Sharing	Mean: Deliberate errors
Bank A	5.376	5.167	6.195	5.900
CredCard	5.696	5.530	6.104	6.167
HealthIns	5.746	5.777	6.422	6.214
LifeIns	5.903	5.581	6.290	6.339

Note: Survey item I-5a measured the concern toward collection; I-5b toward new use; I-5c toward sharing; I-5d toward deliberate errors; and I-5e toward accidental errors. All responses are on a scale of 1 to 7, with 1 representing "not concerned at all" and 7 "very concerned." T-tests here reflect an analysis of research propositions that predicted a higher

tainly, direct observation at several sites and interview data yielded much qualitative data to support the existence of such a gap. Most telling, however, may be the results of the written survey, in which employees had a totally anonymous vehicle for expressing their concerns. One of the written survey items read: "Sometimes, the way that sensitive information is actually handled in a company does not match the company's official policies. In your opinion, how well do the *actual practices and operations* in your company match the official policies regarding handling of sensitive information about your [clients]?" With a value of 7 representing "match very well" and 1 representing "match very poorly," the mean response was 4.79 (with no significant differences across sites). This number indicates a moderate amount of concern regarding corporate practices. But an even greater worry is that, in several categories of Table 4.2 (who can access databases, error detection and correction, how people handle information in the office, and how information is shared with others), quite large percentages of the survey respondents indicated concern regarding the policy/practice gap.

Problems in the Snapshot

In this chapter, we have considered the information-handling policies and practices of seven organizations. This overview served as only a "snapshot," of course, and did not reflect the long-term story. Even so, the snapshot revealed troubling matters: nonexistent policies in important areas and a persistent policy/

Mean: Accidental errors	t-value: Sharing vs. collection	t-value: Sharing vs. new use	t-value: Deliberate vs. accidental
5.386	8.57[a]	9.64[a]	6.34[a]
5.658	3.22[a]	5.07[a]	4.68[a]
5.694	10.25[a]	9.60[a]	6.84[a]
5.758	2.50[a]	4.44[a]	3.70[a]

level of concern regarding sharing than either new use or collection and a higher level of concern regarding deliberate errors than accidental errors. Significance at the .01 level (one-tailed tests) is denoted by [a].

practice gap. Why do these conditions exist? Clearly, the reactive nature of the policy development process (drift–external threat–reaction) contributes to an environment in which ambiguity is allowed to thrive. A function of that ambiguity is a deep split between corporate managers' and others' thinking with respect to information privacy in specific application areas. Those competing views are the subject of chapter 5.

Chapter 5

Different Sides of the Issues

The reactive privacy policy-making cycle of drift–external threat–reaction leaves much room for debate between corporate executives and other stakeholders—who often have quite different agendas—regarding appropriate and inappropriate uses of personal information. In chapter 4 we saw that many internal privacy policies in the corporate environment are inadequate and that even where policies do exist, they are often at odds with the actual practices in the corporation. To a great degree, much of this corporate environment is hidden from the outside world, with consumers and other stakeholders having only a vague idea of what goes on inside. Therefore, until an external crisis makes the corporate policies and practices public, corporate executives resort to incrementalist approaches to policy formulation. Because the policy-making environment is riddled with ambiguity and filled with arguments from different camps, incrementalism often appears a prudent approach. In the short term, it seems, one would be foolish to confront these debates unless one had to. By keeping corporate activities from being evaluated in the light of consumer, media, and legislative scrutiny, executives can work through the information privacy concerns in their own way and with their own time frame. In fact, sometimes for lengthy periods, they can even avoid some of the major discussions.

Since corporate activities are, by and large, hidden from those on the "outside," the debate does not normally see the light of day—that is, until the crisis hits: a flurry of media attention, some legislative scrutiny. Then executives pay the price. They must react, sometimes in painful ways, to the external scrutiny. As the issue of information privacy is becoming a more prominent topic for discussion on the American media and political agendas, the crises will come with greater regularity. Thus, the typical policy-making process, a drift–external threat–reaction cycle, is not a healthy one for corporations for the long term.

One need spend only a small amount of time comparing the statements of privacy advocates and corporate spokespersons in the public media to conclude that there definitely is some disparity in views. Debates are constant and, at times, vitriolic. At the bottom of many of these debates are trade-offs: individuals' privacy gets exchanged for various personal and societal goods. Many of the arguments between privacy advocates and corporations stem from some (often implicit) assumptions about this trade-off. In addition, these debates often involve various implied theories about corporate responsibility. The difficulty with most of these arguments is that the assumptions are, in fact, implied rather than stated explicitly. So when the external scrutiny eventually comes—as it undoubtedly will in the near future—executives and lawmakers may well brace themselves for some heated dialogue and a clamoring for new regulation and legislation.

To best evaluate the possible problems in the coming debates, this chapter considers the following question: if they were informed about the actual corporate policies and practices, would the other stakeholders be happy about those policies and practices? Or, alternatively, would they craft arguments about personal information that differed from those of the corporate players? To some degree, the noncorporate stakeholders hold many views that the employees of the corporation, in some of their most intense times of emotional dissonance and role conflict, also describe. (This chapter considers only their comments in their corporate roles.) But the noncorporate stakeholders experience little of this emotional dissonance. Instead, as they learn more and more about the corporate policies and practices, they simply become angry. This bodes poorly for executives who have in the past relied on secrecy as a defense against a societal privacy reaction. When the media removes that cover of secrecy in the next few years, the stakeholder anger will be waiting.

Dissecting arguments about uses of information requires a framework. Whether made by an individual or a corporation, value-laden policy decisions must take in some mix of ingredients and must evaluate the position of relevant stakeholders; and decisions regarding privacy matters certainly fit in the "value-laden" category. What is that mix of ingredients? Ralph Potter has developed a mechanism known as "Potter's Box" for evaluating such policy decisions. It comprises the following four ingredients for a policy decision:[1]

1. Empirical definition of the situation: a series of judgments concerning facts and potentially falsifiable predictions concerning the outcomes of alternative courses of action. The empirical definitions will not always be viewed the same way by all participants.

2. Primary commitment. Either consciously or unconsciously, decisions are made in light of a primary object of concern. Expressive symbols are used for centers of value, loci of commitment, or sources of identity. In a corporate context, this could be seen as a commitment to shareholders' returns, to the management team's own welfare, to the customer base, to the industry, etc.

3. Mode of ethical reasoning. What constitutes a good reason for choosing one course or another? What factors are to be taken into consideration? What priority and weight is to be given to each?

4. Underlying assumptions. In a corporate context, these might include assumptions about the appropriate roles of business and government, etc. Assumptions regarding the purpose and use of information are common in privacy decisions.

The four elements can be either explicit or implicit in the decision process. Potter claims that the elements are independently variable and that you cannot predict the final decision without knowledge of all four.[2]

An evaluation of each of these items reveals some insight into the arguments from the different sides of the issue.

Empirical Definition

One might think that, even though the other ingredients in a policy decision would be susceptible to argument, at least the *facts*—seemingly subject to empirical verification—would lend themselves to agreement. This assumption is not always true in information privacy debates, however. Clearly, one can represent a set of facts differently depending on one's perspective and interpretation; the "facts of the matter" are subject to much disagreement.

In no situation was this divergence in perception of empirical facts more evident than in the dispute between Neil Day, president of MIB, and Josh Kratka of the Massachusetts Public Interest Research Group (MassPIRG). Since its very charter stated the group's basic aim of sharing medical information between insurance companies, MIB was often attacked by consumer advocates, who claimed that its information was erroneous as well as misused in the underwriting process. Many questioned the very existence of a database that contained medical information and was shared by insurance companies. Kratka's recent report, titled "For Their Eyes Only," called for more stringent regulation of MIB activities. In an interview, he questioned the very existence of MIB: "What right do they have to share information with other insurance companies? There are laws against fraud, so I don't understand the need for the service; remedies are available if people lie on their applications. The information they are sharing is enormously powerful. Even though the application forms reference MIB, most people don't know what MIB is or don't really read the statement." The report called several MIB practices into question and was instrumental in prodding Massachusetts legislators to tighten some insurance-related privacy laws.[3] Excerpts are quoted in Figure 5.1. Figure 5.2 contains excerpts from a letter in which Neil Day responded to some of the criticisms of MIB from MassPIRG and other groups. While the letter was written to Act Up (the "AIDS Coalition to Unleash Power"), an activist group that had been quite critical of MIB, it was also sent to Mass-PIRG.

In this dispute it is interesting to note that although there are some differences in primary commitment on the parts of the two parties (e.g., consumer privacy versus efficient insurance underwriting) and in underlying assumptions (e.g., trustworthiness of corporate entities, the size of the fraud threat), a great part of the debate between Day and Kratka is over empirical facts. How much inaccuracy does exist in MIB? The two observers quote statistics about error rates differently: Day states that only 150 of 10,000 reports that consumers request are disputed,[4] while Kratka maligns MIB's records as inaccurate by noting that "a quarter to one-third" of medical records used in insurance underwriting are inaccurate.[5] How often are MIB records used as the sole source of information in underwriting, in violation of MIB guidelines? Kratka quotes a figure of 15,000 annual violations (a 1975 number), but Day disputes this figure with the observation, apparently more current, that "insurers will not decline an application (or increase charges) based solely on MIB codes." Is inappropriate access to MIB records really a problem? Kratka's report does not confront MIB directly on that charge with any empirical data, but it does include a section entitled "Unauthorized Disclosure of Personal Information," which contains several related horror stories and seems to infer that this problem could involve MIB. But Day, in an MIB document, states, "No legislator, regulator, or other public representative has documented or even alleged wrongful disclosure of an MIB record."[6]

Another empirical fact in dispute relates to the level of informed consent given to MIB by those applying for insurance. Kratka argues that most individuals do not know what MIB is; he uses the fact that only one-tenth of one percent of the individuals who have MIB files request disclosure each year as evidence of consumer ignorance.[7] Yet Day is right when he says that every individual whose information appears in the MIB database has, in fact, consented to having his or her information shared in this way. Each life insurance application form used by MIB's member companies includes the reasonably clear disclosure statement shown in Figure 5.3.

While some, like Kratka, dispute whether the MIB concept is legitimate and whether individuals truly understand the statement they are signing, it is clear that MIB's existence does not in itself constitute a "sharing" violation of privacy. However, one apparently valid criticism is that signing the statement may not truly be voluntary, at least if individuals want to receive life insurance. Yet it is common to hear privacy advocates boast of striking out the MIB disclosure language on life insurance applications and still being approved for a policy. Several computer "bulletin boards" for privacy advocates have included notes to this effect from various individuals. One of the industry observers in this study—an executive at one of LifeIns's competitors—agreed that this scenario might be a plausible one at some insurance companies. This study did not determine how often insurance policies are processed without MIB records being filed. But it does appear, at least if this suggestive evidence is any indication, that there may be some ambiguity regarding the "voluntary" nature of the MIB disclosure statement.

For the record, however, the consumers interviewed in this study did reveal a large amount of ignorance with respect to MIB. Only one consumer in the sample was aware of the existence of MIB, even though all but two of the consumers had applied for life insurance and had gone through an underwriting process. One can only conclude that the consumers had not read the insurance application forms very carefully, since the MIB notification was surely included. However, this lack of awareness may also point to some inadequacies in the notification procedure.

Thus, we see that in the case of MIB and one of its most vocal critics, much of the argument revolves around empirical facts. While it appears that one should be able to easily determine the validity of each party's claims, this evaluation is often difficult in privacy arguments. Each side is presenting its facts on its own terms, so the debate sometimes appears to compare apples with oranges. For example, which is a better indicator of MIB files' accuracy: Kratka's general assertions

Figure 5.1. Excerpts from "For Their Eyes Only"

Insurance companies collect and analyze the medical histories . . . of millions of Americans each year. National databanks then share this highly personal information through a vast, computerized information network. The decisions made on the basis of the network's information are often critical, affecting consumers' ability to obtain insurance, qualify for credit, and advance in employment.

The free flow of information via national databanks guarantees that an error will be repeated many times over, as every report to another institution magnified its impact and makes correction increasingly difficult.

The most prominent repository of medical information is [MIB]. . . . The system is simple, but dangerous. . . . The problems this system creates are serious, and include: storage and disclosure of inaccurate or incomplete information; inadequate provisions for consumer access; and improper use of MIB data by insurers.

Since the MIB does not investigate, the information it provides to its eight hundred member insurance companies is only as accurate as the information reported to it.

MIB will grant consumers access to their MIB file—but only by having a copy sent to a physician, which can be a burdensome, time-consuming, and frequently unworkable procedure. To begin with, this right of access is often illusory, since few consumers even know MIB exists. Of the twelve million people whose medical histories are maintained in the MIB computer, fewer than one-tenth of one percent request disclosure each year.

Secondly, as former Massachusetts Insurance Commission Roger Singer explains, when consumers try to find out what information is in a file, they may spend substantial time and effort for nothing. "Often by the time an applicant is aware of the information, it has already been entered in the MIB's databanks and is being distributed to other companies." . . .

This state of affairs is particularly galling because the computerized codes in MIB files are not medical records in the true sense of that phrase. They are no longer within the medical community; they are handled and seen by lay persons, not medical professionals. They are information summaries, used not for medical purposes but for purposes of underwriting and claims payment.

[MIB rules state] that an MIB report cannot be used, by itself, to make an adverse underwriting decision. MIB information is by its nature very incomplete and occasionally unreliable, since it consists merely of a list of code numbers without explanation of individual circumstances. An MIB report is intended only to alert an insurer to the possible need for further investigation. No application is supposed to be rated, declined, or restricted solely by reliance on MIB reports.

In practice, however, many insurers may in fact rely on MIB information to deny coverage summarily or to increase premium rates with no further investigation. . . . MIB's own 1975 investigation suggested that as many as 15,000 violations of [this rule] occurred in that year alone. Since an applicant often knows little or nothing about the dissemination of his or her personal information to other insurance companies, the application may be rejected by a number of insurers based on what could be the same false report, held in the MIB files, without the applicant's ever knowing that this is occurring.

While MIB contends that this problem has been rectified through greater oversight, it nonetheless still relies primarily on insurance company self-policing for enforcement.

Insurers also use subjective and unreliable information as the basis for underwriting decisions. MIB, for example, continues to have codes for nonmedical information among its two hundred codes for various conditions, a subject of even greater abuse in the past. Nonmedical codes now include "poor driving," "dangerous sports," and similar activities. In addition, MIB classifies "sexual deviation" and "unhealthy appearance" as medical codes.

These codes are particularly dangerous to privacy.

Source: Josh Kratka, *For Their Eyes Only: The Insurance Industry and Consumer Privacy* (Boston: Massachusetts Public Interest Research Group [MassPIRG], April 1990.

Figure 5.2. Response from MIB

On October 9, 1990, Neil Day, president of MIB, wrote a letter to Act Up responding to charges levied by Act Up and MassPIRG. He told me in a letter that he had also sent a copy of this response to Josh Kratka at MassPIRG; he went on to state, "Both groups subscribe to very inaccurate facts and judgments about MIB and insurance." Mr. Day provided me with a copy of his October 9 letter, excerpts from which appear below.

You state that MIB collects information on so-called sexual deviation. The truth is that this practice was discontinued in 1974 when insurers updated their underwriting methods.

You state that MIB means higher premiums. Wrong again. The effect of the MIB system is to lower premiums by reducing losses due to fraud or omission of relevant information by some applicants for life, health, or disability insurance.

You state that the purpose of MIB is to deny coverage. Wrong some more; if the brief codes in the MIB report are not consistent with the application, then the insurer must seek further information about the applicant. Insurers will not decline an application (or increase charges) based solely on MIB codes.

You imply that MIB codes are not very accurate. I challenge this judgment. Last year, twenty thousand consumers asked to see their MIB records. About ten thousand had records, and only 150 ultimately challenged accuracy. This is one example of how MIB meets high standards of accuracy.

about medical records (which do not result from a direct audit of the MIB database), or Day's specific statements about the percentage that are challenged after being reviewed (a self-selected subsample of a self-selected sample)?

But perhaps the most troubling thing revealed in the MIB arguments and this study's consumer interviews is that consumers who have signed insurance applications are not, in general, aware of the MIB database. This is but a symptom of a larger problem, however: this study showed that, in general, consumers are not

You state that MIB hides in obscurity. I say that each applicant receives a written notice describing MIB before her/his application is completed; that notice describes the MIB purpose and gives phone and mail addresses needed to request an MIB record. In addition, MIB promptly and candidly replies to inquiries from legislators, regulators, the media and other public representatives. I challenge your judgment that MIB hides.

You state that there are not restrictions on information reported to MIB. Wrong. The truth is that only information significant to insurability is reported to MIB by insurance companies. MIB does not share credit reports, and MIB reports are not available to employers. I would add that MIB activities have been extensively reviewed and validated by legislators, regulators, and other public representatives.

Groups such as Act Up and MassPIRG want to know the meaning of every code used by insurers to report to MIB. Insurance experts are confident that the two hundred codes now in the MIB system are appropriate and relevant for use to detect and deter fraud, which is the MIB function. MIB has and will make this list available to regulators who have medical and insurance expertise to properly review the MIB system of general codes.

Act Up should get its facts straight and then join the many groups who are actively working for much better delivery of health care through private sector and public sector programs.

---

at all aware of the facts regarding privacy in industries with which they deal on a regular basis. This problem extends beyond the domain of life insurance and into several other areas. Consider the following from the industries in the study:

• Consumers did not realize that the life insurance underwriting process might include an investigation by a private agency or the ordering of a credit report (legal under the FCRA as a "permissible use" of a credit report).

Figure 5.3. Sample MIB Disclosure Statement

As part of the application process, the consumer receives a written notice, which is reproduced below almost in whole:

> Information regarding your insurability will be treated as confiden-
> tial. [Insurance company], or its reinsurer(s), may, however, make a
> brief report thereon to the Medical Information Bureau, a nonprof-
> it membership organization of life insurance companies, which op-
> erates an information exchange on behalf of its members. If you
> apply to another Bureau member company for life or health insur-
> ance coverage, or a claim for benefits is submitted to such a com-
> pany, the Bureau upon request will supply such company with the
> information in its file. Upon receipt of a request from you, the Bu-
> reau will arrange disclosure of any information it may have in your
> file. (Medical information will be disclosed only to your attending
> physician.) If you question the accuracy of information in the Bu-
> reau's file, you may contact the Bureau and seek a correction in
> accordance with the procedure set forth in the Federal Fair Credit
> Reporting Act. The address of the Bureau's information office is
> [address]. [Insurance company], or its reinsurer(s), may also re-
> lease information in its file to other life insurance companies to
> whom you apply for life or health insurance, or to whom a claim for
> benefits may be submitted.

• Consumers were unaware of the extent to which health insurance companies
  shared information regarding employees' health claims with their employers. Most believed that the information on the claims was completely confidential and was never revealed to the employers in any form. While the
  health insurers' policies on this matter differed somewhat, the consumers'
  perceptions are nevertheless incorrect.

• Few consumers realized how much more medical information their health
  insurers are now demanding in their utilization review processes. Most
  clung to a now-outdated understanding of health insurance that viewed a
  health claim form as the full input to the health claims process.

- None of the consumers were aware that credit card issuers sometimes use information about their purchase transactions to place cardholders in psychographic categories. About half the consumers expressed a vague awareness of credit card issuers' "trading names and phone numbers with other companies," in the words of one interviewee,[8] but none were aware of the processes underlying the profiling. None of the consumers were fully aware of the more general concept of psychographics or how they are used in marketing, although two understood some of the concepts.

- Only one of the consumers realized that banks sometimes use information from loan applications to target their marketing activities. Only one of the consumers knew that banks' platform automation systems sometimes allow employees to input identifying customer information, such as number of children. None of the consumers were aware of banks' ability to purchase additional information about customers from an outside vendor. And, in fact, only one of the consumers seemed to understand the broader market for consumer-targeting information—of which the banks' vendor's offering was only a small part—and the various databases involved in that market.

Thus, the focus groups often turned into an educational experience for the consumers. The consumer stakeholder interviews began with some general questions about privacy in today's society. Then, through the course of the discussion, consumers were asked about a number of policies and practices in the various industries. It quickly became apparent that most of the interviewees were not aware of how information was being used.

As they learned more about the various policies and practices, many consumers became angry. For example, one focus group participant began the discussion by noting that she "didn't think privacy was a big issue." By the end of the discussion, some ninety minutes later, she stated that she was ready to "become a consumer advocate." Several times during the discussion, she became quite agitated, her face reddened, and she raised her voice, saying things like, "I can't believe they're doing that with our information! I never knew it!" Other interviewees left with a resolve to talk with their bankers about their uses of information. One stated that he was "going to go home and look at an insurance application to see about that MBI [sic] statement." Two members of one group stated that they were going to write their senators, although they were rather vague as to what they were going to say.

But probably the most overt reaction to the information came from an interviewee in Winston-Salem, North Carolina. She said:

I probably won't have the guts to go through with this, but it makes me want to just cut up all my credit cards and quit buying anything that anybody can trace to me. I'll pay all my bills in cash and become a hermit. [Interviewer: You seemed upset about the medical records. What about that part?] I'm not sure. I have to use my insurance when I go to the doctor. It makes me want to just pay for most of my medical stuff myself to keep it from being record-ed [in a database].[9]

The reader should not infer that all the consumers interviewed exhibited such a strong response to the corporate policies and practices. Two of the interviewees, for example, seemed to be unfazed by what they learned in the discussion and ex-hibited no greater concern for privacy after the discussion than before. It should also be noted that the information about corporate policies and practices was not presented to the consumers in a prejudicial or "gee, ain't it awful" manner. In-stead, the information was put forth with a balanced approach that highlighted benefits as well as risks. Even so, the average interviewee's concern for privacy seemed to increase somewhat during the discussion. Furthermore, it appeared that focus group members reinforced each others' growing privacy concerns. Once a particular group member became enraged by a particular policy or prac-tice (for example, a bank's buying additional information about its customers), he or she was usually able to convince other members that the practice was offen-sive, even if they had not originally perceived it that way. Occasionally, another member was able to dampen the emotion by presenting a "voice of reason" argu-ment to the group (e.g., "Can't you see that this kind of program keeps the prices down?"), but the general rule was this: once the consumer became angry, the con-sumer stayed angry.

These findings stand as a stark reminder to industries handling sensitive per-sonal information: if policies and practices are deemed offensive by consumers, simply providing consumer education about existing policies and practices may be a counterproductive endeavor. Many executives, especially those who are en-gaged in targeted marketing activities, fall into an "education trap," in which they argue that consumers do not understand their activities and would be more sym-pathetic if they did. This problem will receive additional attention in chapter 7, which will describe some recommendations for improving this environment. Consumers certainly deserve to understand the facts of the industries with which they deal. However, before embarking on an educational campaign, executives must first ensure that their policies and practices can withstand the scrutiny of outsiders.

Primary Commitment

Every organization and individual embraces some sort of stated or unstated commitment when arguing. As the second component of Potter's Box, these commitments also explain much of the diversity in opinions on the different sides of the question. In this study, the executives' primary commitments were to profitability and the law,[10] but these commitments were sometimes defined through indirect concepts such as "protecting the customer base." The other stakeholders rarely felt any commitment to corporate profitability, however; in fact, only one interviewee—whose father had been an insurance company executive—noted any concern for the corporations' profitability, viability, and well-being. Instead, the interviewees' implied commitment was to consumers' rights and, since it was clearly the focus of the discussions, to consumers' privacy. A representative exchange with a consumer follows:

> They should not be able to do that [referring to a policy under discussion] because it puts us [consumers] in a bad position. We should say how that information is to be used. [Interviewer: Wouldn't their policy lead to a win-win situation, where both the company and the consumer got something they needed . . . the consumer would get a good or service that was targeted to them, and the company would increase their profits?] As a consumer, it doesn't really matter to me if they make money or not. And I don't want their product if that's the way they sell it.

While this interviewee exhibits some ignorance of the economic system, it is nevertheless instructive to consider this attitude as representative of those facing many executives. It is unsafe to assume that consumers understand the importance of corporate profits, particularly when they perceive that those profits are coming at the expense of any concept they personally find important—like their own privacy. The concept that corporate health is linked to societal well-being or employee job security is somewhat foreign to many consumers. Instead, these consumers seem to evaluate corporate efforts in selfish ways: what will the corporation give me, and what will they take from me? For example, this study's consumer interviews revealed that many consumers, once fully informed about the corporate policies and practices, are quite unwilling to give up much information about themselves if the only benefits they receive are additional offers of products and services. An analysis of the consumer interviewees' comments suggests that by the end of the interviews, twelve of the eighteen interviewees (67 percent) fell into this category.

This finding is somewhat similar, though not identical, to Alan Westin's results from a recent public opinion poll, in which he determined that Americans could be grouped into three different categories with respect to privacy: "Fundamentalists," who favor new privacy laws and who generally choose privacy controls over consumer-service benefits when they compete with each other; "Pragmatists," who weigh the benefits of various opportunities and services against the degree of intrusiveness of the information sought and who believe that business organizations should "earn" their trust rather than assume they have it automatically; and the "Unconcerned," who do not favor any additional privacy laws and who are generally trustful of organizations collecting their personal information. According to Westin, Fundamentalists comprise 25 percent of the population; Pragmatists, 57 percent; and the Unconcerned, 18 percent. Westin noted that the Pragmatists were the most dynamic group with respect to public opinions. If they are unconvinced that their privacy is being protected properly, they act like Fundamentalists, creating a 75–80 percent majority in favor of regulation. On the other hand, if the Pragmatists are convinced that Fair Information Practices are being followed, they act more like the Unconcerned and accept voluntary action by corporations.[11]

In this study's sample of consumers—admittedly much smaller than Westin's and drawn with far less randomness—only two individuals (11 percent) could be reasonably viewed as Unconcerned, and only three (17 percent) as Fundamentalists, *prior to* the focus group discussions. Thus, one could argue that thirteen (72 percent) of the sample were Pragmatists before the discussions began. However, by the end of the discussions, nine of these thirteen were exhibiting opinions that were better classified as Fundamentalist. Furthermore, and perhaps more interesting, no amount of coaxing from the interviewer or other focus group members could calm these nouveau Fundamentalists down once they reached their apex of emotional concern. It is unclear whether Westin's research examined this somewhat temporal phenomenon, in which Pragmatists seem not only to think like Fundamentalists on particular issues but, over a period of time, to actually *become* Fundamentalists. Of course, this study included only a small amount of follow-up with the consumer interviewees: eight of the eighteen—seven of whom were acting like Fundamentalists by the end of the sessions—were interviewed again by phone two weeks after the initial discussions, and all of those eight were still exhibiting the same attitudes they had at the end of the meeting. Whether those attitudes dampened over time was not tested in this study, but it is possible that, as months pass, one's concern about privacy might decline in the absence of additional horror stories.

In contrast to the consumer stakeholders' commitments, which centered almost exclusively around notions of consumer rights and individuals' privacy, corporate commitments sorted into two very different categories: profitability and the law. With respect to the first category, executives did not always frame their arguments using "profitability" or related words, although such terminology was used occasionally. Instead, executives commonly referred to profitability indirectly by using phrases such as "a tighter bond with our customers" or "increased efficiency in our marketing." This was especially true when executives discussed uses of customer information for targeted marketing.

The secondary corporate commitment, to the law, encompassed all uses of information: corporate interviewees exhibited a remarkable respect for the legal boundaries around every aspect of their business processes. Although some bank personnel were unsure at times about the legal prohibitions on certain uses of customer information—and at times even asked me whether *I* could tell them about the law—all of them expressed a desire to adhere to the law, and many framed their arguments about policies and practices in terms of their legal prerogatives (e.g., "It's legal for us to buy that information, of course").

Interestingly, the corporate commitment was not only to obeying current laws but also to avoiding new laws. On numerous occasions, corporate interviewees noted that they wanted to temper their actions so that "we don't get a lot of new legislation" or "wind up with some onerous regulations." One high-ranking bank executive said, "If you could tell me which of our current activities would lead to a clamoring for new laws, I'd walk downstairs right now and say, 'Stop that project, it's not worth it!' The last thing we need are a bunch of new privacy regulations on top of the stuff we already have to deal with for [capitalization and real estate guidelines]. I'd give up half of our marketing to avoid having to deal with another OCC-like [entity] picking over everything we do." An insurance executive said, "Probably the smartest thing we could do as a company and an industry is to behave so that the legislators think we are the finest privacy-respecting organizations they have ever seen. I'm not saying that we're doing that today, mind you, but that it would be our smartest move. We should act as though our every move could contribute to a legal backlash."

What the corporate interviewees often missed in looking at present and potential laws, however, was that when it comes to information privacy, adhering to the law is only a *necessary* condition for societal acceptability; it is by no means a *sufficient* condition. The law has not kept up with the technical possibilities, and consumers are applying their own senses of right and wrong, which often go beyond the legal dictates. For example, the bankers in the study often argued that buying information about their customers was acceptable because it was legal. However, consumer stakeholders brushed across the legal questions and added their own analysis:

> Maybe there are companies out there that legally sell this information, but I would be pretty mad if I found out my bank was buying information about me. [Interviewer: Would you move your account?] I'm not sure, but I would certainly complain if I knew they were doing it. [Interviewer: Why?] It doesn't seem like they're respecting me and my business. There have got to be some banks that realize I don't give them my account so that they can go snoop around behind my back. If I can figure out which banks those are, I might move there.

Thus, the commitments of corporate executives—to profitability, to existing law, and to avoiding additional legislation in their industries—differ greatly from those of many other stakeholders.

Mode of Ethical Reasoning

The third ingredient in Potter's Box is the mode of ethical reasoning: what constitutes a good reason for choosing one course or another? What factors are to be taken into consideration? What priority and weight are to be given to each? Philosophical theories offer a clear and distinctive framework for evaluating these arguments: *teleological* (or consequentialist) versus *deontological* (or categorical) thinking. Before turning to the ethical reasoning used by the different parties in this study, we should first consider the differences between teleological and deontological thinking.

So named because it relies on a conception of *telos* (the good), the teleological approach starts with an assumption of what is good. This assumption can vary greatly depending on the observer's viewpoint; some claim that pleasure is the good to be pursued, while others argue that the good should be a relationship with one's community. Furthermore, proponents of various subtheories differ as to how the good should be ethically distributed. The distinguishing feature of teleological theories is that they establish a normative position regarding what is good and what constitutes the "good life." Once one settles on the definition of the good, one can evaluate particular actions as either right or wrong, depending on whether the action increases or decreases the total amount of good from a particular perspective—usually that of an individual or organization. Thus, to define an action as right or wrong requires that one evaluate the consequences of the action to determine the amount of good the action produces; hence, teleological arguments are often called "consequentialist."

Of course, there are many different kinds of consequentialist thinking. One can choose actions with consequences that maximize the good from different perspectives: for example, from the perspective of a single individual (ethical egoism); from the perspective of all human beings affected by the action (utilitarianism); or from the perspective of all living beings, including nonhuman animals (ethical universalism).

At the other end of the spectrum is deontological thinking. Deontological thinking does not define right actions in terms of maximizing a good. Rather, these theories prescribe duties that human beings must fulfill *regardless* of the consequences that flow from their actions. This is the ethical approach commonly associated with claims of "rights," such as a right to property, a right to political equality, or a right to distributive equality. Under deontological theories, something other than the consequences following from an action must be considered before one can ascertain whether the action was right or wrong. Immanuel Kant, one of the best-known deontologists, developed the concept of "categorical" analysis, a label now often applied to deontological arguments.

In this study, many stakeholders exhibited a different mode of ethical reasoning from that displayed by many corporate decision makers. However, the evidence on this item is mixed, since the corporate decision makers were not unanimous in their own approach to such decisions.

In general, executives were far more likely to use consequentialist argumentation than were other stakeholders, who tended to embrace a categorical mode of reasoning. When arguing for or against a particular practice, executives tended to define the validity of the action in terms of its results. Particularly with respect to customer complaints and defections that ultimately translated into profitability reductions, executives argued in an ethically egoistic manner. Occasionally an executive would invoke a utilitarian argument; for example, one bank marketing executive claimed that "targeting consumers directly will eventually lead to a more efficient economy, which benefits everyone," and a health insurance executive defended the sharing of claim information with employers by saying that "the more we can do to make employers aware of these costs, the more they will manage and lower them, which will benefit everybody in society." Sometimes corporate managers would put themselves in the shoes of the individual consumer, but even then they embraced a consequentialist viewpoint, as in this written comment from a corporate survey respondent:

Generally, I think an individual would object to companies' storing and sharing [his or her] private information . . . [especially] if the person has in his [or her] background negative information (e.g., bad credit rating, jail sentence). If a person has a positive background, he [or she] can often profit by companies' sharing this information. Many companies target such items as advance notice of sales, high CD rates, low credit card interest to such individuals.

Over 85 percent of the relevant comments made by corporate interviewees were of a decidedly consequentialist nature. Consumer stakeholders, on the other hand, were much more willing to define particular corporate actions as either right or wrong—regardless of the consequences of those actions. Consumer stakeholders seemed to ground their categorical arguments in a presumed right to privacy, which then allowed them to label particular practices.

This distinction was most visible in interchanges regarding the use of some customer information for marketing purposes. Most consumer stakeholders felt, for example, that the quality and nature of the products being marketed were irrelevant; they simply felt uncomfortable with the fact that the information was being used for what they considered an unintended purpose. This point was confirmed in the consumer interviews by their answers to the following question: would it make any difference if the offering was for a high-quality insurance product or for a pornographic magazine? Most stakeholders claimed that it would not, but when a similar question was put to several corporate interviewees, they claimed that it provided a critical distinction in the debate. Corporate executives often defended the targeting practices by noting that the products offered were always of "high quality." The stakeholders were arguing from a categorical perspective: this use of information is clearly wrong. The executives, in contrast, were arguing in a consequentialist mode: this use of information is wrong if it leads to offers for offensive products; otherwise, it is acceptable.

In addition, executives were more prone to argue in terms of gradations, while the consumers preferred absolutes. A certain use of information might result in "a little loss of privacy" or a "slight intrusion," according to executives. Consumers, on the other hand, viewed information uses in black-and-white terms: this use is right, this use is wrong. One representative interchange will illustrate this distinction. As we saw in chapter 3, a CredCard executive explained that the practice of using transaction information for marketing purposes was not viewed as a major violation of privacy, since the cardholders' purchases were not evaluated by humans. "Only the computer sees it," he noted. "It's not like people are looking at your purchases." He also said, "The process is not very individualized. Only broad categories are used." This distinction was not a convincing one to the stakeholders, however. Without exception, they found the *use* of the information to be the issue; they brushed off as unimportant the distinctions of whether the information was seen by human eyes or was finely honed. The executive director of a consumer advocacy group said, "It is irrelevant whether the scrutiny of the transactions is through automation or is done manually. The issue is that I'm placed on a list at all because of what I have purchased, when I had an expectation of privacy in the transactions." A consumer in a focus group said, "I don't care if they have two categories or two hundred. I don't want them to look at my purchases to put me into categories. Period."

However, broad findings regarding consequentialist and categorical thinking can be somewhat misleading. In fact, some executives—particularly in the insurance industry—*did* embrace categorical argumentation. A LifeIns executive said:

> Sometimes, you just have to do what is right, even if it loses business. That's happened to us several times in deciding on releases of AIDS test information and in dealing with disclosures to agents. You have to keep in mind, though, that we can *afford* to be ethical in this business. It's like in Las Vegas—the house never loses! We know the underwriting statistics, and we know what death rates will be. Unless we do really stupid things, we will make money. So, I can make decisions about what to do with information just because they're the right decisions. If we lose a little business in some particular situations, so what? We won't starve.

Similarly, health insurance executives—especially at HealthIns B—often referred to the "right way to handle sensitive information" and the "special nature of the health care relationship." The consequences of actions were mentioned far less frequently at HealthIns B than at other sites. When they were discussed, it was usually in the context of "the potential for legal action."

In addition, there was a splinter group of consumer stakeholders—two among the study's sample—who fell into the consequentialist mode. Typically, these same individuals believed that total disclosure in society would be a good thing, since "only guilty people need to worry about privacy." When evaluating corporate policies, these individuals often looked to the outcomes of the policies in order to render their opinions. For example, with reference to use of customer information for marketing, one person noted, "It doesn't make any difference to me if they use information like that. The only thing is, I don't think we should get as much junk mail as we do. If their policy is making more junk mail, then it's probably bad."

It is interesting to note the argumentation that surrounds targeted marketing activities. Executives focus almost exclusively on the *ends* or consequences of the process: the mailed or telemarketed offers. If those offers are not in poor taste or excessive in number, the campaign must be an inoffensive one. Most (but not all) consumer stakeholders focus on the *means* through which they were selected for the mailing or telemarketing. If they felt that the method of collection of the information was secretive or deceptive, that the information was being used for a different purpose from that for which it was collected, or that the categorizations were based on faulty inferences (e.g., "Just because I bought one product doesn't mean I'd want a different one and, besides, I'm offended by being categorized, anyway"), consumers would deem an action as categorically wrong, irrespective of the amount of mail or phone calls it generated. This distinction, while not an absolute one, could be an important one for executives to remember. Confusion over ends and means, when wrapped around issues of information privacy, could lead in short order to more external threats.

Assumptions

Now consider the final ingredient in Potter's Box: underlying assumptions being used by the different parties. We might expect that stakeholders would dispute the corporations' assumptions regarding information ownership. However, this issue was seldom quoted as a pivotal factor in the arguments. In fact, a consumer advocate said: "I don't see who *owns* the information as the big issue. Rather, the question is: what's the *expectation of privacy* on the consumer's part when entering into a transaction? Who should be allowed to set this expectation? The consumer!" This advocate's assertion was confirmed by the focus groups and individual consumer interviews. In only a few cases did a stakeholder argue against an action because "the company doesn't own that information." Rather, arguments were most often framed around inherent intrusiveness and the consumer's right to know how information would be used.

Intended Purpose. This item generated much concern among the stakeholders. What is the intended purpose of information that consumers give to corporations in the course of doing business? A bank executive argued that consumers provide information "so that we can serve the customer's needs," and the executive broadened this definition to include the use of the information for targeted marketing.

Consumers often saw this matter in a different way: they believed information was given to the bank to process a *specific transaction*. In fact, they were often flabbergasted to find that the information was being used for any other purpose. In commenting on a new system that would have platform personnel ask new customers some personal questions for the database, one consumer said, "If the banker asked me some of those questions [especially how much I make], I would not tell them unless I was applying for a loan. It's none of their business. . . . [Interviewer: why do you say that?] Because the reason you give them information is so you can get a *specific* [emphasis added] thing you want. They are wrong to say 'Well, if she ever told me for any reason, then I can use the information for anything I want to.' Dead wrong." Another consumer said, "I don't think the banks should use information I give them on a loan application to sell me stuff. The only reason I told them that information [for example, my income] was to get a loan. As for the balances on my accounts, maybe they think they have a right to use that for marketing, but I don't really like that, either."

Similarly, once they understood how the system worked, many stakeholders disagreed with the sharing of medical information through MIB, even though they agreed that it improved the underwriting process and led to reduced insurance rates for many applicants. They claimed that the intended purpose of this information was to enable a single insurance company to make a single underwriting decision, even though the MIB disclosure statement was undoubtedly included in the application.

Some stakeholders also disagreed that intended purposes for health insurance claim information might include reports to employers—even if specific individuals' medical procedures were not disclosed. "They shouldn't even tell the employer how much an individual's charges are in a given month," said Kratka at MassPIRG. Many focus group consumers agreed with this assessment and felt that claim information was only intended for paying claims—not for reporting. Arguments that such reporting helped employers to reduce health care costs were not convincing to most interviewees.

In addition, although most interviewees at CredCard disagreed, most stakeholders maintained that the intended purpose of credit card transaction information was the processing of charges—not the creation of psychographic categories for targeted marketing. One consumer advocate said:

I think there are certain expectations of privacy on the parts of consumers. It's not so much a question of prohibiting certain activities, like credit card issuers' uses of transaction information. Rather, it's a matter of telling the consumer what is going on and giving them the option of participating or not. The consumer should be the one making the decision about this use of information—nobody else. . . . I think that, to the extent that credit card issuers use transaction data, they are creating a potential public relations nightmare when people realize what they're doing. If they want people to think of credit cards as being somewhat equivalent to cash, they are not giving the consumers an even deal.

Several other industry observers agreed that such uses of personal information were in a "gray area."

Consumers interviewed were usually offended to learn that credit card transaction histories were being scrutinized, because their assumptions regarding the intended purpose of the information did not include such scrutiny. This comment was typical: "I knew that the credit card company's computer processed the charges onto my bill, but I thought that was it! I don't think they have any reason to look at what I'm buying, because it's really none of their business."

Voluntarism. One additional area in which corporate and noncorporate stakeholders hold different assumptions is related to the policy-making process itself: when corporations do change their policies in response to a threat, their employees usually assume that they are doing so voluntarily. A CredCard interviewee, for example, referred to their renewed policy-making efforts as being "voluntarily undertaken in response to [a combination of] internal and external forces." Noncorporate interviewees, however, view very few of the corporate policy-making activities as being truly voluntary and instead regard them as being undertaken under duress. A focus group interviewee said, "These companies won't ever change unless they're made to. They won't do anything of their own accord."

With respect to the use of AIDS test results in life insurance underwriting, industry interviewees repeatedly referred to changes that had been made in a "voluntary" manner. An industry observer who participated in some of the task forces said, "In only a few cases were we *required* to make the changes we made. We were concerned about what was being said, and we wanted to *voluntarily* [emphasis added] move to a more acceptable level. Nobody made us do it." But the "voluntary" nature of the responses was questioned by some interviewees. One lawyer who often dealt with gay and lesbian issues replied, "Voluntary? Who are they kidding? If they hadn't changed their approach, they were about twenty minutes away from legislation that would have forced their hand. We weren't about to let them get away with the [information management] scheme they were using. [Interviewer: Do you mean MIB?] I mean *all* of the insurance people who thought they could just decide for themselves to perform tests and create databases that could really hurt people." A gay activist remarked, "You'll never get anywhere with [big corporations] by being nice and hoping they just decide to change. You've got to make noise. They *won't* decide to change on their own. They won't do it voluntarily."

To some degree, the issue may be one of semantics: if a corporation acts in response to an external threat—and none of the corporate interviewees ever really denied that this happened—many consumers are unwilling to ascribe noble intentions to the action and do not really view it as voluntary. Executives, on the other hand, are fond of remarking that their organizations made changes "without being forced to." This attitude may be simply a matter of pride and control: people prefer to feel that they are in charge of situations. But one can reasonably ask, as the advocates and consumers often do, how an action can be classified as voluntary if it was in fact undertaken solely to head off a threat from legislators or regulators.

Although they did not necessarily occur at the sites in the study, some examples from the public press fuel this suspicion. In 1992, American Express reached an agreement with the attorney general of the state of New York: the company agreed to inform its cardholders about the extent to which it was using transaction information in compiling mailing lists that were shared with various service establishments. Although the agreement was clearly reached under pressure from the attorney general, an American Express vice president, James E. Tobin, took great pains to note, in a letter to the *Privacy Times*, that the agreement was "voluntary and reaffirms our role in protecting consumer privacy."[12]

In another set of widely reported cases, the major credit bureaus came under extensive pressure from several state attorneys general, again led by New York State's attorney general, to change their credit-reporting practices. At the time of this writing, both TRW Credit Data and Equifax have signed agreements that they will improve accuracy of credit reports, make them easier for consumers to understand, and improve their customer service procedures. Although pressure from the outside was clearly evident in each case, both credit bureaus have repeatedly portrayed their agreements as merely reflecting changes in their practices that they had already embraced. Although New York's attorney general, Robert Abrams, stated that Equifax was "compelled" to implement the measures, Equifax's vice president, John Ford, disputed that statement. "Ford . . . said the agreements were reached voluntarily with the states and in the best interest of the consumer."[13] Furthermore, Equifax "was quick to point out that [the] firm reached an agreement in a voluntary, congenial manner, while TRW only came to the table after a lawsuit was filed."[14] TRW, however, stated that the provisions in the settlement agreement merely "encompass processes and procedures that we already have in place or that have been planned for some time."[15]

Perhaps even more telling is the debate about Equifax's 1991 decision to stop renting targeted marketing lists based on information in credit reports.[16] When Equifax announced the decision, Abrams said that it was "the pressure created by our investigation of the credit industry that prompted this major company to do the right thing and change its ill-guided and illegal policy of selling confidential information about consumers to direct marketers." He also claimed that Equifax's decision was made "in response to negotiations" with his office. But Equifax's senior vice president said that a discussion with Abrams's office was merely a "factor" in reaching the decision and that Abrams's office "never threatened" to sue Equifax. He also stated that the company had already decided to pull the lists off the market before ever talking with Abrams's office.[17]

In all fairness, it should be noted that Equifax has made a major investment in attempting to lead on privacy issues, including sponsorship of annual public opinion polls. TRW Credit Data also has devoted significant additional resources to improving its customer service and now offers consumers one free copy of their credit report each year—a service for which Equifax still charges eight dollars. But changes at both credit bureaus were clearly prodded by the attention the industry and their corporations were receiving from legislators and regulators, which, if nothing else, created an external threat of sufficient size to get executives' attention.

A Right to Privacy. Finally, there is one additional area in which some corporate and noncorporate interviewees made varying assumptions: whether or not there *is* a right to privacy in a commercial context. With respect to the U.S. *government*'s involvement with its citizens, a judicially recognized right to privacy is grounded in several amendments to the U.S. Constitution and stated explicitly in several state constitutions. (This right was the basis, for example, of the famous *Roe v. Wade* decision that legalized most abortions.) But the existence of a right to privacy with respect to *commercial* transactions is much less clear. Consumer protections in such transactions are much narrower, and constitutional protections do not apply in the same way that they do between citizens and government.

Even so, and almost without exception, consumers were quick to claim such a right to privacy in commercial transactions as though it were guaranteed constitutionally. Corporate interviewees in the insurance industry also referred to such a right with great regularity. But managers and executives who often dealt with targeted marketing campaigns—particularly at the banks and CredCard—sometimes seemed to question whether Americans had a valid claim to a right to privacy. A total of eleven corporate interviewees made one or more comments that questioned the existence of such a right. Here are representative comments from three different interviewees:

> People often say they have a right to privacy, but what they really have is a right to be a consumer. Other than protecting the consumer-merchant relationship, I'm not aware of any other duty we have in that regard. Of course, consumers can *force* us to do some other things, but I don't acknowledge the God-given right to privacy that they claim. You give that up when you buy things. . . . You can have a right to privacy if you are a hermit.
>
> [Interviewer: So, you don't acknowledge a general right to privacy?] Well, I was hoping I wouldn't get pinned down that way, but . . . no, I don't really. That's just a code word or phrase for something that a bunch of loud advocates like [names of well-known privacy advocates] are screaming about a lot. But they don't understand that the economy is a complex system that has lots of trade-offs, and you can't just say, "Oh, but I have a right to privacy, so stop all the commerce."
>
> If people have a right to privacy, then they also have a right to hide their bad deeds. If someone is a deadbeat, then anybody who has to deal with them should know about it. We don't need to have that kind of right in our society, and I'm glad we still have a few intelligent people out there who agree with me.

This variance in assumptions—over whether or not a right to privacy really exists in commercial transactions—is an issue of such great importance that it goes far beyond the present study. We will encounter it again in chapter 6, when we discuss the driver for most of the privacy arguments we hear today: ambiguity.

Implications

Thus, wherever we look with respect to privacy arguments, consumers and other stakeholders are usually on the other side of the fence from their corporate counterparts. An examination of each of the ingredients in value-laden debate, as defined by Potter's Box, revealed that there was much disagreement between the parties, and these disagreements all bode poorly for the current approach to information privacy.

- With respect to empirical facts, the biggest problem is consumer ignorance regarding corporate policies and practices. Although there were exceptions, most consumers became angry as they learned more about the policies and practices, and attempts to calm them down afterward were usually unsuccessful. Since it is reasonable to expect that consumers will become better informed about policies and practices in the future, given the increasing media and legislative attention to information privacy, the current path is a dangerous one for corporations. While "what they don't know won't hurt them" may have been a workable moniker for the past, it will work less dependably in the future. Note also that among the better-informed consumers and advocates who *did* seem to understand some of the corporate policies and practices, there is a real gap between the manner in which corporations often portray empirical facts (e.g., the number of errors in a database) and the way an opposing advocate might.

- As for primary commitments, corporate commitments revolve—not surprisingly—around profitability or one of its surrogates. But executives and policymakers should be troubled to learn that most consumers were far less committed to such notions than to their own consumer rights, which in the context of this study usually meant a right to privacy in commercial transactions. It is particularly surprising that very few consumers indicated any concern as to whether or not the corporations succeed in their quests. To the extent that we should all be committed to a successful, interlocked economy, the consumers' position indicates either a misunderstanding of the economic system or a frustration with it. Nevertheless, their attitude reveals a very real gulf between corporate and consumer positions.

- The mode of ethical reasoning, while not consistent for all interviewees in either the corporate or noncorporate domain, differed a great deal with respect to the growing field of targeted marketing: corporate interviewees like to argue in terms of the *consequences* of personal information use, whereas consumer interviewees prefer to argue in more categorical ways about the *means* in which they are targeted for offers. Consumers are much more likely to say that a particular use of information is either right or wrong, whereas corporate executives will define that use in terms of its ultimate outcome: for example, did the use of information result in consumers' receiving offers for high-quality merchandise? In general, we can say that corporate executives embrace an ethically egoistic mode of argumentation, whereas most consumers prefer a categorical mode based on an assumed right to privacy.

• And, finally, the assumptions underlying various parties' arguments are also
at odds. In particular, there are many differing assumptions about what actually constitutes the intended purpose for gathering personal information.
Corporate interviewees are inclined to assume a quite broad "intended purpose," whereas consumer interviewees define this matter much more narrowly. Furthermore, with respect to corporate responses to external threats,
corporate interviewees like to assume that their responses are "voluntary,"
whereas consumers and other advocates are far less charitable in their interpretations. And, finally, we find that there is some amount of dispute over
whether a right to privacy really even exists in the commercial arena.

These differences, which span the whole domain of privacy issues encountered
in this study, are symptoms of a deeper problem: the ambiguous privacy domain
in the United States. In general, these disputes from different sides of the issue are
hidden from view until they erupt in a public dispute. Corporate decision makers
very rarely poll the public to find out their opinions before taking an action that
has privacy implications[18] and, certainly, very rarely ask the public *why* they feel
a certain way about information uses. Many executives avoid the debates highlighted in this chapter, because they require confrontation of some issues that
may ultimately affect the corporate bottom line. Most executives prefer, as long
as possible, to keep their arguments about privacy issues hidden inside their own
corporate boundaries and to keep their logical arguments under wraps. Consumers and other advocates are much more willing to expose their arguments to
public scrutiny, but they are often limited in their knowledge, and—although
their opportunities to raise their concerns are increasing—they traditionally have
had few venues for voicing their arguments. But, without these debates, determining which actions are right or wrong is difficult, since each group is working
with its own set of empirical facts (often incorrect), its own commitments, its own
mode of reasoning, and its own assumptions.

The fact that corporations lounge in the drift period means that these arguments will often be based on outdated policies and unreconciled practices. But it
also reveals that corporations are in many cases as confounded as the consumers
about what constitutes "good and bad business" in the new world of databases
and privacy. Several underlying, systemic problems in the American privacy domain exacerbate both the corporations' reliance on a drift period and the conflicting arguments from many different perspectives. The drift and the arguments are
merely symptoms. The real problem is the ambiguous environment created by the
country's ambiguous approach to information privacy itself. In chapter 6, we examine that ambiguity in greater detail.

Ambiguity All Around

So far we have observed several troubling phenomena in the U.S. corporate privacy domain: a reactive policy-making cycle that relies on an external threat for impetus to action, resulting in a set of inadequate policies and a troubling policy/practice gap, along with a clear break in argumentation between corporations and noncorporate stakeholders. But none of these problems exist in isolation; rather, they are symptoms of a more systemic disease: ambiguity in the U.S. corporate privacy domain. We cannot proceed to discuss solutions for the problems of the current environment without first considering the underlying drivers for those problems. Thus, in this chapter we examine the ambiguity from which the other problems originate.

The ambiguous corporate privacy domain fuels a poor policy-making dynamic—the drift–external threat–reaction cycle. Because corporations are not forced to, they do not confront privacy issues in a proactive fashion. This passive approach provides ample opportunity for an ill-suited set of policies to develop and for a policy/practice gap to evolve. The ambiguity also provides the quicksand on which the corporate privacy arguments are crafted, and it offers little incentive for corporations to confront the differing stakeholders' arguments in a forthright fashion. Thus, either directly or indirectly, we can trace all the problems uncovered in this study to this single driver.

Despite some heroic efforts in the 1970s to chart an explicit set of principles for behavior—witness the Fair Information Practices described in chapter 1—there has been a remarkable lack of clarity in translating those abstract principles into day-to-day corporate operations. Furthermore, as the focus on privacy ebbed and flowed during the 1980s, much of the momentum for increasing privacy protections diminished. Ironically, this slowdown happened during the same years that technological advances were spurting forward with the greatest velocity in history, making the protection of privacy all the more necessary but, at the same time, all the more complex. The 1990s dawned with a renewed concern for privacy on the part of consumers and legislators but also with an aura of uncertainty that reflected diffusion and confusion on all parts.

The greatest evidence of this ambiguity is the great confusion surrounding assertions of privacy intrusions: it is often not even clear when—or if—a privacy intrusion has occurred. What we are most often left with, instead, are *claims* of intrusion on the parts of individuals and privacy advocates, which are counterbalanced by *denials* on the parts of corporate decision makers. For example, the Lotus MarketPlace: Households product discussed in chapter 1 was widely assailed by privacy advocates as intrusive. However, corporate spokespersons maintained that consumer concerns were based on "misunderstanding of the product" and ignorance of the "actual data content and controls built into the product."[1]

While the technology and the increasing value of information both drive the renewed focus on privacy, we must look to several underlying, systemic factors for a full explanation of the ambiguity in the corporate privacy domain. First, there is confusion regarding the place of commercial sector privacy in U.S. public policy. Second, there is much dispute about the role corporations have in dealing with any societal issue, including privacy. Third, the explosive growth of technology has created a vacuum in many areas with respect to appropriate and inappropriate behavior. This chapter will examine each of these factors and will then pinpoint the specific areas in which the ambiguity will cause problems for corporations and for the privacy coalition over the next few years if actions are not taken to resolve the ambiguity.

Privacy in American Public Policy

Our societal values and our mores are represented, to a great degree, by our legislative and judicial responses to privacy concerns. We see in those responses an evolving societal concept of privacy—one that began before the earliest settlers arrived in the U.S. and that continues to evolve in the 1990s. A full treatment of this evolutionary process is far beyond the scope of this book, but a brief synthesis follows.

Origins of U.S. Privacy Values

All cultures value privacy in some form, and the United States is no exception.[2] But "there has been no particular moment of decision in the country's history when the populace suddenly declared *de novo* that privacy was a good thing. . . . [Such a value has] certainly been with us since the foundings," writes David Flaherty.[3] Early settlers brought European privacy values to the new world, and though the new environment forced them to modify their views a bit, their desires for personal autonomy, emotional release, self-evaluation, and limited and protected communication[4] remained strong components of their value system.[5] These values could be observed in their homes, communities, churches, and other societal infrastructures, as well as in their legal system.[6]

To a great degree, the growth of technology, and our society's response to it, have molded our concept of privacy in the subsequent 350 years. Telegraphs, telephones, newspapers, cameras, etc., have all altered our views.[7] During the nineteenth and twentieth centuries, the growth of cities, enabled by improved communication technologies, has spurred a migration from the more isolated rural environment to the more concentrated urban environment. As a result, many individuals are now living more closely together than they did previously, and this new arrangement has redefined the notions of both "personal space" and "intrusion." The concept of community has changed, and our concept of privacy has evolved along with it.[8]

Privacy as a Basic Right

As our society and concept of privacy have evolved, so have our public policy approaches. Privacy now occupies a unique position from a legal perspective, as Robert Ellis Smith has summarized:

> Privacy is unique . . . in the fact that it can involve either constitutional law or tort law. Privacy invasions may also arise under contracts, criminal law, civil procedure, and administrative law. . . . The concept is confusing . . . because it is found in both tort law, as when one private party harms another by invading his or her privacy; and in constitutional law, as when an arm of the government conducts a criminal-investigation search or infringes upon one's private beliefs, conduct, or the control of one's own body. . . . Depending on the nature of the intrusion, it can involve criminal procedure (whether to admit improperly seized evidence, for instance), substantive criminal law (prosecution of a Peeping Tom), civil procedure (the doctor-

patient privilege), torts (spreading malicious gossip about someone), family law (access to adoption information), or contracts (failing to keep a fact confidential after having agreed to do so). Privacy protections are found in statutory law . . . , in administrative law . . . , and in case law.[9]

In many cases the confusion is grounded in a blurry distinction between *governmental* intrusions into citizens' private lives and privacy problems in *commercial* transactions. Of course, legislators are free to pass specific laws that provide specific consumer protections against governmental privacy intrusions (e.g., the Privacy Act of 1974) or improve the privacy domain in commercial transactions (e.g., the FCRA). Such laws act somewhat as trump cards in privacy arguments. But many privacy disputes are in the somewhat vacuous territory outside these specific laws. In those cases, resolutions must be based on the underlying legal frameworks for privacy protection.

These frameworks differ depending on whether the relationship is between 1) a citizen and the government or 2) two or more citizens—the category most applicable to commercial exchanges. In the former case, the Constitution gives citizens rights vis-à-vis their government, and it protects citizens against governmental intrusions into their lives. But in the latter case, marketplace transactions are not generally addressed by constitutional privacy protections unless the transactions are of a very unusual nature. Instead, these transactions *could* fall under the domain of contract law, which could address privacy concerns *if* a contract included provisions for protecting privacy; few contracts do. More often, the venue for pursuing nongovernmental privacy intrusions would be tort actions. When one human being has injured another in some way (including invasion of his or her privacy), tort actions can offer relief to the injured party. A brief examination of these two approaches to privacy—constitutional protections and tort law— will demonstrate the distinctions.

Constitutional Law. The U.S. Constitution defines the relationship between the U.S. government and the citizens of the United States. Citizens are given certain rights, and certain restrictions are placed on the government's power. The Constitution does not specifically define a "right to privacy." Even so, over time the Constitution has been interpreted to acknowledge such a right, despite the fact that the word "privacy" was not explicitly written therein. Many Supreme Court rulings (e.g., *Griswold v. Connecticut*, *Roe v. Wade*) have acknowledged this right in a judicial sense. The First, Third, Fourth, Fifth, and Fourteenth Amendments each contain a number of protections for citizens and are often used in court cases to demarcate some boundaries around individual privacy claims.[10] The right to privacy vis-à-vis the government is of course not an absolute one—for example, citizens cannot invoke the right in refusing to provide income data to the Internal Revenue Service—but it does provide a legal foundation for protecting citizens against governmental intrusions into their lives.

Torts. Unless the government is a party to a transaction, though, the constitutional protections are usually moot ones. The other broad protection for privacy comes in the tort action of invasion of privacy. Grounded in a societal movement of the twentieth century—likely beginning with a famous 1890 *Harvard Law Review* article by Warren and Brandeis[11]—the tort action of invasion of privacy encompasses four distinct wrongs: 1) appropriation of a plaintiff's name or likeness; 2) intrusion upon a plaintiff's privacy or private affairs; 3) public disclosure of private facts about a plaintiff; and 4) placing a plaintiff in a false light in the public eye.[12] In many cases, consumers might find grounds for a tort action in one or more of these categories. Lacking that, consumers must rely on either a contractual clause that guarantees their privacy will be protected in a transaction—a clause rarely included in consumer contracts—or a specific law that gives privacy protection in a specific transaction (e.g., the Video Privacy Protection Act), or both.

Distinction. The distinction between governmental-sector and commercial-sector privacy protections is often a confusing one. A key question, of course, is this: is there a general right to privacy in commercial transactions in the United States? Of course, numerous privacy laws (at both state and federal levels) do address the boundaries within which commercial transactions occur, and the number of such laws is growing.[13] (In 1992, for example, over one thousand bills were being tracked by the Direct Marketing Association [DMA].)[14] But having specific laws that address specific business practices is quite different from having a general right to privacy in a commercial context in the same sense that such a right exists in a governmental context. Contrary to what some observers have claimed, the Constitution does not provide such a general right for commercial transactions.

To be sure, consumers have some measure of privacy protection in the commercial arena, but it is not rooted in the same principles as their constitutional protection from governmental intrusions. For example, if one were upset because one's life insurance application had been rejected by an insurer due to a sloppy underwriting process (a problem in a commercial transaction), one could not argue convincingly that this violated a constitutional provision for due process, a right provided for defendants in criminal cases being prosecuted by the government.

This distinction between the governmental and commercial sectors is, admittedly, a confusing concept with blurry boundaries. "Privacy is a rarity in American law in that it is both a tort *and* a constitutional right. It is not unusual for lawyers to confuse the two and use constitutional language in tort cases and vice versa," writes Robert Ellis Smith.[15] One often finds public arguments about a right to privacy stepping into this same quagmire, particularly in debates about targeted marketing, the sale of mailing lists, etc. The polarization is exacerbated by the use of constitutional terminology in arguably inappropriate situations (e.g., target marketers who refer to their "First Amendment rights" to sell lists of customer names and addresses).

Adding to the confusion, furthermore, is the fact that a constitutional right to privacy—even within the governmental domain where it applies—is a judicially recognized right rather than an explicitly stated right. Exactly what type of right it is—a specific right unto itself or a composite, derivative right that encompasses other concepts like reputation and protection from emotional distress—continues to be debated by philosophers and legal theorists.[16] And the fact that it is not specifically listed as a right by our founders is upsetting to many. A 1990 public opinion poll included the following question: "Do you agree or disagree with the following statement? If we rewrote the Declaration of Independence today, we would probably add 'privacy' to the list of 'life, liberty, and the pursuit of happiness' as a fundamental right." Seventy-nine percent of the public agreed with the statement.[17] This paradox—that something deemed so important by a large majority of Americans is not included, per se, in our Constitution—reflects the uniqueness, the complexity, and the dynamic nature of the construct called "privacy."

Commercial Sector Privacy. Even if we ignore the confusion regarding the specificity of the right and the distinction between the governmental and commercial sectors, we find some dissonance in the legislative approach to privacy *within* the commercial sector. When crafting specific commercial laws, the U.S. has been quite contradictory in its approach to privacy. When an issue has caught the eye of lawmakers and appeared to represent an immediate threat to lawmakers and their constituents—as in the Video Privacy Protection Bill (the "Bork Bill") regarding video rental records—some limited legislation has been quickly passed. Yet legislators have also seemed sympathetic on many occasions to claims that certain steps taken in the cause of privacy would hurt U.S. commercial trade. For example, lobbying by the DMA, among others, seems to have convinced lawmakers that very restrictive changes in the FCRA would have a detrimental effect on commerce.[18]

It appears that federal lawmakers have acknowledged not an absolute right to privacy in the commercial sector but, instead, an implicit societal objective: a reasonable trade-off between citizens' right to privacy and the efficient functioning of society. Few in the United States—whether corporate executives, legislators, or consumer advocates—would argue with this objective in the abstract. In fact, after presenting such an abstract objective to over four hundred different audience members—from consumer, executive, and legislative ranks—in various venues, I have never had anyone challenge this abstract objective in any serious way. Perhaps this objective mirrors much of the ambiguity in American society: most of the privacy arguments we encounter are, indeed, over what constitutes a "reasonable trade-off." For example, in the Blockbuster Video case discussed in chapter 1, the various stakeholders apparently agreed that the release of video rental records violated individuals' rights to such an extent that the improved efficacy of targeted advertising campaigns based on such records would not be worth it. On the other hand, such an objective does not provide a trump card of a right to privacy in all circumstances: for example, one cannot claim that credit bureaus should be abolished because it would lead to greater privacy; although the statement itself would be true, one would also have to consider the negative effects on the lending process and the concomitant implications for the economy as a whole.

Of course, having such a societal objective in the abstract does not resolve the disputes about privacy. Each player still perceives his or her position as more meritorious than another's, and each argues differently regarding reasonable versus unreasonable trade-offs. Corporations still wish to maximize their own profits, and some of the most ardent privacy advocates still pursue their agendas with little regard for the economic impact of their claims on either individual corporations' profitability or the economy as a whole. But it is fairly clear that actions of the legislative branch have been more in line with this broad, abstract objective than with the establishment of an absolute right to privacy in commercial transactions.

Thus, the role of privacy in the United States is an ambiguous one. There is confusion regarding whether or not we have a general right to privacy in commercial transactions, although—despite some claims to the contrary—the law contains little evidence to support such a direct claim. Instead, the law reflects a more ambiguous societal objective involving complex trade-offs in specific situations.

Is it any wonder, then, that U.S. corporate executives dodge debates about privacy issues and allow their corporations to drift until forced to react? With such ambiguity at every turn, they might argue that there is little to gain from confronting any of the arguments. After all, they are following the same approach as their national legislators, who also react to specific threats. Furthermore, it is not immediately clear in any case that corporations have any role in U.S. society with respect to such social issues as privacy. We now turn to this additional area of ambiguity.

Role of Corporations

The role of corporations in American society is as blurry as the role of privacy. Certainly, corporations form the infrastructure of our economy. To a great degree, corporate profitability equals societal well-being, especially when one considers the impact of corporate success on jobs, community growth, and the like. But it is much less clear what responsibility corporations have with respect to social issues like privacy: should corporations play some role that dictates a responsibility for increasing the level of socially desirable "goods" like privacy? Or, alternatively, if they obey the law and make profits, have they fulfilled their responsibility?

The impact of these questions on the privacy domain is fairly deep. If corporations have a responsibility only to obey the law and make profits, then the solutions to corporate privacy problems must lie in either additional legislation or methods that reduce corporate profits for activities that violate privacy. Under this argument, unless their violation of individuals' privacy in some way reduces those profits, corporations have fulfilled their charter. On the other hand, if corporations have some additional social duty to be "good citizens," then society can expect them to take proactive steps through self-initiated endeavors. Unfortunately, it is unclear just what duty corporations have in confronting the privacy issues.

On one side, there is the argument that corporations themselves have a social responsibility to assess societal needs and to meet them. Chief proponents of this approach are Kenneth E. Goodpaster and John B. Matthews, Jr., who argue in "Can a Corporation Have a Conscience?" that a corporation performs the same tasks as individuals in making moral decisions, so one can "morally project" attributes onto a corporation just as onto an individual. Thus, it is appropriate to view corporations as ethical actors and to judge their actions as though they were individuals.[19] This view holds that the responsibility of corporations—just like that of individuals—is to be good, ethical citizens. By this argument, corporations would be responsible, not only for making profits but also for protecting a socially accepted right to privacy, just as they are expected to be environmentally aware in their packaging and disposal of waste materials. In many cases, even without laws requiring them to do so, corporations would be expected to voluntarily take actions furthering the cause of privacy, even if those actions sometimes reduced their own profits. In a parallel way, of course, we expect individuals to occasionally take actions that offer them no economic gain but represent "the right thing to do."

Competing with this view is a concept most notably linked with economist Milton Friedman, who disputes the assertion that corporations should be viewed as ethical, humanized actors. His 1970 article "The Social Responsibility of Business Is to Increase Its Profits" is widely quoted:

> Only people can have responsibilities. A corporation is an artificial person and in this sense may have artificial responsibilities, but "business" as a whole cannot be said to have responsibilities, even in this vague sense. . . . A corporate executive is an employee of the owners of the business. He has direct responsibility . . . to conduct the business in accordance with their desires, which generally will be to make as much money as possible while conforming to the basic rules of the society, both those embodied in law and those embodied in ethical custom.[20]

Note that Friedman has provided a convenient escape hatch in his argument—one that is often ignored—when he calls for conformance to the basic rules of society. However, Friedman does not feel that, given conformance to those rules, corporations have any responsibility other than to make profits. The other ethical considerations are the purview of other societal parties, such as government and individuals. Under this view, corporations would be expected to acknowledge a right to privacy only if they were forced to by the law or by ethical custom. It should also be noted, however, that ethical customs with respect to privacy in the corporate context would usually entail industry-wide customs that would often be at odds with the most profitable uses of information. Thus, it is unclear how privacy customs would develop under Friedman's model except through law.

There is no clear national consensus as to which model actually describes our economy in the 1990s. Over time, there seem to have been two shifts: increasing regulation in most industries, coupled with an increasing view of corporations as having social responsibilities. The former is confirmed by an examination of the many law publications now available for almost every industry and the growing size of the legal code. There is also evidence for the latter shift, however: shareholders are often losing fights in which they argue that socially responsible actions are reducing their own returns from corporations—an argument they often won in the courts just a few years ago—and, in many cases, shareholders themselves are now calling for socially responsible actions from their directors. The concept of "shareholder activism," made popular by many calls for divestiture from South Africa, has taken hold across the country. One need only examine the yearly stockholders' meeting announcements of most major U.S. corporations to see a number of proposals for social responsibility put forth by various shareholders.

The evidence regarding corporate responsibility in the specific area of information privacy is also conflicting. Within this study, much ambiguity was evident. In chapter 5, we noted that corporate interviewees tended to exhibit commitments primarily to profitability and the law. However, some insurers, in particular, seemed to be committed to privacy as a value in and of itself. Some Cred-Card interviewees also noted that consumers often had standards for information use that were stricter than the law, and CredCard tried to be sensitive to those higher standards. It was obvious that few executives wanted to be *leaders* in privacy issues, but few expressed a desire to be laggards, either.

Executives nationwide seem equally ambivalent about their role. In the 1990 Equifax opinion poll, executives were asked whether they wanted to be pioneers in adopting new privacy policies, to adopt only after an industry-wide consensus developed (but before applicable laws existed), or to wait until laws were passed. In every industry surveyed, the majority preferred the more voluntary approach of industry consensus (though as we have seen, the word "voluntary" can have many meanings) and did not want to wait for a legal mandate (see Table 6.1). One could interpret these results according to either the Goodpaster/Matthews or the Friedman model: executives might be willing to take socially responsible actions, along with their colleagues in other companies, *or* they simply might wish to wait for the "ethical custom" of Friedman's model to develop. All we really know is that there is no clear consensus.

As we have already noted, the actions of the corporations in the study conformed with the law, but there is scant evidence that the organizations are taking any additional steps to further the cause of privacy except when it appears that those steps will lead—in the very short run—to a protection of corporate profitability. Thus, with a few exceptions they seem to be adopting the Friedman model in their dealings with privacy issues. Had they adopted the Goodpaster/Matthews model, they would have often taken overt and self-initiated actions to increase the societal level of privacy and would have gladly foregone their own profits to further that goal. Instead, as a rule, they relied on their adherence to the

Table 6.1. Executives' Roles

	"We want to be a pioneer in adopting company policies that provide new privacy protections."	"We want to adopt new privacy policies when a consensus is developed in our industry about what is right to do."	"We want to wait until laws are passed that define what is proper and improper to do, and would then comply as good citizens."
Insurance	22%	46%	29%
Credit grantors	16%	41%	37%
Banks and thrifts	19%	43%	32%
Direct marketers	23%	50%	20%
Human resources	19%	44%	30%
Consumer affairs	31%	41%	20%

Source: Adapted from Equifax Inc., *The Equifax Report on Consumers in the Information Age* (1990): Table 11–5, p. 101, courtesy of Equifax Inc., 1600 Peachtree Street, Atlanta, Ga. 30302.

law as their shield against privacy problems and worked solely to maximize their own profitability, even at the expense of personal information privacy. However, some counterexamples from the insurance industry were also noted, so this conclusion must be regarded as somewhat partial or tentative.

Yet because our society has not clearly embraced either model of corporate responsibility with absolute clarity—indeed, corporate directors still often find themselves being sued if they take any actions that further social responsibility but reduce profits for the shareholders—it is difficult to assess the duty corporations have in protecting personal privacy. This ambiguity often leads to societal debates: indeed, the rancor directed toward the companies in the opening examples of chapter 1 could not exist under the Friedman model of corporate responsibility, since all the actions were arguably legal under existing law. Consequently, the problems experienced by the Lotus MarketPlace: Households product,

Blockbuster Video, and so forth must have been grounded in some assumptions about corporate responsibility that were closer to the Goodpaster/Matthews model. In public debates about privacy issues, executives are increasingly adopting language that mirrors this latter approach and are less frequently referring to the legality of their actions.[21] This book obviously assumes that corporations are responsible for protecting personal privacy even in areas that are not dictated by present U.S. law. As we will see in chapter 7, however, the long-term mechanisms for ensuring a socially responsible stance from all corporations are complex ones.

Thus, the ambiguity of privacy itself is further exacerbated when the discussion moves into the domain of U.S. corporations. Since we cannot state conclusively what duty the corporations have, it is difficult to define how the problems should be corrected. This difficulty is further exacerbated by the very quickly moving field of information technology, which is leaving a vacuum in place of clear rules for appropriate and inappropriate behavior with respect to privacy.

A Vacuum

Most of today's privacy laws and business customs were crafted almost two decades ago, in the early and middle 1970s. Those two decades have seen an unprecedented revolution in the power of information technology resources: computers, databases, and telecommunication facilities. Many applications of information technology that are commonplace today—easily merged relational databases, interorganizational computer systems, and so on—were mere fantasies in 1975. Moreover, technological improvements are occurring at an accelerating rate. In terms of data storage and communication, what was impossible just a few years ago can now be accomplished with little effort. In fact, over the past few years, the price/performance ratio for computer hardware has improved at an annual rate of almost 40 percent.[22] Note the implications of the price and speed data contained in Table 6.2. As a summary statistic, consider the time and cost for large IBM computers to complete a fixed regimen of 1,700 typical data processing instructions. In 1955, the set of instructions took 375 seconds and cost $14.54. By 1965, these numbers had declined to 29 seconds and $0.47. And in 1987, an estimate for the same set of instructions was four-tenths of one second, with a cost of $0.04![23]

Table 6.2. Hardware Trends

	Early to mid-1950s	Late 1950s to mid-1960s	Mid-1960s to early 1970s	Early 1970s to early 1990s	Later in 1990s
Size (typical computers)	Room size	Closet-sized	Desk-sized mini-computer	Typewriter-sized micro-computer	Credit card–sized micro-computer?
Density (components per circuit)	One	Hundreds	Thousands	Hundreds of thousands	Millions?
Speed (instructions per second)	Hundreds	Thousands	Millions	Tens of millions	Billions?
Reliability (time between failures of circuits)	Hours	Days	Weeks	Months	Years?
Memory (capacity in characters)	Thousands	Tens of thousands	Hundreds of thousands	Millions	Billions?
Cost (per million instructions)	$10	$1.00	$.10	$.001	$.0001?

Source: Adapted from James A. O'Brien, *Management Information Systems: A Managerial End User Perspective*, 2d ed. (Homewood, Ill.: Richard D. Irwin, 1993): 112. Used by permission of the publisher.

Software

Yet the technological movement in hardware—impressive in its own right—can be viewed as merely an "enabling event"[24] for another story: a changing software environment. Between the 1940s, the age of the earliest computers, and the early 1990s, there have been several generations of operating systems, with attendant generations of applications. Over time, the technological environment has progressed to a point where collection and sharing of personal data are quite easy and, at times, uncontrolled.

Harvey M. Deitel has distinguished several generations within the history of information technology. Those generations can be summarized as follows:[25]

- The Zeroth Generation (1940s): computers without operating systems. Users hand-coded all instructions with complete access to the machine language. Information could not even be stored, much less used or shared.

- The First Generation (1950s): batch processing developed. A computer could be shared, but a great deal of time was lost between the completion of one job and the initiation of the next. Any attempts to build a large database of personal information would have been foolhardy, as the technology would not support it.

- The Second Generation (early 1960s): shared systems with multiprogramming and multiprocessing capabilities. Time-sharing systems were developed; the use of terminals in conversational modes became possible. A watershed development was the first transaction processing system (American Airlines' SABRE). For the first time, it became possible to store some amount of information, albeit in a fairly inefficient form, and to share it between processes on a computer. Yet the speed and capacities of computers were still quite limited, and personal information was still somewhat protected by these technological constraints.

- The Third Generation (mid-1960s to mid-1970s): general-purpose computers, with a software layer between the user and the hardware. This necessitated complex job-control languages. This generation also signaled the beginning of software engineering as a field: a disciplined and structured approach to creating reliable and maintainable software. This period marked the beginning of database systems, the major enabling event for applications that made extensive use of personal information.

- The Fourth Generation (mid-1970s to present): the era of virtual machines, large database systems, PCs, and networks. Cooperative processing—movement of information between microcomputers, minicomputers, and mainframes, with transparency for the user—became possible. This generation also saw the beginning of expert systems applications. During this period, large quantities of personal information began to be stored in large, complex database systems. However, the databases were not always centralized, as the technology also provided for distributed storage on networks of minicomputers and PCs. This meant that there were fewer controls on the use of personal information, since it was no longer under the domain of computer operators but, rather, that of end users themselves. Storage and processing costs both declined exponentially, thus enabling a number of heretofore impractical applications.

Major trends of the early 1990s include the growth of large, global networks. Electronic data interchange (EDI) operations—initiated as long ago as 1972[26]— are expanding, so that paper financial transactions are being replaced by electronic ones. This development should lead to new, electronic marketplaces, but it also means that more information about individuals is being collected, stored, and shared. The increased capacity of PCs continues to fuel the PC applications software industry. Also, the traditional, centralized approach to storing information is giving way to an abundance of distributed databases, which are now under the control of individuals, not centralized management. Thus, the ability to control the proliferation and spread of personal information storage is becoming more problematic. This matter was, in fact, one of the major privacy concerns leveled against the Lotus MarketPlace: Households product: since the database was to be sold on CD-ROM, there would be major difficulty in controlling its distribution after the initial purchase. Interorganizational systems (IOSs) are becoming more commonplace as data are easily shared between different divisions and companies; the growth of the "information highway" enables further developments in this area. The rising standards for the exchange of data are quickly reducing the incompatibilities between computer systems that, for many years, prevented corporate computers from "communicating."

The rapid acceleration of the technological "art of the possible" makes the impact of information technology on privacy issues all the more pronounced. Even if it had been theoretically possible to evaluate and to move the same information in the precomputer age, it was not practical or achievable. However, given the speed of change in technological advancements, the venue is shifting rapidly. "What once rested in a manila folder now [can] be transferred at great distances, analyzed more cheaply, stored in a fraction of the space and retrieved instantaneously."[27] And it is reasonable to believe that such changes will be even faster in the future.

But the growing preponderance of computers in our society raises many new ethical questions. As Deborah Johnson, in her 1985 book *Computer Ethics*, writes, "Our increasing use of computers has raised ethical questions which, while not fundamentally unique, have never been posed in quite the form they are now."[28] Of course, one can argue that computers have had little effect on the issue of privacy and that privacy issues were around long before computers were. Any privacy violations that occur with computers could have occurred without computers. The ability to move large amounts of information quickly has, of course, been created by the computer technology. But some people argue that the same information could have been moved without such technology; it would just take longer. Computers merely improve the efficiency.

The problem with this view, of course, is that it sees computers' effects on privacy as being only a difference in *degree* and not a difference in *kind*. This view might be true in abstract, but it is not true in reality, for our society has not yet developed mores for dealing with all the new uses of information that are being made available by improvements in technology; our social contract has not been renegotiated to account for these new developments. For example, we have not yet developed societal norms regarding the sharing of information about our purchases between our credit card issuer and mail-order retailers: until just a few years ago, the technology for sharing such information did not exist. Similarly, we do not have societal norms (or clear laws) dealing with the use of information from credit reports in targeted marketing databases. This vacuum occurs because the technology for using such credit data did not exist until recently. We are dealing today with the technology of the 1990s but the social norms of the 1970s. It is tempting to conclude that, given time, the social norms will catch up. However, the technology seems to be changing much more quickly than society can recalculate the parameters around new uses of information—more quickly than our societal infrastructure and our ethical base are changing. John Ladd writes, "The traditional concept of privacy itself . . . has no application in the modern world of computer technology, where detrimental information about individuals can be easily collected without violating physical barriers. In view of new developments, the very definition of privacy needs to be revamped."[29]

Computers enable new applications that store, use, and share large amounts of personal information. Even if this development does represent a change only in degree, not in kind, it dictates that we must make new value judgments that we have not previously considered. The question is no longer a technical one—for example, *can* we look at individuals' credit card purchases to put them in psychographic categories for targeted marketing?—but rather an ethical and legal one: *should* we?

Johnson suggests that new technologies often offer a vacuum containing no explicit or agreed-upon specific rules.[30] And it is in this vacuum that most of the drift occurs during the corporate policy-making cycle. After all, if society cannot decide what is right or wrong, why should corporations devote great resources to doing so? From this perspective, one should be able to feel as much pity for executives in today's computerized world as disdain for their decisions. Confronted with competitive pressures, a working technological solution that offers strategic advantages, and an environment that does not seem to prohibit certain activities even if they are, as an executive interviewee put it, "gray from a privacy perspective," executives will often choose the gray alternative. That gray area is most obvious in the targeted marketing arena, where consumers often reveal what appear to be conflicting desires about privacy and benefits. The 1990 Equifax survey asked two questions and received very different responses:

- "Businesses marketing goods and services directly to consumers are now able to buy from mailing list–making companies information about your consumer characteristics—such as your income level, residential area, and credit card use—and use such information to offer goods and services to you. Do you feel this is a good or bad thing?" Only 28 percent of the general public said this ability was a "good thing," while 69 percent said it was a "bad thing."

- A follow-up survey asked: "Companies try to learn which individuals and households would be the most likely buyers of their products or service. They buy names and addresses of people in certain age groups, estimated income groups, and residential areas with certain shopping patterns so they can mail information to the people they think will be most interested in what they are selling. Do you find this practice acceptable or unacceptable?" Sixty-seven percent of the general public said it was an "acceptable" practice; only 31 percent labeled it "unacceptable."

It could be argued that in asking the second question the survey moved the goalpost by referring to the more general "names and addresses" of groups that appear to be based on demographic information, while the first question asked about "your consumer characteristics," which are more individualized and perhaps more ominous. However, even with this discrepancy, there is clearly a remarkable distinction and dissonance in the responses. Which targeted marketing practices are acceptable, and which are not? Executives can only guess, since to a great degree their actions are occurring in the vacuum.

This vacuum is not restricted to targeted marketing, of course. Each of the industries in this study has confronted some areas of ambiguity in societal expectations for privacy: to what extent health claim data should be shared with employers, to what extent AIDS test results should be stored and shared in industry databases, to what extent the growing access capabilities of bank databases should be made available to tellers and other personnel, to what extent banks should augment their customer databases with outside information, etc. Each of these industry dilemmas is to some degree enabled by the technological capabilities of the 1990s: for example, sharing health claims with employers is much easier with interorganizational computer systems (e.g., the health insurer's computer terminals can be placed in the employer's personnel office), and banks' augmentation activities become trivial endeavors with modern database merge programs.

It appears, then, that even if organizations did acknowledge their own social responsibility regarding privacy, and even if they did agree that a right to privacy existed and should be protected in the commercial sector, they would often be hard-pressed to define exactly how they should behave in specific situations. The privacy domain is so wrought with ambiguity that it is difficult to perceive a future without substantial tension as these matters are sorted out.

The Future of Ambiguity

This ambiguity in the privacy domain, which leads to the reactive corporate and legislative policy-making cycles, large holes in privacy policies, and gaps between policy and practice, will undoubtedly wreak havoc later in the 1990s if it is not soon curbed. The sites and industries in this study are only proxies for the real world of privacy concerns. As we look outward into the broader domain, we see that several forces, unless checked, will explode later in the decade in a series of privacy debacles. Before moving to a suggested solution for reducing the ambiguity and resolving many of the problems, we should consider the pressure points for U.S. privacy in the later 1990s—the areas in which the ambiguity stands poised to cause the most damage in the information realm.

Marketing

One area in which the ambiguity will prove especially troublesome during the 1990s, as the move from generalized to targeted marketing continues, is the collection and use of data about one's purchases. As this study showed, consumers and merchants have great disputes over the intended purposes for data collection. Such arguments will continue for the next few years, as the implicit assumptions of the 1980s lead to more and more vocal disputes and, eventually, some legally enforced definitions. But even more troubling will be a growing number of arguments over the ownership of the data. While this item did not seem to be a strong point of dispute in this study, there are growing indications that it could erupt in the near future as a pivotal issue not only between consumers and companies but also between the companies themselves. Even if the arguments are between two corporate entities, the issue of information privacy becomes inextricably interwoven into the other debates.

AT&T announced in 1991 that it would begin scrutinizing the records of calls to toll-free 800 numbers to determine which customers called certain types of numbers most often. It planned then to send special directories to frequent callers. In October 1991, the company was to send a directory to 200,000 consumers whose calling patterns indicated an interest in gift and specialty items. It planned to follow in later months with directories for travel-related services, senior citizen products, health and fitness items, and sports merchandise. Although the plans are still in effect as of this writing, they have come under tremendous attack from direct marketers who use AT&T's 800 numbers. The marketers cite consumer privacy as one issue but, more importantly, argue that AT&T has no right to use information about who is ordering from them. An article in *Privacy Times* reported:

> "I don't believe that who calls me is any business of AT&T," said Phil Staples, president of Names and Addresses of Northbrook, Illinois. AT&T "should have asked for my permission as a businessman, and I definitely don't think they have the right to use my customers' names without that permission," he said. . . . "Direct marketers have a legitimate concern" over data ownership, Tim Lytle, chairman of Lytle and Co. credit card processing firm, said . . . [but] an AT&T spokesman dismissed charges that the directories infringe on direct marketers' property. "This is AT&T data, and we can make use of it in this fashion," Bob Nersesian, AT&T spokesman, said . . . "We see the directory as a customer need we are trying to meet," Nersesian said. "I don't see what the controversy is except that we are competing with direct marketers."[31]

Some weeks later, a trade publication reported that the Chicago Association of Direct Marketing had condemned the AT&T plans in a resolution that read, in part: "The Chicago Association of Direct Marketing believes this program constitutes an invasion of privacy and strongly urges AT&T to either cancel the program or to include names in their data file only after written permission has been obtained from both the caller and the call recipient."[32]

In another incident, Citicorp announced that it would begin selling lists of its credit card holders sorted according to their purchase patterns. Again, a number of complaints from direct marketers arose: in addition to raising issues of personal information privacy, the direct marketers maintained that their customer lists were their property, not Citicorp's, even if the customers had used a Citicorp credit card to make their purchases.[33] The debate is unresolved as of this writing.

In both the AT&T and Citicorp cases, different corporate entities are arguing over the ownership of customer data. AT&T and Citicorp are assuming ownership because the data flows through their "data pipes," so to speak; the other corporate entities are disputing that assumption. Because it strengthens their case, the other parties are often raising the issue of personal information privacy, but this issue may not be driving their concerns. As computer networking capabilities continue to increase over the next few years, these sorts of debates will become much more common. The AT&T and Citicorp cases are probably the first of many in this category.

And as the corporate ownership debates intensify, the media publicity will no doubt increase consumers' awareness of different uses of data about them. As that occurs, their own claims of data ownership will also no doubt increase. To date, such claims have held little credence under U.S. law. But there may now be a general societal mandate for such a position. Judging from the consumer interviews in this study, it is safe to say that consumers do not acknowledge that merchants have sole ownership of data about their purchases. Alan Westin, a long-time scholar of privacy, predicts that individuals' claims to ownership of this information will become so intense during the 1990s that the law will be changed. He notes that when the issue of commercial use of a person's likeness first came about in the early 1900s, changes in the U.S. law resulted in compensation for such uses (celebrity endorsements). He predicts that "American law in the 1990s will construct a similar concept for consumer personal profile data acquired by businesses from consumer submissions and transactions. . . . All consumer data bases used for direct marketing will be consensual, based on the consumer's knowing agreement to their use and the payment of fair market value."[34]

Unfortunately, the path from the present situation—in which both the law and tradition assume that merchants own data about their customers—to the new one will be a painful one. While the law is not especially ambiguous at present (it allows almost all merchant uses), it is somewhat out of step with the realities of the marketplace and, apparently, the expectations of consumers. Thus, the ambiguity comes from a consumer expectation that differs from the law. Consequently, corporations wishing to engage in "good business practices" may well find that adherence to legal precedents in this area is an insufficient protection throughout the 1990s. Since the legal policy-making cycle is reactive, laws will need considerable time to catch up with the real world.

In addition to ownership issues, the later 1990s will see continuing debates regarding new uses and sharing of purchase data. As the intended purposes for collection are ultimately sorted out, the pressure to protect against additional uses will increase. Increased pressure on data collectors to offer opt-out and opt-in provisions, under which consumers can say whether or not they want their names used for particular purposes, will be commonplace. A 1992 legislative debate surrounding the FCRA amendments addressed one measure, that would have required credit-reporting agencies to obtain consumers' approval before providing their names to direct marketers. Although the measure lost by a 26–23 vote before the House Banking, Finance, and Urban Affairs Committee,[35] the slim margin suggests that there is a moderate amount of support for such opt-in procedures in some federal legislative circles.

In addition, officials at the state level are exerting much pressure toward this end. In late 1991, the New York State attorney general's office was considering proposing legislation that would stop the release of information in credit card files without prior cardholder approval via an opt-in authorization.[36] In April 1992, the Virginia governor signed into law a bill prohibiting the sale, rental, or other disclosure of consumer transaction information without notification and an opt-out option for the consumer. Prompted by a local supermarket chain's introduction of a "frequent shopper" club that tracked purchases, the bill was amended in committee to apply only to merchants with fixed retail locations in Virginia. A *Washington Post* article reported, "Supporters of the measure in the House of Delegates said it makes Virginia a leader in the emerging backlash against what they consider invasions of privacy on a mass scale."[37] Assuming that states like New York and Virginia really are leaders in this backlash, then a number of similar restrictions may be considered and implemented in other states.

Also, as we discussed earlier, the EC privacy initiatives strongly favor overt consumer consent for the use of transaction data. Although the matter was not fully resolved at the time of this writing, the European privacy commission had tended toward an opt-in requirement, under which consumers would have to give their express consent each time their names were rented. Furthermore, it was unclear what the initiatives' impact on international direct marketing would be, since there would also be prohibitions against trading customer data with any country whose laws were viewed as deficient.[38] Given the trends in the industry, the growing consumer dissatisfaction, and the international pressure, the 1990s will probably see many more initiatives like those of Virginia and New York, and similar action can eventually be expected at a federal level.

Another trend for the 1990s, buoyed by the ambiguity surrounding privacy and targeted marketing, is the blurring of the line, in debates, between physical and information privacy. In targeted marketing, arguments about the delivery of the offer are often confused with those about the use of the database itself. In an abstract sense, the former represents *physical* privacy concerns (intrusions into one's physical space or solitude) while the latter represents *information* privacy concerns (inappropriate access to identifiable information about oneself). Since the issues are increasingly being raised in the same breath, however, it is likely that the distinction cannot be maintained over time. Just like information privacy issues, physical privacy laws are getting increasing attention in targeted marketing. For example, telemarketing will be restricted in some measure by the Telephone Consumer Protection Act, which was passed by the U.S. Congress in late 1991 and signed into law shortly thereafter. This act gave the FCC responsibility for investigating methods of limiting telemarketing calls to individuals who did not want to receive them. Although it was widely reported at the time of the congressional debates that the bill would create a national "do-not-call" database, the FCC did not embrace that specific approach.[39] However, the lawmakers' intent was clear: they wanted to reduce the physical intrusion of telemarketing calls. While their debates often included references to privacy in general, and the use of consumer databases in particular, their actions ultimately affected the physical end product of the marketing: the calls themselves. As with phone calls, concerns about mailed offers are rising and will continue to rise through the 1990s. The problem is often referred to as "mailbox clutter," and individuals are now intermingling privacy concerns with environmental concerns in calling for a reduction in such targeted mail. Los Angeles mayor Tom Bradley even urged the city's residents to ask mailers to remove their names from lists—and supplied postcards to aid them in their task—to reduce the quantity of paper being added to the city's landfill. So targeted marketers can expect a two-pronged attack during the 1990s: on one hand, their use of consumer information will increasingly come under scrutiny; on the other, the manner in which they contact potential customers will also be derided and regulated. Both information and physical privacy concerns will be raised, but the arguments may not always distinguish between the two. Instead, the industry may be attacked simply for "privacy problems," which may in themselves become intertwined with some "environmental problems." The ambiguous privacy environment will allow plenty of room for these debates to continue.

Marketers should also recognize an important trend for the 1990s with respect to the specific external threats they will experience: increasingly, these will come not just from the media and the legislatures but also from the competitive arena. Such competitive volleys will take the form of campaigns in which companies claim, "Buy our product, and we will protect your privacy better than our competitors will." In this study, one such company was a credit card issuer that ran a series of television commercials touting the "Privacy Protection Plan" accompanying its credit cards. Examples are also beginning to be noted in other arenas, as outlined in chapter 1: in the early 1990s, MCI began to offer a "Friends and Family" plan, which provided reduced long-distance calling rates to the members of one's "calling circle," as long as they were also MCI customers. In early 1992, AT&T began to run commercials in which actors ridiculed the MCI plan for its alleged privacy violations and noted that AT&T provided calling discounts *without* requiring customers to provide a list of their closest friends and relatives.[40] It is only reasonable to expect that privacy will be used more often as a competitive weapon as it becomes a more and more vital concern for consumers.

As privacy increases as a consumer issue and as these debates flourish, another ambiguous privacy line—the one separating the public and private sectors—will also be bent and twisted, particularly with respect to targeted marketing information. On one side, information collected by governmental entities will increasingly find its way into the private sector's marketing activities. This phenomenon appears to have two drivers: increasing technological capabilities, which make such exchanges possible; and tight governmental budgets, which make the sale of existing governmental data seem a painless method of securing additional, much-needed funds.

For example, a controversial but continuing practice finds the U.S. Post Office sharing information from its NCOA program with several targeted marketing database owners. Under an agreement, information about individuals who fill in standard NCOA cards to have their mail forwarded is shared with the database owners, who use the information to update their own databases. The information is also used, in many cases, to create lists of "recent movers," which are then sold for targeted marketing purposes. Hearings in the early 1990s led to the proposed Postal Patron Privacy Act of 1992, which would have officially legalized such licensing of NCOA data to outside companies, as long as the forms included an opt-out provision for consumers. However, privacy advocates continued to argue that the licensing was illegal.[41]

Also falling in a troublesome area of ambiguity, but apparently legal in many states, are the lists being synthesized from driver's license data and sold for targeted marketing. Under such arrangements, lists of individuals who are, for example, wearers of corrective lenses, over a certain weight or height, etc., are compiled from driver's license data, which is legally available, and sold by private firms. And the sale of CD-ROM disks containing voter records—including name, address, telephone number (often unlisted), occupation, birthplace, birthdate, and political affiliation—has recently come under fire in California, although it has not been directly intended for targeted marketing purposes. Offering records on 1.25 million voters from San Diego County for ninety-nine dollars, Sole Source Systems is breaking new ground. Although Sole Source says the CD is to be used only for "election purposes, . . . election, scholarly or political research, or government purposes," and that the disk is only sold after one presents an ID and fills in a form, there is much speculation that the data will soon be used by targeted marketers.[42] While the data in most of these products are technically public, and the products therefore legal, it is unclear whether the definition of "public" was ever intended to include such easily transferred compilations. Our traditional norms for "public" and "private" are, like so many other concepts, falling victim to the ambiguous boundaries of the information age.

Although examples of the private sector's procuring governmental records have been more common to date, the line is also beginning to blur in the other direction: governmental bodies are increasingly seeking private-sector data for their purposes. In the 1980s, the U.S. Selective Service bought a list of children who had registered for an ice cream chain's "Birthday Club"; it then wrote to club members eighteen or older, reminding them of draft registration mandates.[43] In 1992, the FBI reportedly tried to buy several mailing lists for use in its investigations. *DM News*, an industry newspaper, reported that both Metromail and Donnelley Marketing had been approached by the FBI, which was seeking access to compiled consumer databases for investigatory uses. Donnelley said that it would not sell to the FBI, because such a sale "would be an inappropriate use of lists," but the FBI had apparently gained access to some lists through other firms. The FBI request reminded many of the 1984 IRS attempt to use rented lists to catch tax cheats, which reportedly had been a failure.[44]

Thus, the line between public and private data in targeted marketing is blurring in both directions. Many governmental bodies understandably wish to take advantage of the data in their possession, and the technology allows them to generate some new revenues. Governmental agencies like the FBI often find that private databases contain information that would be helpful in their tasks. But individual Americans may rightfully be troubled by this trend as it continues throughout the 1990s, because in the past one could safely assume that one's per-

sonal, commercial dealings were within one sector and one's governmental dealings—often mandated by law—in another. When the legal requirements for a
typical American life-style—for example, securing a driver's license or voting—
required that one provide information to the government, one could traditionally
assume that the information would stay in that realm. Similarly, one could usually assume that one's purchase patterns were accessible, at most, to members of
the commercial sector. That those patterns may now be scrutinized by a federal
investigatory agency is indeed a frightening thought for many. And yet, the ambiguous privacy domain does not provide any clear legal boundaries to prevent
any of these exchanges. Unlike many European countries, which have federal
commissions or boards to oversee governmental data-handling tasks, the United
States has allowed its agencies much greater freedom. Chapter 7 will address this
concept further.

Across the marketing milieu, then, the ambiguous privacy domain will prove
increasingly problematic in the 1990s. Arguments over intended purposes for collection, information ownership, the line between physical and information privacy, and the appropriate boundaries between the public and private sector will all
increase in scope and frequency as the ambiguous rules around information collection, use, and sharing fail to keep pace with the technological capabilities. But
the problems in marketing, while quite big ones, are not the only areas in which
the 1990s will see privacy issues erupt. Credit and financial affairs will also feel
a strong impact.

Credit and Finance

Ambiguity is currently breeding problems in the credit and financial industries,
and that trend will undoubtedly continue throughout the decade unless it is
stemmed in some way. There are three large areas of concern: errors, reduced
judgment, and new use/sharing.

Errors. Mistakes in credit reporting and credit decisions are causing, and will
continue to cause, much concern. As we discussed in chapter 5, recent efforts by
several state attorneys general (AGs) had brought both TRW Credit Data and
Equifax to out-of-court agreements regarding their policies and practices. A
prominent driver for the AGs' actions was repeated instances of errors in individuals' credit reports—errors that reportedly have been almost impossible for
the individuals to correct. The most prominent fiasco occurred in 1991, when a
subcontractor hired by TRW Credit Data recorded all taxpayers in Norwich, Vermont, as tax *delinquents.* The information was entered into TRW's computers,

and many of Norwich's citizens began to be refused credit. A *Wall Street Journal* article described the problem:

> A doctor couldn't use his credit card on vacation in Alaska. At the annual town fair, a banker found himself cornered at the bumper-car ride by an anguished jewelry-store owner whose mortgage application had inexplicably run into trouble. The town clerk's office was deluged with calls from worried banks around New England.
>
> When Karen Porter, a quilt maker who serves as town clerk, heard that so many people seemed to be having sudden credit problems, she called TRW, leaving six urgent messages over the course of a week. A week later, TRW called back, and the mystery began to clear up.
>
> Ms. Porter thinks Norwich's family finances are back to normal now, but she's not sure. A TRW spokesman told the local newspaper that "no huge number, probably less than 3,000 people," were affected by the error, small comfort to the town of 3,100.[45]

Even in isolated cases where only a few individuals are involved, correction of the errors has often proved problematic. Consider the experience of Joseph Pazos:

> Pazos of West New York, N.J., . . . says he checked his credit report in 1987 after he was turned down for a credit card. He found the report was littered with negative information about his father, Jose Pazos, who lives at the same address. The younger Mr. Pazos obtained letters from more than a dozen of his father's old creditors, stating that their dealings were with Jose, not Joseph. He even changed his mailing address to a post office box in another town.
>
> But four years later, he says his father's data is still cluttering his reports. Meanwhile, he has been turned down for two more credit cards and a student loan. The loan fell through just before he was going to start bachelors-degree night courses, and he had to postpone them for a year.[46]

As we noted earlier, the actual frequency of such errors is open to debate: Consumer Reports' study showed that 48 percent of the reports were in error, while a spokesperson for the credit-reporting industry claimed that, of the reports challenged by consumers, only one-half of one percent would actually have resulted in an adverse credit decision.[47] But the industry clearly has a problem with consumers' and legislators' perceptions, if nothing else. It is doubtful, though, that simply providing free credit reports, as TRW is now doing, will actually solve this problem.[48] The real solution must come from a repositioning of values within the industry, so that accuracy in credit reports and respect for consumers receive strong consideration. To date, the credit-reporting industry has seen the commercial purchasers of reports as its customers and the consumers represented in the reports as a distant entity. However, there is some indication that, at least in some quarters, this approach may be changing. According to a 1991 *Business Week* article, Equifax's new president decided in 1989 to reposition his company as the one most responsive to consumer concerns. "We had to start treating the consumer like a customer," he said. Equifax has now added additional customer service representatives; TRW claims that they had already taken that step.[49] It may well be that competitive pressures eventually cause the credit bureaus to improve the accuracy of their reports through additional edit checks and verification procedures. If not, there will probably be a legislative mandate, perhaps with an audit oversight provision from governmental authorities, to force that result. Either way, the problem of inaccuracy stands as a visible challenge to the industry during the 1990s.

Reduced Judgment. Another challenge to creditors is the perception of reduced judgment in decision processes. As expert systems technology has increasingly permeated the industry, many companies have begun using computer models to make decisions about granting credit. Instead of the traditional model, in which an analyst considered each application in paper form, relying somewhat on established tables but also using his or her own intuitive sense regarding probabilities of default, today's credit decisions are often made through the use of computerized credit-scoring models. Based on an individual's previous credit history, the computer assigns a certain number of points, and credit is granted to individuals with scores above a standard cutoff point. Although many lenders compute their own scores, the three large credit bureaus also offer a service in which they calculate and sell risk scores to purchasers of their credit reports. Such scoring has been in use for over a decade, but it has become much more complex and precise as computer techniques have been refined over the years. The system has also led to some amount of concern on the part of consumers, who sometimes feel as though they are being treated, in the words of a person interviewed in this study, "as just a bunch of numbers." The concern became problematic for Equifax in its recent agreement with the state AGs. In that agreement, Equifax promised to make its risk scores available to consumers when they order their own credit reports. Previously, the risk scores had been sold to the credit bureau's customers, but they were not made available to consumers.[50] Yet providing consumer access to risk scores may actually *increase*, rather than decrease, the overall level of concern during the next few years. Mirroring some executives' perception that "what they don't know won't hurt them," many consumers were previously unaware of the scoring practices and were therefore not inclined to complain about them. As the practice becomes more public, it is likely that an even greater backlash will occur. Furthermore, if it becomes apparent that some creditors' scoring models are including information that applicants deem inappropriate (such as their purchase histories or other psychographic data purchased from outside vendors), the concerns may be heightened.

Credit-granting institutions will also find that the new use and sharing issues are prominent in the 1990s. Use of credit data in marketing—a bone of contention to privacy advocates for many years—will remain a prime issue. Also, the banking industry's increasing use of its customers' financial information (e.g., data supplied on a loan application) for internal marketing purposes will likely come under increased scrutiny. When the banks go outside to buy additional marketing information about their customers—as some banks in this study were doing—customers will increasingly rebel. Whether this rebellion will eventually prompt a legislative response is yet to be seen, but the banks' many years of uninterrupted drift will come to an end in the 1990s when they feel their own external threat.

Sharing. In addition, the credit-reporting industry will face a major hurdle with the sharing issue during the mid-1990s. As the number of super-bureaus (secondary companies that resell credit reports to small businesses) continues to increase, problems with establishing responsibilities for the administration of FCRA guidelines remain somewhat blurry. Many individuals and organizations who would like to purchase credit reports would be turned down, under the FCRA guidelines, if they approached one of the Big Three credit bureaus. Yet some groups continue to allege that the same credit reports are available with very little scrutiny from any number of super-bureaus across the country. Often all it takes—according to investigative reports in various publications and media—is a statement that the reports will be used for employment verification.[51] In other cases, filling in the super-bureau's application only in part—but enclosing the required fee—gains one access to all the credit reports in the country.[52] As the network connecting providers of credit data, sellers of credit reports, and resellers of reporting packages becomes a more intricate web, it becomes unclear exactly which party has responsibility for which part of the FCRA. Is the super-bureau required to check the validity of each application for its services? Some credit bureaus are certainly assuming that duty.[53] On the other hand, are the Big Three credit bureaus in some way responsible for ensuring that their credit reports are not ultimately put to some improper use? In addition, the FCRA requires that consumers be told the identities of each entity purchasing copies of their credit reports. But if the initial purchaser is simply a super-bureau, then the super-bureau alone may appear in the consumer's record. The ultimate purchaser of the report thereby keeps his or her identity a secret, thus undercutting the FCRA's intent. As the world of telecommunications makes sharing data more feasible, the ambiguity of the privacy domain once again becomes a problem. And yet, especially as Congress continues to reconsider the FCRA, the credit industry's responsibilities for enforcement will become even more critical.

So the credit and financial industries will have their share of privacy worries during the remainder of the 1990s as their accuracy rates, decision processes, and sharing and new use protections come under scrutiny. However, an even bigger challenge to privacy protection may come from the use of medical data, to which we now turn.

Medical Data

The mid- and late 1990s will see a tremendous upsurge in concerns about information privacy in medical records as technological gains make new collections and uses of data possible. The collection, sharing, and new use of medical data will become pivotal points of argument. Technological gains in both the medical and computer worlds, buttressed by business pressures that prompt their use, are causing the environment to change much faster than the law and societal norms. Consequently, the ambiguity becomes increasingly problematic, and it may well lead to a number of reactive legislative curbs inhibiting technological gains that could ultimately benefit society as a whole.

With respect to the collection of personal medical information, problems with AIDS test results, so prominent an issue in this study, should be seen as foreshadowing even more complicated issues. A newer technology with even more potential for danger is emerging: genetic testing. The Medical Section Committee on Genetic Testing of the American Council of Life Insurance (ACLI) has defined genetic tests as "laboratory tests used to determine the presence or absence of abnormal or defective genes and/or chromosomes. Such tests are direct measures of such defects or abnormalities, as opposed to indirect manifestations of genetic disorders."[54] Genetic testing is becoming a more prominent topic of discussion primarily because of the Human Genome Project, a fifteen-year effort initiated in 1988 and sponsored by the National Institutes of Health and the U.S. Department of Energy. The project's goal is to determine the location and chemical sequence of the genes in human DNA. At the same time, DNA tests are increasingly being used in the courts, since they provide a sort of "fingerprint" for individuals. Certainly, society could experience many positive benefits from an understanding of genetic backgrounds and from better identification of criminal suspects. However, the technology can also present a number of dangerous privacy exposures, since results of genetic testing reveal not actual diseases but only a *probability* that one might, at some time, contract a disease. Consequently, the collection, storage, and use of such test information pushes the arguments about AIDS test information to an even greater depth. Genetic tests reveal only a potential problem for the future, and some privacy advocates and medical ethicists assert that they could easily be abused.

A 1991 House subcommittee hearing heard witnesses discuss questions like these:[55]

- Should a health insurer be allowed to charge more for a policy sold to someone who carries a disease gene, because of the chance that the person's child will have the disease?

- Should employers be allowed to order the testing of a prospective employee for genetic traits as part of gathering "job-related medical information"? (A 1991 survey of five hundred companies by the Office of Technology Assessment found that one percent had policies on genetic testing but that 62 percent of the companies' health officers said the decision to perform genetic tests should be the employer's.)

- Can a doctor who discovers that a patient has a gene for a treatable inherited disease ethically tell the patient's relatives they should be tested, even if the patient objects?

A 1991 task force sponsored by the ACLI and the Health Insurance Association of America (HIAA) found that genetic testing was not yet in use in the insurance industry nor about to be embraced. Furthermore, the task force argued that, for several reasons, genetic testing might never find a home in the industry:[56]

- Only 3 percent of life insurance applications are currently declined, and no studies have shown that any more applicants would be denied life insurance if genetic tests were used. Insurers can already predict some medical conditions based on existing factors, like high cholesterol for heart disease. Furthermore, insurers understand that genetic testing only deals with probabilities, and that environmental and life-style factors are also important. Researchers estimate that the average person carries six to eight genes that could lead to diseases; thus, insurers are obviously not going to deny coverage to all who carry such genes.

• Because about 85 to 90 percent of health insurance is currently purchased through group plans, for which individuals are not underwritten, these employees' health insurance would not be affected by genetic testing. If HIAA-sponsored legislative reforms were to be implemented, other individuals who are not now insured under such plans would receive additional protection. They would not, then, be subject to any discrimination from genetic testing.

• Genetic testing is costly. Researchers anticipate that it will be several years before genetic tests are inexpensive enough to be economically viable for insurers to use. However, even if they do not perform genetic tests themselves, insurers might have to deal with an "adverse selection" phenomenon if individuals have their own genetic tests. Under that scenario, individuals whose risks were higher than their insurers thought might become disproportionately heavy purchasers of insurance. Thus, even if they did not pay to run genetic tests on applicants, insurers would need access to any test results that were already known to the applicant, so that they could avoid any potential "adverse selection."

The cost of testing might also have great impact on employment-related decisions, since the cost of genetic tests could limit the frequency with which they were administered.

Despite the insurance industry's attempts to minimize the impact of genetic testing, concerns about the testing clearly run deep. Even Nobel laureate James D. Watson—one of the two researchers who described DNA's structure—has indicated some fear: "Speaking as a citizen, I think genetic information should be absolutely private. The idea that there will be a huge bank of genetic information on millions of people is repulsive. . . . I shudder at the thought of all this information in the hands of a malicious head of the FBI."[57] News reports about genetic testing have become quite common in the early 1990s, with the *Wall Street Journal*, *Consumer Reports*, and many others devoting space to the topic. Individuals' awareness of the potential for benefits and abuse of genetic testing will grow over the next few years and, consequently, so will calls for legislative curbs. By mid-1992, some states had already placed prohibitions into effect: Arizona and Montana have laws that prohibit insurers from excluding individuals based on their genetic traits; California and Pennsylvania had similar bills under consideration. In April 1992, Florida's governor signed a bill requiring not only insurers but also employers, lenders, and schools to notify individuals who had had DNA analysis that their results had been used in granting or denying loans, education, coverage, or employment. The New York legislature was considering a far-reaching bill that would prohibit discrimination in employment, insurance, housing, training, credit, or education on the basis of genetic predisposition. A few other states had laws against insurers' using specific genetic conditions (e.g., sickle cell anemia) in underwriting. At a federal level, the Human Genome Privacy Act was considered in both the 101st and 102nd Congresses. This act would have barred government agencies from disclosing genetic information about individuals who were involved in the federal research, and its sponsor indicated that it might be amended to include insurance and employment concerns.[58] Attention to genetic testing issues can be expected to accelerate later in the 1990s. Since genetic tests push the boundaries of existing societal values and laws, they increase the ambiguity of the privacy environment.

Concerns about new uses and sharing of medical information will also increase during the 1990s. The use of medical records for marketing purposes was widely assailed after a *Wall Street Journal* article on the topic in February 1992.[59] According to the article, many physicians and pharmacists regularly permit organizations to dial into their computers and retrieve patients' prescription records, which are then used for aggregated marketing purposes. In most cases, the pharmacy or physician is remunerated through a discount on his or her computer. It is unclear whether any of the prescription records are actually associated with particular patients' names, but the potential certainly existed, since the collecting organizations have full access to any and all records on the computers. (One organization had been collecting patients' Social Security numbers but recently discontinued the practice.[60]) In response to this story, the American Medical Association disseminated a statement warning doctors about the ethical implications of giving patient data to marketers. At the same time, a member of the U.S. House of Representatives introduced a bill to ban disclosing prescription records without a patient's consent. If passed, this bill would become the first federal privacy law covering such medical information.[61]

But reactive responses like these do not solve the overall problem: given the improved technological sharing capabilities and the strong financial incentives to share such data, additional threats will continue to rear their heads. For example, one industry observer who had been an executive at a health insurance company told of being approached in 1991 by an entrepreneurial start-up venture, which was introduced to his firm by one of the Big Six accounting firms. The entrepreneurs proposed to take over his company's processing of health claims for a ridiculously low fee—far less than what it cost his firm to process the claims in-house—in return for access to the health claim data. The entrepreneurs proposed to sell mailing lists gleaned from the data; for example, they might peddle a list of individuals taking Prozac, an antidepressant, to manufacturers of competing medications, and they would include the names and addresses of the individuals' physicians in the list. The executive reported that the lists could also be sold to private hospitals, who could write to the families of ailing individuals and offer their services (e.g., "Dear Mr. and Mrs. Warren: We note that your son, Mike, has been depressed for some time, and our treatment facility . . ."). While this executive declined the entrepreneur's offer ("I told them they'd better get out of my office in a hurry, but I suspect they'll find some other executives more inclined to listen to them"), such entrepreneurial efforts are only the tip of an iceberg that will become more and more problematic during the later 1990s. The trend toward employers' self-insurance of health claims means that employers will gain freer access to employee medical information, which could potentially be misused. It is reasonable to expect that a spate of well-publicized incidents in which employers are alleged to have taken discriminatory personnel actions based on such medical information will eventually lead to a reconsideration of the employers' access rights for this information, even in a self-insurance situation. The existing state insurance laws have primarily been based on an assumption of traditional insurance relationships, with the risk being borne by the insurance company. The trend diverges from this model, but the norms surrounding the new self-insurance model fall into the ambiguous privacy zone.

The increasing computerization of health care claims for both payment and research purposes will also fuel concerns about sharing and new use of medical data during the 1990s. In an attempt to address the health care crisis in the U.S., four pilot regional health care databases are being created through which one's health claims would be transmitted on-line directly to one's insurer. In addition, the database would provide researchers with an ideal access point for studying health trends and, most important, a means of tracking expenses for various procedures and providers. Thus, for example, the hospitals in a particular city could be ranked from most to least efficient, based on the expenses filed in their claims. A bill introduced in June 1992 in the U.S. Senate would amend the Social Security Act to provide for a nationwide system of this type. The bill gives the secretary of health, education, and welfare substantial responsibilities for investigating various alternatives of implementation. In addition, the secretary would become responsible for translating the NAIC Model Act into workable guidelines for the system.[62] The bill acknowledges the need for privacy considerations—and, in fact, a task force under the auspices of the National Academy of Sciences is examining privacy issues; but the overall plan for computerizing health claims in centralized databases will undoubtedly cause concerns as the implementation becomes more concrete. How will individuals' privacy be protected as records are shared electronically and used for new venues of research? Once again, the technological and economic solution breeds new privacy concerns.

For various reasons, medical information—arguably for many individuals the most sensitive information collected and stored in a database—will likely serve during the later 1990s as an emotional lever for greater privacy protection. The medical and insurance industries have done a marvelous job in the past of controlling their own activities and, to a great degree, ensuring the confidentiality of patient information through a number of basic ethical norms. But these protections are beginning to splinter, often not because of any ethically improper behavior on behalf of the medical community or the insurers (e.g., intentionally releasing a medical record to a newspaper) but rather because of technological possibilities and market pressures. Self-insurance by employers, for example, places much of the burden for appropriate use of medical data not on the insurer —who has traditionally protected it well—but on the employer, who may have other pressures. As new, centralized databases are created to facilitate the control of health care costs and the more efficient processing of claims, yet another privacy exposure develops, since additional players are involved with the data. Thus, the traditional protections surrounding medical information will prove insufficient as the caretakers of the data shift.

Workplace

In addition to problems in the marketing, financial, and medical arenas, privacy concerns will also arise in the general workplace during this decade. Several technologies are providing ample ground for reinterpretation of the boundaries between appropriate and inappropriate management practices. As this happens, the ambiguity surrounding these behaviors will erupt in a societal backlash.

Most workplace concerns for the 1990s will involve information collection. There will continue to be much ambiguity regarding which types of data are appropriate for an employer to collect before and during the employment relationship. While polygraphs have been outlawed as a preemployment screening technique for almost all nongovernment jobs, the use of "honesty tests" and other psychological screening tools will continue to be controversial throughout the decade.[63] Employers' preemployment use of credit reports—a permissible use under the FCRA—will also receive scrutiny during the 1990s, as will their queries to workmen's compensation databases, which track the claims filed by employees, thus allowing employers to check on whether prospective employees will likely be accident-prone. Genetic tests as well will come under fire when used in the employment relationship.

The greatest concerns for the workplace, however, will be those regarding surveillance of employees in their day-to-day jobs. It is already widely alleged that monitoring of workers causes increased levels of stress. Sometimes this monitoring occurs during telephone conversations, as supervisors listen in to ensure that operators are handling calls properly. Increasingly, monitoring is being tied to computerized tasks, with measurements of each employee's productivity embedded in the system, and such measurements will become more common over the next few years. Since the law—not anticipating such technological capabilities—is virtually silent on the appropriateness of such monitoring, this activity falls among those that are legal but often attacked as intrusive. Most common are systems that check how quickly workers are performing a task, sometimes ranking the workers or sending messages like "You're not working as fast as the person next to you."[64] One user called a "computer spying hotline" to report on her job: "It's a nightmare. Everyone knows how many seconds you spent in the bathroom. It's like kindergarten."[65] Other systems, not widely implemented but growing in popularity, actually track employees physically within the workplace: each employee wears a badge that allows his or her location to be monitored. While such systems have extensive benefits—for example, they can enable phone calls to be automatically routed to an individual's current location[66]—they also provide a sense of Big Brother surveillance.

Exacerbating concerns about surveillance are new technologies like electronic mail ("e-mail"), which are technologically ahead of societal norms and laws. In particular, a troublesome question about e-mail messages in the workplace will persist for several years: are the communications between employees their own private property, or do they belong to the corporation? If the latter, the corporation appears to have every right to examine the messages; if the former, it does not. At present, the law is silent on this question. While messages via both e-mail and "voice mail" (a telephone system that takes messages) are protected in their transmissions by the Electronic Communication Privacy Act of 1986, the act does not address an *employer's* access rights. However, several lawsuits have been filed to test the boundaries: both Epson America and Nissan Motor Corporation

U.S.A. have been defendants in actions by present and former employees who alleged that their privacy had been violated by corporate snooping into their e-mail.[67] While the boundaries remain unclear, there is no question that conflicting corporate policies increase the ambiguity. (Some consider in-house e-mail to be private, like phone calls, while others call it company property; the situation is just as complicated for messages sent outside the corporate walls.[68]) It is even unclear whether e-mail messages are a form of corporate archive that must be preserved, or whether they should be destroyed as quickly as scratch paper: in a governmental example of this dilemma, the Bush administration tried to destroy a number of computer backup tapes containing e-mail messages related to the Iran-contra scandal, but a number of historians, librarians, and public interest groups were able to block the administration's quest.[69] As newer technologies—such as one allowing employees to read documents and add "voice notes" that are then appended to the document—are unveiled and diffused across the corporate world in the next few years, additional questions about ownership and norms will continue to spring up. In terms of legislation, the heat is bound to increase: state bills to limit monitoring have already been introduced in several states, and federal bills to require companies to use "beep tones" when monitoring workers' conversations were introduced in both the U.S. House and Senate in 1992.

Anonymity

Finally, one additional trend will increase the ambiguity in privacy norms: anonymity in many transactions will be reduced. This phenomenon is especially pointed because of technological advances in the telecommunications industry, where Caller ID and Automatic Number Identification are now being used to identify callers. Thus, when one places a call to an 800 or 900 number, one's phone number may be captured, enabling the organization receiving the call to look up one's name and address through a computerized "reverse phone directory" and use or sell this information. Readers of *DM News*, a direct marketing industry publication, frequently find advertisements for lists of callers to 900-number services such as dating clubs. In the past, one could generally assume that one's phone calls would remain anonymous unless one chose to reveal one's identity during the conversation. Now, in many cases, that anonymity is being removed. Caller ID, offered by many telephone companies, provides the phone number of calling parties on a small screen attached to one's phone. Different state legislatures have passed a bewildering array of laws either outlawing Caller ID (a recent Pennsylvania court case seemed to do this but left some ambiguity);

providing "per-call" blocking (before dialing one can type a code that prohibits the called party from knowing one's identity); or, as under New York's law, providing "per-line" blocking (all calls made from one's line are labeled "private," and the number is not revealed to the called party).[70] Voice mail callers are also finding that they cannot leave an anonymous message: the system often captures their calling extension information and reports it to the called party. The intermingling of cable television and telephone services, made legal by an FCC ruling in July 1992, can only increase the potential for one's life-style purchases to be scrutinized in a nonanonymous fashion.[71] Thus, all the technological pieces for changing anonymous transactions into identifiable ones are quickly falling into place. Predictably, the reactive legal policy-making cycle has not addressed these trends, but the pressure to do so will rise during this decade.

Social Security Numbers

Finally, and ironically, one item will *not* become as pivotal an issue as one might expect. Since the 1960s, there has been much debate about the use of the Social Security number as a personal identifier in the United States. Proponents claim that use of a unique identifier enables society to be more efficient in its record-keeping, but opponents argue that having such an identifier merely enables many intrusive databases to be formed and merged more easily. With provisions that were sensitive to this concern, the Privacy Act of 1974 offered some constraints on the collection and use of the Social Security numbers. However, it is not clear whether the spirit of that law has been obeyed; for example, several states now use the Social Security number as the driver's license number for their citizens. Lawsuits over requirements to provide one's Social Security number are common.

During the 1990s we will see that the Social Security number is becoming not more but *less* relevant as an identifier, primarily due to the growth of relational database technologies, which allow one to locate a record with any combination of pieces of data (e.g., name, address, phone number). This database technology differs noticeably from those of the 1960s and 1970s, in which records were often retrievable solely through a primary key like the Social Security number. As more and more databases are converted to the relational technology, it will be increasingly possible to find and merge individuals' records almost as easily without the number as with it. In fact, some of the major credit bureaus already use the number as only a secondary field in their databases, making it no more important than other pieces of data.

The real keys to privacy debates in the later 1990s will not be such particular matters as Social Security numbers but, rather, the managerial decisions made about the actual collection and use of personal information. Operations that required a Social Security number in the 1960s will be quite achievable without it in the 1990s. The true privacy problems will come not from the number's role in merging databases but from the appropriate and inappropriate uses of the data themselves. Of course, the Social Security number debate is not totally irrelevant, as the number will always be a good source of identification and will enable a better matching system in databases. But its importance in privacy debates is dwarfed by the huge ambiguities surrounding marketing, financial, and medical uses of information; the workplace surveillance issues; and the reduction in anonymity provided by new technologies. Even if the Social Security number *does* receive the protected status that some argue it should, most of the managerial uses of personal information that were uncovered in this study will continue unabated. These are the concerns that deserve—and will ultimately receive—the most attention in the 1990s.

A Big Task Ahead

The ambiguity in the U.S. privacy domain provides much room for debate in almost every industry that handles personal information. Whether or not there is a right to privacy in the commercial sector in the United States, how much responsibility corporations should bear in administering that right, and which behaviors are appropriate and inappropriate all contribute to the ambiguity. As we look into the later 1990s, we see ample fodder for debates and reactive legislation that in one way or another will affect almost all industries in the United States: employment, medical records, financial affairs, etc. Clearly, the current system of reactive corporate and legal policy-making, which stems from the ambiguous privacy domain and leads to substantial problems both inside and outside corporations, cannot effectively address the growing technological challenges to privacy for the rest of the decade. A new approach is needed.

Chapter 7

Solving the Problems

In their book *Databanks in a Free Society* (1972), Alan Westin and Michael Baker presented the results of an important study in which they examined the record-keeping policies and practices of several organizations. At that time, they found that privacy advocates' fears of extensive and intrusive databanks had not yet come to pass. They stated: "Our basic finding is quite strong—*the organizations that we visited have not extended the scope of their information collection about individuals as a direct result of computerization* [italics in original]." But they also noted that technology was making the sharing of records much more feasible, and they offered several insightful recommendations to help organizations prepare for the future.[1] By 1977, when the PPSC conducted its exhaustive study of numerous industries, computerization had enabled quite a few instances of intrusive corporate behavior, and the PPSC detailed a number of recommendations for improving the balance between society's needs and individuals' privacy desires. However, during the 1980s most of the PPSC's recommendations were ignored, although the technological strides of this decade made the commercial collection, use, and sharing of individual-specific information even more economical and feasible. Consequently, corporate uses of personal information grew by leaps and bounds during this period, with relatively little governmental control and with large zones of ambiguity regarding appropriate and inappropriate behavior.

By the late 1980s and early 1990s, when the latest "privacy scare" began to erupt and when this study was conducted, many corporations' policies were outdated, and their practices were often inconsistent with the policies they did have in place. Having been awakened to varying degrees by the growing power and vocal expression of the privacy coalition, they now find themselves taking defensive positions. But because the privacy domain still remains ambiguous, they are not sure how to solve the problem. At the same time, privacy advocates are clamoring for more laws, since these advocates usually operate on the assumption that each particular privacy infraction in each industry can be identified and regulated with few negative consequences for society as a whole. Lawmakers often seem confused by the debates: many want to be responsive to citizens' growing concerns about privacy, but many are also sensitive to the arguments about the economic instability that can be created by a number of overly restrictive laws. Indeed, all parties—acting from different perspectives but with the best of intentions—seem to be reaching a position of gridlock in which some, or all, will lose. The technology and its applications have outstripped our ability to govern them, and reeling them back in will be a painful process.

However, we have no choice but to confront them. This country's existing approaches to privacy are serving no one well: not executives, who are forced to make decisions about new applications without any real appreciation for their responsibilities or for society's expectations; not consumers, who are increasingly seeing their privacy eroded by the sometimes well-intentioned (but often not fully considered) collection, use, and sharing of personal information by the corporations and government; not legislators, who continue to react to specific and visible privacy invasions rather than confronting the overall problem with an overall solution; and not by privacy advocates, whose arguments are finding a warmer reception but still a somewhat confused response from society as a whole.

As the PPSC anticipated in 1977, things are not going well in the U.S. privacy domain of the early 1990s. This study utilized a somewhat limited sample, and generalization from such a sample can be dangerous (see Appendix). But the stories across the sites were, for the most part, internally consistent, and the evidence from areas outside the study for the most part confirmed the study's findings. We can reasonably state, then, that the U.S. corporate privacy domain faces the following problems in the early 1990s: ambiguity regarding privacy rights, corporate responsibilities, and appropriate activities; a lack of proactive efforts by corporations; the likelihood of a consumer backlash; and the prospect that legislators will react by imposing regulations that may do as much harm as good.

These findings are not discrete ones; rather, they are all indicative of the piecemeal approach to information privacy that has been embraced in the United States. This fragmented approach often leaves executives in a quandary as to which actions are appropriate, prompting them to abdicate responsibility to mid-level managers until forced to do otherwise; leads to widely divergent thought processes and differing assumptions across society; and causes significant emotional dissonance for many corporate employees. Because the legislative response to privacy issues has tended to vacillate with the political environment, corporations have generally ignored the issue until forced to do otherwise. This course has often seemed prudent, at least in the short term; after all, roughly a decade (1977–86) passed with very little federal attention being paid to privacy issues. Now, however, the tide has turned.

Of course, a concept as fundamental to human dignity as privacy should not really be subject to the changing political winds. Instead, it should receive constant attention, not only from consumers and advocates but also—especially—from corporate executives. The current system does not encourage this focus, however. Instead it encourages corporations to "do whatever we can get away with," in the words of one executive. When the alarm finally rings, the corporation responds. Until then, though, the concept of information privacy stays in limbo.

How can this problem be solved? One reaction, of course, is to call for more laws—specific prohibitions of certain uses of information. For example, one might call for laws prohibiting credit card issuers from using transaction histories for any purpose other than billing, or prohibiting health insurers from revealing to employers any information, even in summarized form, about their employees' health. But such an approach would treat symptoms rather than the problem itself. It relies on a "regulatory fix," a fallacy described in one study on automobile pollution.[2] The regulatory approach implements reactive prohibitions based on the perception of present and past infractions. However, it does nothing to prepare us for the future. Furthermore, this approach is quite likely to kill some programs that, in a utilitarian sense, have a net benefit to society. Instead, what we need is a *systemic* fix. We need a way to reduce the ambiguity in the U.S. privacy domain and to prompt the appropriate corporate behaviors over the long haul. We need a change in approach consistent with the unique qualities of the U.S. governmental and economic systems.

The U.S. System

In this country, three interlocking societal mechanisms work in unison to create the climate in which corporate decisions are made. These three mechanisms have been defined as 1) economic and social factors in the market system, felt through the "invisible hand" of the market; 2) self-generated initiatives undertaken by executives, exhibited as the "hand of management"; and 3) legal constraints, felt through the "hand of government."[3] These three "hands" interlock to determine the boundaries on appropriate behavior in the privacy domain. However, the hand of government is often described as the mechanism of last resort,[4] which kicks in when the other two fail to achieve an acceptable solution. A brief examination of the other two "hands" will reveal why this description might be true, especially in the case of information privacy.

To say that the invisible hand of the market will produce acceptable corporate behaviors assumes that consumers can and will exert economic pressure on societal institutions. For example, a consumer might tell a merchant, "I will not buy anything else from you until you change your policy." Christopher Stone, in his book *Where the Law Ends*, argues that for individual consumers to apply economic pressure to corporations, the following four conditions must be met: people must *know* they are being injured; people must know *where* to apply economic pressure; people must be in a *position* to apply pressure; and the pressure must be *translated* into warranted changes. Stone argues convincingly that these four conditions will rarely be met.[5] When privacy considerations come into play, the first condition is especially troublesome: often, consumers do not know that they are being injured by certain policies and practices. In those situations, the remaining conditions become somewhat moot.

Of course, Stone's analysis assumes that the consumers are acting as individuals instead of as a collective group. In general, that assumption is fair, especially in the privacy domain. For individual consumers to band together to exert group pressure, they would all have to realize that they were being injured; find each other; organize their attack; and implement their plan. Given the difficulty of achieving even the first step, such a plan seems unlikely. Yet there are existing consumer advocacy organizations that could exert some economic pressure. Those advocacy organizations were not very effective during the 1980s, but with the increasing media and legislative scrutiny of the 1990s, their clout is increasing.[6]

So, given that individual consumers might have a difficult time in exerting power through the invisible hand of the market, the only other alternative to a legal response is self-regulation by managers. In other words, managers must, of their own accord, modify their behavior so that it meets the approval of society's other elements. This expectation is rather large. As already noted, consumers' opinions are difficult to assess, because there are few direct mechanisms for soliciting them. Moreover, executives can through the design of many corporate structures become somewhat insulated from outside environmental influences. In addition, corporate pressures toward profitability—usually stressed in a short-run context—can make long-run considerations of other stakeholders' positions quite difficult. And, finally, executives must normally make their decisions long before the other societal infrastructures have addressed the issues. Consequently, they are forced to make decisions with quite limited input. Not surprisingly, then, their assumptions and arguments often differ from those of the other parties.

Thus, with the hand of the market and the hand of management both facing major obstacles, the hand of government seems an attractive alternative. However, legal proscriptions may not necessarily be a better solution. Stone notes three reasons: laws are always reactive and therefore lag behind the problems they purport to solve; even when laws are crafted, they are created under the partial control of the corporations themselves, which have substantial lobbying and public relations power; and implementation of the laws is difficult and expensive. In addition, it is hard to punish a corporation for wrongdoing. Fines provide economic disincentives, but they are seldom effective deterrents for corporate managers, as the shareholders bear the brunt of the punishment. Threatening to jail the executives leads to additional problems, because in a bureaucratic structure it is usually difficult to fix culpability on individuals.[7]

If new laws come to pass in the 1990s as a last resort, what form will they take? They will likely be quite specific—perhaps of the nature of the Video Privacy Protection Act. Such has been the tradition of U.S. privacy laws: they address rather narrow issues and are usually crafted in a reactive response by anxious legislators. They do not fit together into a cohesive pattern or represent an omnibus solution to privacy problems. Furthermore, they often do not reflect a realistic understanding of the specifics of the industries they propose to regulate. Instead of adopting such an approach, the United States should instead move toward a more cohesive approach that reduces the ambiguity by acknowledging the validity of an updated set of Fair Information Practices, clarifying the corporate responsibility for protecting privacy, and establishing a new legislative infrastructure that creates proper incentives for industry and corporate actions.

Fair Information Practices

As we have already discussed, the biggest problem in the current corporate privacy domain is ambiguity. Society has lost its footing with respect to the specific boundaries surrounding the collection, use, and protection of personal information. Later in this chapter I will outline a number of steps for improving the privacy protection process. First, however, it will be useful to reexamine the foundations of privacy protection established over two decades ago.

Figure 1.2 displays the first set of Fair Information Practices, presented by a Department of Health, Education, and Welfare committee in 1973. The Fair Information Practices formed a solid baseline for privacy protection. However, the changing information environment has brought new challenges and opportunities. The results of this study indicate that some new Fair Information Practices should be added to the list. I would suggest the following additions:

• There must be no deception in data collection practices. When asked to provide information, a person should be told, in clear language, the purpose for collecting the information and all the ways in which the information will be used.

• On a regular basis, a person should be given the opportunity to opt out of any information practices he or she finds inappropriate. Such an opportunity should be clearly communicated.

• Within any organization that uses the personal data, only individuals with a legitimate need to know—narrowly interpreted—should have access to the data. Such data should not be shared with other organizations unless the above provisions regarding clear description of purpose and opportunity to opt out have been met.

• Disparate data files should not be combined unless the above provisions regarding clear description of purpose and opportunity to opt out have been met.

• Decisions about use of the data should be made through appropriate judgmental processes. Although many of these decisions can be made through automated processes, exceptional situations should be subjected to human scrutiny.

We must acknowledge, in the case of privacy, that corporations have an overt duty to ensure their adherence to the Fair Information Practices. This corporate responsibility requires constant attention, just like environmental protection, affirmative action, etc. All of these responsibilities must be balanced against the most fundamental duty of a corporation: to make a profit for the shareholders. To achieve this balance requires that a structure be developed throughout the economic and governmental system to stimulate the necessary response from corporate decision makers. That response should be one with a long-term perspective.

So rather than crafting small, reactive laws that regulate corporate behavior at a "micro" level, we should consider the totality of evidence at hand. The study revealed an interesting phenomenon: the realistic possibility of either a consumer backlash or legislative scrutiny was often enough of an external threat to spur a corporation to reexamine its privacy policies. While a *single* consumer's concerns might be overlooked, the threat of extensive negative publicity—as in the case with AIDS test results at LifeIns—was enough to spur corporate action. When consumer concerns became part of a legislative inquiry, as they did regarding CredCard, corporate attention was often immediate and intent.

The importance of such a threat cannot be overstated. Executives are, in general, people of integrity who wish to adhere to society's expectations for proper behavior. But executives have two very limited resources: time and attention. To the extent that such a threat becomes a consistent and visible one, executives will devote more of their limited resources to consideration of these issues. Thus, a major threat will shorten the drift period and make the policy-making effort a continuous and proactive one rather than a reactive one. The key is to establish a consistent threat of retaliation for privacy intrusions.

What are the options for effecting this new plan? According to Colin Bennett, there are five basic models for regulating privacy. While none has been empirically observed in its pure form, each has been embraced by one or more countries to some degree. Bennett's description of the five models can be summarized as follows:

1. The Voluntary Control model, which relies on self-regulation on the part of corporate players. The law defines specific rules and requires that a "responsible person" in each organization ensure compliance.

2. The Self-help model, which depends on data subjects' challenging inappropriate record-keeping practices. Rights of access and correction are provided for the subjects, but they are responsible for identifying problems and bringing them to the courts for resolution.

3. The Licensing model, which requires that each databank containing personal data be licensed (usually upon payment of a fee) by a separate governmental institution. This institution would stipulate specific conditions for the collection, storage, and use of personal data. This model anticipates potential problems and heads them off by requiring a prior approval for any use of data.

4. The Registration model, which acts much like the Licensing model with one exception: the governmental institution has no right to block the creation of a particular information system. Only in a case where complaints

are received and an investigation reveals a failure to adhere to data protection principles would a system be "deregistered." Thus, this model provides more remedial than anticipatory enforcement of principles.

5. The Data Commissioner model, which utilizes neither licensing nor registration processes but instead relies on the ombudsman concept through a commissioner's office. The commissioner has no powers of regulation but investigates complaints from citizens. The commissioner is also viewed as an expert who should offer advice on data handling; monitor technology and make proposals; and perform some inspections of data processing operations. This model relies to a great degree on the commissioner's credibility with the legislature, the press, and the public.[8]

In these five models, the level of governmental involvement in corporate privacy matters seems to vary as shown in Figure 7.1. The Voluntary Control and Self-help models place very few preemptive restrictions on corporations and allow them to manage their own affairs. The Self-help model is the most laissez-faire in its approach: short of specifying a few rights of access and inspection for citizens, it relies on the citizens to police the corporations and pursue their own remedies in the courts. The Voluntary Control model provides only a small additional requirement: that each organization have an internal compliance officer, whose viewpoint, one might argue, could be tainted by his or her corporate relationship. The Data Commissioner model does provide for an external governmental ombudsman who acts to some degree as an advocate for citizens; however, there is no overt governmental management of the internal data handling processes at the corporations, save the inspections that the commissioner might conduct (but with no real enforcement authority). The Registration model goes far beyond this scenario by adding the somewhat bureaucratic requirement that all databanks be registered and by giving a government agency the authority to regulate corporate record-keeping activities directly—and to "deregister" those it finds inappropriate. The Licensing model goes even further, making regulation a "before the fact" rather than "after the fact" determination: this model effectively prohibits all uses of personal data without the prior approval of the governmental agency.

In looking across the international privacy approaches, one finds Sweden at the far right of the diagram, with a structure very close to the Licensing model. The British policy is one of Registration, while Germany has embraced the Data Commissioner approach. The United States has been at the far left of Figure 7.1, with a system that combines Voluntary Control with Self-help.[9] The obvious

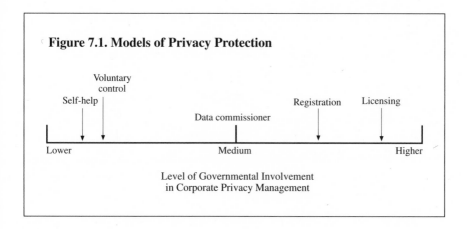

Figure 7.1. Models of Privacy Protection

question for consideration now becomes: which model is right for the United States in the 1990s?

If the results of this study and other evidence from the media tell us one thing, it is this: our country's existing approach of Self-help and Voluntary Control is not working.[10] The latter model was never really embraced in the United States for commercial enterprises, but even if it had been, one could not have realistically expected internal corporate monitors to properly police their own organizations' data-handling activities; in fact, this approach could only lead to more of the emotional dissonance observed in this study. The Self-help model, which underlies most of the United States's approach to privacy in commercial enterprise, makes several problematic assumptions: that citizens are aware of their rights, of corporate encroachments on those rights, and of how to pursue remedies;[11] that citizens are willing to expend the energy to undertake these roles; and that "an inexpert judiciary" is able to decide "quite technical issues."[12] Priscilla Regan calls the concept of self-help an "advertising gimmick that bureaucracies use to 'symbolize' their concern with these issues."[13] It is certainly true that few, if any, privacy debates have been clearly resolved through the Self-help mechanism in the United States.

Thus, we are left to decide which of the competing models is the appropriate one for the United States to embrace in the 1990s. As guidelines in making this decision, I offer three assertions that are buttressed by this study's results:

1. The biggest challenge is the reduction of ambiguity in the U.S. privacy domain. This ambiguity drives the reactive policy-making cycles and leads to most of the problems uncovered in this study.

2. Corporations will only pay attention to privacy concerns when they perceive a realistic threat of retribution for inattention. In each case where privacy concerns were addressed by the corporations in this study—and, for that matter, in each case reported in the media over the past few years—that threat was a visible trigger for corporate action.

3. It is unclear how much regulation is necessary to ensure that such a threat is effective. Therefore, legislators should initially avoid implementing more regulation than is necessary to solve the problems. However, should corporations prove to be uncooperative in their voluntary responses, additional regulation should be embraced.

This third assertion deserves a fuller explanation. The results of this study are inconclusive regarding the need for explicit regulation as an external threat in the corporate cycle. In some cases, it appeared that corporations were reacting to the mere *threat* of regulation, negative publicity, or competitive pressures when they entered their reaction periods. CredCard, for example, had been hit with no new regulations regarding its cardholder histories at the time of this study; the fact that a congressional subcommittee was conducting an investigation of the credit industry was enough to spur an enlightened response. The life insurance industry undertook its changes in AIDS testing less as the result of any specific law at the state or federal level than as a response to a perceived threat of *future* legislation. The health insurers were responding to a state law but acknowledged that this law was not onerous in and of itself. Instead, they were reconsidering their policies in light of the threat of *additional* legislation. Looking outside this study, we see that many of the widely reported corporate actions on privacy also fall into this category. Though the Lotus MarketPlace: Households product had been the subject of some discussion by legislators, it was withdrawn from the market not because of regulation but as a response to the threat of legislation and continued negative publicity. Equifax withdrew its credit-based mailing lists from the market not as a result of new regulation—although the New York State attorney general's office had clearly indicated displeasure with the practice—but in order to improve its public image and ward off future legislative threats.

On the other hand, there are also some examples in which corporations appear to react only when regulation—or some sort of judicial retribution—is eminent. For example, a few interviewees in this study seemed to believe "If it's legal, it's okay," but they were certainly in the minority. It has also been alleged—though those of us outside the corporations do not know for sure—that some changes at Equifax and TRW Credit Data were prompted not by a spirit of voluntary change but rather because of state AGs' threats. We saw in chapter 5 that the arguments of many corporate interviewees indicated a real commitment to the law; on several occasions, though, a commitment to profitability led them to adopt even higher standards, because customers often had higher standards than the laws, and profitability depended on a continued and trusting relationship with customers. Furthermore, the interviewees' commitment to the law involved not only adherence to existing laws but also the avoidance of new laws that could be crafted in response to perceptions of corporate misdeeds.

At a national level, opinion polls of executives leave some doubt about how much regulation will be required to solve the privacy problems. In a 1990 poll, the majority of executives (from 41 to 46 percent, depending on the industry) preferred to adopt new privacy policies voluntarily when the rules were clarified in their industries, without waiting for new laws and regulations. However, from 20 to 37 percent of executives preferred to wait for laws to be passed before taking action.[14] What is unclear, of course, is how many of the executives in this category would still change their corporate policies if 1) the ambiguity regarding industry rules were reduced and 2) there were a real threat of laws being passed if they did *not* adhere to those rules voluntarily. Most would probably comply voluntarily under such a scenario, though the 1990 public opinion survey did not test this question.

In general, then, there is no clear-cut answer as to how much regulation is required to effect a privacy solution. Clearly, though, regulation comes only with a societal price: it requires that an investigative and enforcement mechanism be created and supported within the government and that corporations devote some portion of their resources to dealing with that mechanism. Once they focus on and devote time to problems, corporations can sometimes craft solutions that are more clever and efficient than those that regulators and legislators would suggest. As long as those solutions satisfy the requirements for an improved privacy domain, they represent a more effective use of societal resources. Thus, an ideal solution should be geared against devoting corporate and governmental resources to an extensive regulatory infrastructure if such a system can be avoided. Although some observers have argued convincingly for a regulatory U.S. Data Protection Board, their arguments have often been constructed around governmental abuses of privacy, in which the privacy agency is regulating the activities of other government agencies. While the agencies being regulated probably resist such a system, the model actually represents nothing more than one layer of government overseeing another. To move from that scenario to one in which the governmental agency regulates the activities of *corporations*, however, requires a larger leap: under that model, the free enterprise system's assumptions are challenged significantly as the government assumes an overseer role over certain business activities. While this may yet prove to be the only suitable mechanism for achieving a healthy privacy environment, evidence has not yet shown that such a step is necessary.[15] To the contrary, there is reason to believe (although the evidence is not conclusive) that a set of clear and unambiguous principles of behavior in each industry, coupled with a credible threat of regulation if those principles are ignored, could result in an acceptable solution. This solution would clearly represent the cheapest one for society as a whole. If the corporations refuse to cooperate with such a plan, regulation still stands as an attractive alternative.

Consider each of the models in light of these three assertions. Some might argue that the tendency of executives to react only to external threats in confronting privacy issues would justify a quite heavy-handed mechanism such as the Regulation or Licensing models. But such mechanisms have a tendency to quickly evolve into bureaucratic governmental structures that prove a burden to efficient societal functions. When I interviewed several Swedish businesspeople in Fall 1990, their views of the Swedish Data Inspection Board (DIB)—the licensing office—were less than congratulatory: "It's nothing but a bureaucracy charging fees to push paper around," "They don't even do inspections anymore, they're so busy tinkering with their rules," etc. Similarly, David Flaherty's study *Protecting Privacy in Surveillance Societies* shows the dangers of bureaucracy under the Licensing model.[16] Furthermore, the time lags that would naturally evolve in any such licensing scheme—dictated by the organizational constraints of the licensing agency—could quickly cripple any strategic, competitive uses of information technology.

The Registration model, particularly as implemented in Britain, has some appealing characteristics: the registrar has worked with industry and governmental associations to develop "codes of practice" that are unique to each group, thus providing some measure of guidance regarding appropriate behavior and reducing the ambiguity; to businesses guilty of noncompliance the registrar can issue "enforcement notices" and, in extreme cases, "deregistration notices." This British system was developed only after years of often acrimonious debate,[17] but it appears to have many features that could serve the United States well, particularly with respect to clarification of industry-specific data boundaries. Yet the British model still remains problematic for the United States in another regard: the registration of databases still ranks as a bureaucratic requirement that would be troublesome for U.S. business. It is not clear what such registration accomplishes; registration is not likely to cause the citizenry to be better informed about data usage. While it does provide a "check and balance" in the sense that organizations could be denied registration if they did not adhere to the rules, punitive measures could be taken against offending organizations even *without* the existence of a register. The processing of registrations appears to be rather routine and without careful scrutiny of each application, so the registration process itself may not be doing much more than generating paperwork and incurring costs. Bennett reports that while the British law provided for only twenty employees in the registrar's office, at one point there were as many as ninety-four employees, sixty-six of whom were working on registration tasks, as the paperwork took on a life of its own.[18] Far more important, it seems, are the ombudsman and research tasks undertaken by the registrar. The United States desperately needs these features in its own privacy system.

The German implementation of the Data Commissioner model is also relevant for the United States. Flaherty describes the commissioner's role as one of education rather than enforcement: "If the commissioner discovers infringements of the law in the processing of personal data, he or she can submit a complaint,"[19] and the commissioner has the right to consult the Bundestag (the lower house of the legislature) at any time.[20] Bennett also describes this system: "The BfD's [German equivalent of the Swedish DIB] primary role is that of an adviser who can investigate and try to persuade but who does not have the authority to issue binding regulations. . . . The office also takes pride in the fact that it serves an educative and advisory function: it shows the authorities that data protection can be in their interests as well and educates the general public about its rights under the law."[21] The German BfD focuses on governmental rather than commercial uses of personal data. But there is reason to believe that this approach of convincing and reporting, rather than dictating, may be a very good first step for the United States to take in solving its own privacy problems in the commercial sector. However, the German solution is not fully appropriate for the United States without some modification. In fact, none of the models or international implementations seems, in and of itself, to satisfactorily address the three assertions above. Thus, a new approach melding many of the features of the other models appears to be required.

The best solution for the United States appears to rest on the continuum shown in Figure 7.2. A Data Protection Board, based on the Data Commissioner model, should be created with advisory powers. Such a board, when fully implemented, would be expected to assist corporations in developing codes of acceptable practice, as the British registrar has, and to field citizen complaints. This board should serve in an educational role, as does the German BfD. It should always stand

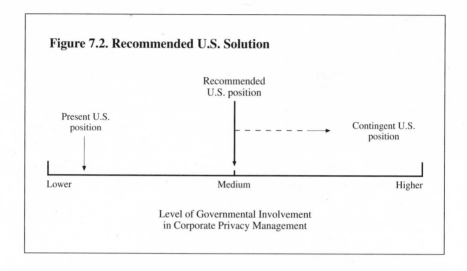

Figure 7.2. Recommended U.S. Solution

ready to expose corporate policies and practices that are inappropriate and to lobby with the legislatures when attention is needed. In its initial form, the board should *not* have any regulatory powers. However, should corporations refuse to cooperate with the board voluntarily, the legislatures should stand ready to move the board somewhat to the right on the continuum by granting some measure of regulatory power. Alan Westin, a prominent privacy observer, believes that by the year 2000, "business leaders in all the privacy-intensive industries will join consumer groups in supporting the addition of a national-standards and regulatory-oversight function for [the board]. They will want to assure uniformity of rules and practices throughout each industry, and to hold the least privacy-observant firms to what will then be the mainstream standards."[22] This desire for regulatory oversight on the part of business leaders seems somewhat unfathomable now, since such oversight would strike most business leaders as more a threat than a savior. But this view is in large part due to the ambiguity surrounding privacy, and as that ambiguity is reduced, it is conceivable—though I believe unlikely—that the business leaders themselves could desire regulatory authority for the board. A more likely path is that regulation continues to be seen as a threat, but that this threat serves as a potent reminder to corporations that their cooperation is expected.

With this framework in mind, we can consider the particular pieces of this U.S. privacy solution. A new system is depicted in Figure 7.3. Society must ensure that consistent pressure and scrutiny are leveled against industries that use personal information. That pressure can best be effected through the Data Protection

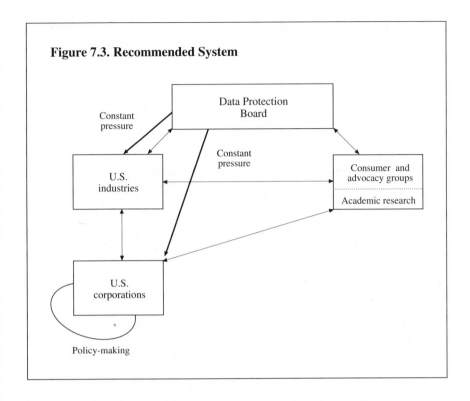

Figure 7.3. Recommended System

Board with advisory powers and the potential for additional regulatory powers if needed. U.S. corporations should then band together in industry associations to develop, in concert with the board, a set of "generally accepted privacy principles" for the industry. Corporations should implement these principles in their own operations through a continuous policy-making cycle that does not rely on an external threat for motivation. The constant visibility and pressure of the board should ensure the operability of this cycle. Consumers and advocacy groups continue to have a watchdog role in this new system, and academic researchers remain responsible for providing independent analyses of privacy questions. Each of these components will now be examined in greater detail.

Data Protection Board

The expanded set of Fair Information Practices discussed earlier in this chapter reflects a societal foundation for privacy practices. But if the discussion were to end there, individual corporations in different industries would still be left with ample ambiguity regarding specific uses of personal information. For example, some bankers might draw different conclusions regarding the legitimacy of buying additional customer data than others would. Consumers would likely continue to disagree with many of the practices. While Fair Information Practices do provide a set of principles, there is a danger that organizations will interpret them as fanciful ideals and that they will hence spark countless disputes.

Thus, as a second facet of the recommended approach, the Fair Information Practices should be undergirded by a societal mechanism for ensuring a consistent focus on corporate policies and practices: a federal board. Supported by professional groups such as Computer Professionals for Social Responsibility[23] and the Association for Computing Machinery,[24] such a board should act as a focal point in information privacy debates. The board could provide an ideal venue for providing leadership on information privacy issues. The board should sponsor information privacy studies, ensure that legislators are aware of existing corporate policies and practices, and increase consumers' awareness regarding uses of personal information. It should also be available to consult with corporations as they craft their own approaches to information privacy issues. "The United States carries out data protection differently than other countries, and on the whole does it less well, because of the lack of an oversight agency," writes Flaherty.[25] This board would provide not only an oversight function but also the capacity for helpfulness and leadership.

Despite its positive attributes, though, the creation of the U.S. Data Protection Board will no doubt garner opposition from several parties. Opposition has attended all the previous proposals for such an oversight mechanism, which date back to Senate subcommittee hearings of the late 1960s. While some prominent legislators, such as Senator Sam Ervin, supported a board, there were many arguments to the contrary. For example, the 1973 study by the U.S. Department of Health, Education, and Welfare argued that no new mechanisms were needed to protect privacy. Even so, by 1974, the Senate was considering a bill to provide for a five-member Federal Privacy Board that would regulate federal, state, and local agencies. Spokespeople from these agencies argued vehemently against the board, on grounds of both cost and bureaucracy. By the time the bill worked its way through the House and Senate, the oversight function was given to the Office of Management and Budget, and the board was reduced to the Privacy Protection Study Commission, which went on in 1977 to produce the well-researched and well-written report discussed earlier.[26] But the concept of a permanent board received little attention for several reasons, according to Bennett: "A number of pressing factors forced Senator Ervin to back down on his insistence that an independent commission with oversight and investigative powers was a sine qua non of effective Privacy Act implementation; the most commonly cited factors are the pressures on congressional time, the drive to pass some privacy legislation in the wake of the Watergate affair, the resistance to the creation of more bureaucracies, and the risk of a presidential veto."[27] Following these experiences, and consistent with the ebbing attention to privacy protection during most of the 1980s, attempts to create a board languished until the late 1980s. But proposals have been generated in various bills before the last several Congresses. Consistent with the shift in focus on other privacy fronts from governmental to commercial activities, the attempt by Congressman Robert Wise (D-W. Va.) in 1990[28] would have provided for a board that monitored "both governmental and private sector activities."[29] Opposition to this proposal was quickly noted. In a DMA publication, the chief DMA lobbyist wrote: "The board would be advisory only, but as anyone who knows government will tell you, it is only a short step from an advisory board to a regulatory board. Wise's bill is a rehash of similar bills introduced several times. . . . DMA was asked to testify. . . . DMA did not take an official position on the bill itself, but in the question period following the testimony, expressed doubt that another agency was needed."[30] But not all executives are opposed to a board. One executive in the credit bureau industry who recently testified before a congressional subcommittee supported the creation of such a board, provided its duties were to "provide analysis in a confidential manner; consider consumer interests; recognize industry initiatives in privacy protection mechanisms; and provide a balanced viewpoint of privacy interests, industry initiatives, and overall economic issues of resource allocation and global competitiveness."[31] In addition, the 1990 public opinion survey conducted by Equifax showed some support for a board across a broad spectrum of Americans. The survey asked the following question: "Which of the following do you think is needed at the federal level to protect consumer privacy?" Respondents were offered an option of "the present system," "a nonregulatory privacy protection board," and "a regulatory privacy protection commission." The percentage of respondents choosing each option are shown in Table 7.1.

Not surprisingly, support for a board is stronger among the public than among executives in any of the surveyed industries, who favor the present system of "specific laws, congressional oversight, and individual lawsuits."[32] More respondents favor a regulatory than nonregulatory board; but this preference, though interesting, should not be taken as a ringing endorsement or assurance of support for such a plan. In fact, the larger percentage of executives in each category supports the "present system." Without question, this group would strongly oppose a

Table 7.1. Preferred Regulatory Options

	"Present system"	"Nonregulatory board"	"Regulatory commission"
Total public	31%	24%	41%
Insurance executives	49%	20%	28%
Credit grantors' executives	55%	17%	25%
Banks and thrifts' executives	43%	23%	30%
Direct marketing executives	39%	28%	29%
Human resource executives	51%	20%	25%
Consumer affairs spokespersons	33%	31%	33%

Source: Adapted from Equifax Inc., *The Equifax Report on Consumers in the Information Age* (1990): Table 11–7, p. 106, courtesy of Equifax Inc., 1600 Peachtree Street, Atlanta, Ga. 30302. The full texts of the options were: "Stay with the present system of specific laws, congressional oversight, and individual lawsuits"; "Create a nonregulatory privacy protection board to research and publicize new controversies over privacy for public policy consideration"; and "Create a regulatory privacy protection commission with powers to issue enforceable rules for businesses handling consumer information."

regulatory board and would much more quickly accept a nonregulatory entity, despite some possible reservations. Given the complexity of the American legislative process, with its reliance on lobbyists and corporate influence, it would clearly be easier to implement a nonregulatory than a regulatory board at the present time.

Of course, even if its role were nonregulatory, the board could not be effective if executives viewed its opinions as toothless. One of its duties, therefore, must be to challenge inappropriate uses of personal information when they are observed. To some degree, the board would solicit citizen complaints, which would generate such challenges. The board should attempt to resolve the complaints through consultations with offending corporations. But challenges to policies and practices could also involve lobbying legislators for new laws and, on occasion, pursuing remedies through the court system. However, an important element of this system is that the actual remedies are to be enforced not by the board itself but rather through the existing legal infrastructure.

Perhaps the board's greatest potential contribution would be the drawing of boundary lines around certain information-handling practices, thus reducing the ambiguity of the privacy domain. As this study discovered, few executives wish to be industry leaders in setting privacy policies; for this reason the usefulness of the board in determining definitions of appropriate and inappropriate information uses cannot be overstated. To the extent that executives could call on it to evaluate proposed projects and offer balanced opinions, the board could provide the information privacy leadership so badly needed in many industries. Yet the board need not perform this function in isolation. Assistance can come from both academic research and specific industry initiatives.

Future Research

Like the board and the consumer advocacy groups, academic researchers have an important role in the new privacy domain, as Figure 7.3 shows. They are responsible for bringing an independent and thoughtful approach to empirical questions of privacy, in discussing both how things now work and how things could be improved. Their studies should not only confront the existing corporate environment but also consider how that environment is at variance with the perceptions of other stakeholders. This study represents an exploratory first step on this path, but much additional work clearly needs to be done. Based on this study's findings, a few specific tasks lie ahead for academic researchers.

First, this study suggested that personal data are handled in different ways by corporations in various industries. However, because the study was of an exploratory nature, it is difficult to say with absolute certainty whether the findings at the particular sites in the study—admittedly limited by the number of sites that could be examined in the depth required—can be generalized to all the sites in each industry. An ideal study would examine a much larger number of sites in great depth and would also include a broad-based written survey for additional companies. Now that we are becoming better informed about the specific issues in each industry, we are in a better position to ask pointed questions and to establish the extent to which each policy and practice is embraced across the industries. Such studies would be ideal for collaborative efforts between industry associations and academic researchers; the former could ensure access to the necessary data, while the latter could ensure the objectivity necessary in such efforts.

Second, this study suggested that the type of information a company handles may have some impact on the formality of the company's policies and employees' perceptions. Note, however, that the hierarchy of such information types, if it indeed exists and applies to corporate policies, has never been fully investigated.[33] A survey of consumers, privacy advocates, and executives would be useful in considering this perceived hierarchy. In addition, administering the existing questionnaire more broadly, in environments handling other types of personal information, might yield illuminating results.[34]

Third, the study results indicate that there may be a presumed hierarchy in the offensiveness of certain information practices: sharing of information is associated with more formal policies than collection and new use of information. Similarly, deliberate errors are associated with more formal policies than accidental errors. While this study addressed the phenomenon with an exploratory written survey, this hierarchy deserves a more rigorous examination, with specific hypotheses and an extensive survey instrument. Such an instrument should contain several items measuring each of the issues and threats, and the researcher should develop scales for measuring each construct.[35]

Fourth, much work needs to be done in additional industries to establish their approaches to these issues. In particular, the direct marketing industry—with its attendant list brokerage services—will likely experience much scrutiny in the next few years as the impacts of targeted marketing become apparent. As technology enables the collection and cross-categorization of more information, the marketplace will inevitably find ways to tighten this segmentation by collecting more information and merging additional information sources. Without question, the industry offers fertile ground for additional research on the cutting edge of information privacy issues. Also, the symbiotic relationship between insurers and medical providers deserves additional attention. While this study focused on the insurer's side of the equation, there are also a significant number of privacy concerns on the side of the medical providers. An exploratory study of hospital record-keeping, for example, would undoubtedly be enlightening.

Of course, in addition to these, other academic research projects addressing privacy questions undoubtedly need attention. Academic researchers have the responsibility to provide a rigorous, objective, and creative perspective on privacy questions and to publish their conclusions, thereby informing the ongoing debate and assisting the board in its tasks. A fully informed board, armed with the threat of legislative action, should serve as a sufficient trigger to spur responses from industry groups, who can provide leadership within their industries in concert with the board.

Industry Initiatives

Almost all industries that handle personal information have industry associations. These associations can take the lead in developing clear, industry-specific statements regarding appropriate and inappropriate uses of information. If these statements are socially responsible and if industry players adhere to them, the threat of legislative action—made more tangible by the board's existence—will diminish appropriately.

How should the industry groups approach their task? As a model for this effort, consider the concept of "generally accepted accounting principles" (GAAPs) in the financial accounting profession. The GAAPs represent the accounting profession's efforts to establish a body of theory and practice—a common set of standards and procedures that serves as a guide. The GAAPs have several sources, but one of the most important is the Financial Accounting Standards Board (FASB), a seven-member body that issues statements on financial accounting standards, including interpretations of those standards.[36] The GAAPs and the FASB stand as examples of an industry's voluntary effort to provide guidelines for its members. The guidelines have a quasi-legislative flavor, since audited financial statements can be considered valid only if they have been prepared in conformance with the GAAPs. Thus, the government recognizes the validity of the GAAPs and the FASB; for example, the Securities and Exchange Commission would expect accounting statements included in annual filings to be compiled in accordance with the GAAPs. There is, therefore, a partnership or symbiotic relationship between the financial accounting industry and the government. The industry makes its own rules, in accordance with existing laws, and the government works with these industry rules rather than creating its own.

Consider the potential state of the financial accounting industry *without* the FASB and GAAPs. Each accounting firm would be left to interpret the law on its own and to create its own principles of accounting where the law was silent. This situation would lead to a nonstandard accounting environment, and the government would undoubtedly pass an increasing number of laws to bring some standardization to the field. These laws would not necessarily be the best ones for the business and accounting communities, however. The accountants and businesspeople know far more about their environment than the lawmakers, who would have to interpret the needs from their own perspective. Far better, of course, is the present system, in which the industry creates its own set of rules, which are then cross-checked by the government and given almost the weight of law.

This hypothetical example of an accounting community without the GAAPs and the FASB comes quite close to describing the privacy environment in some industries today. Lacking a clear set of definitions regarding right and wrong behavior in personal information matters, each firm is forced to develop its own principles. There is often no governing body in place from which to seek assistance. Eventually a set of industry practices evolves, but these practices are often inconsistent and are embraced without a cohesive industry reflection as to their impact. Ultimately, when complaints about the practices reach some critical mass, the government steps in with new laws. This move has already taken place in some industries (for example, the credit industry) and can be expected in others in the near future.

Associations in privacy-intensive industries should act in a form analogous to the FASB by creating "generally accepted privacy principles" (GAPPs)—guidelines of fairness in using personal information—for their industries. However, unlike the FASB, which draws exclusively from the accounting ranks for its membership, the industry groups should have a broader composition. This expansion of membership should ensure that relevant opinions are solicited and should also give the principles additional credibility outside the industry. The GAPPs should be crafted as a joint effort by the industry associations and the board, as in Britain, where the registrar has worked with industry groups to develop various codes.

While the GAPP and GAAP concepts are similar, they are not identical. GAAPs primarily address the reporting of financial results. A particular reporting practice might change a firm's financial statements, thereby altering its ability to raise funds in the capital markets. Thus, executives might sometimes factor the accounting implications into their management decisions, because, for example, a judgment as to whether a certain outflow was viewed as an "expense" or a "capital investment" might color the particular alternatives. Taken to an extreme, a change in GAAPs might mean that a line of business that previously was profitable would no longer be, and executives might be forced to abandon it. However, this sort of consequence would be rare. Most GAAPs would have rather routine implications for accounting reports.

In contrast, GAPPs have the potential for closing off large sectors of business for different companies in one fell swoop. For example, if GAPPs for targeted marketing dictated no re-use of individuals' names by new businesses, then the U.S. list brokerage industry might unravel. The varying perspectives on empirical facts, commitments, modes of argumentation, and assumptions—the bones of contention in privacy arguments—are much more heated in most privacy debates than in accounting disputes, since the privacy domain is much more ambiguous than the accounting domain. Furthermore, the accounting profession has a long history of established precedents, but there is no "privacy profession"; the relevant precedents are confusing; and the history, at least regarding specifics of computerized information flow, covers at most thirty years.

But the knowledge that the climb will be an uphill one should not deter us from starting the trek. The development of GAPPs will provide badly needed guidance for U.S. privacy policies. Just as each corporation drifted until it experienced an external threat, the nation as a whole continues to drift, with little privacy direction. The expanded Fair Information Practices, while useful as guidelines, are too abstract to be helpful at an operational level in most industries. Those Fair Information Practices must be translated into operational language, and the GAPPs should perform that task.

How should industries enforce their GAPPs? The best mechanisms would be self-policing by industry members; development of an industry "seal" indicating compliance with the principles; and an acknowledgment of the validity of the principles by the government. When deviations from the principles occur, members of the industry should reprimand their own members for violations—far preferable to a strictly governmental response.[37] In addition, a visible reminder of each firm's conformance to the principles will be a useful tool. An industry "privacy seal," modeled after the Good Housekeeping Seal of Approval, could be attached to the advertising and literature of industry players who complied with the principles. Eventually, this seal should create a competitive disadvantage for firms that violate the principles. The government can also assist in this effort by acknowledging the validity of the principles defined by the industry. This validation will probably take place in the courts, where decisions can cite the official industry principles as guidelines. If all of these mechanisms fail, there is still a fallback plan: a regulatory board with enforcement powers.

Thus, the new societal system would feature an expanded set of Fair Information Practices, undergirded by a Data Protection Board that provides a constant threat of consumer and legislative scrutiny, leading to an industry response of "generally accepted privacy principles." In this environment, and with this constant pressure, American corporations using personal information will be forced to consider their own approaches to information privacy.

Corporations' Actions

As the threat of negative publicity or legislative scrutiny becomes stronger and more continuous, executives will undoubtedly become more aware of their own organizations' privacy approaches. Will they take action to improve those approaches, will they continue along their present paths, or—the worst possible alternative for privacy protection—will they adopt contentious attitudes and attempt to fight all attempts to improve the privacy domain? This study discovered few examples of the fighting attitude and several examples of the conciliatory one. In the broader privacy domain, there is an indication that the DMA is raising funds to counter some privacy legislation;[38] however, the association is also devoting an enormous amount of resources to prodding the voluntary cooperation of its members: "Its leadership is constantly haranguing members . . . to comply with DMA's own middle-of-the-road privacy policies so that at each legislative threat DMA can point to 'voluntary compliance,'"[39] writes *Privacy Journal*'s Robert Ellis Smith. Both this study and the outside evidence suggest that the increased external threat created by the new privacy infrastructure will lead to an enlightened internal response from companies and industries. While this self-regulatory response may be accompanied by some antilegislation lobbying, a claim, like the DMA's, of voluntary self-regulation indicates that corporations will probably become somewhat introspective about their own privacy approaches.[40] This scenario is not assured, of course, but it appears likely.

However, it is rather troubling that this study showed few examples of companies that had *effectively* transformed their overall privacy environments. The earlier part of this chapter outlined a societal mechanism for creating the external threat that seems to be required before corporations will address privacy concerns. If we assume that this mechanism—and the threat of a more regulatory approach looming in the background—force a renewed appreciation for privacy on the parts of corporations, we must then offer some realistic advice for those corporations as they begin to act on this newfound enlightenment. They should focus on the differences between policy and practice illustrated in the survey results, as these differences call for careful consideration of the existing control structures. Similarly, the numerous areas in which policies either do not exist, or exist only in implicit form, deserve attention.

Thus, in concert with the industry initiatives, executives must take their own self-directed actions to effect change in the privacy environment. The hand of government, embodied in the Data Protection Board, will provide the incentive for executives to pay attention to privacy issues. The hand of management must take up this challenge by providing a continuous focus on privacy issues; if it does not, regulators and legislators will provide unwanted guidance. The mechanisms described below should assist executives in this quest. In many cases, these recommendations would fit a rather large organization. For smaller companies, of course, the scope of many mechanisms will be reduced.

Obviously, the approach to be embraced will vary depending on an organization's own values and habits. Some organizations have a strong culture of *compliance*, and those organizations will probably choose to implement a fairly rigid set of mechanisms (for example, audits and other explicit checks/balances). Other organizations may instead embrace a culture of *commitment*, operating more flexible assumptions.[41] These organizations rely less on a compliance structure and more on the individual members' commitment to the organizational purposes. While sharing the concerns about privacy issues, these organizations may opt for a less rigid approach. Some of the following sections provide options from which executives can choose. In all cases, executives will undoubtedly wish to tailor their responses to their organizations' own values and habits.

The following recommendations revolve around these assertions: senior management should consider privacy issues carefully on a continuing basis; analysis and appraisal of the information environment is necessary for framing appropriate policies and actions; and executives should take actions that let consumers and employees know that the corporation is concerned and is taking steps to provide privacy safeguards. To that end, I have provided some guidelines for a company's self-analysis, which would involve performing an initial audit to create a new base line; examining existing practices and codifying them into policies as appropriate; and creating a long-term program for maintaining the privacy environment.

Initial Audit

As we have seen, many organizations—through unintentional neglect—have not considered the totality of their own information policies and practices in several years. While they have invested in computer access and integrity controls, this investment has to some extent been made at the expense of the broader policy-making effort. Now it is time to evaluate the whole "state of the privacy environment."

In performing this evaluation, executives should consider their policies and practices in light of a "sunshine rule." What if these policies and practices were to be evaluated in the "sunshine" of full disclosure? If consumers or other stakeholders were fully aware of the corporation's policies and practices, would they be satisfied? Most consumers in the study were not well educated about the information policies and practices of the organizations with which they dealt. However, when they became more aware of these policies and practices through the course of the interview, they became angry. During the next few years, executives can reasonably expect additional media scrutiny of their policies and practices. As this scrutiny occurs, consumers will undoubtedly become more aware, and the "sunshine" will fall on the corporate policies and practices.

During the study, one corporate participant noted that "consumers will never really know we used the information in this way." Such statements will become less accurate as media scrutiny makes policies and practices more visible. In the future, consumers *will* know. And, as one financial industry executive noted, consumers' standards for information use are often higher than the law's. It is reasonable to expect that as they become more aware, consumers will often demand that their own higher standards supplant those codified in the law. Thus, merely noting that a corporation's policies and practices are legal under existing law—the defense used by many executives—will be insufficient in the future environment. Executives should instead ask, "Is my organization ready for scrutiny on an order *higher* than that of the existing law?"

The increasingly interconnected nature of our information environment complicates this assessment: the organization must consider not only its own employees and their approach to privacy but also the other entities that share in the organization's information resources. In some situations these entities can include customers and suppliers of the firm, who may be connected into the firm's information flow. A successful privacy policy must reflect an assessment of all these parties and their roles.

To begin this self-analysis, a list of policy focus points should be prepared by a task force, a senior staff member, or a responsible executive. Based on the framework and findings from this study, the following focus items should be useful in developing the list:

1. *Information in the files.* Are there pieces of information that either have been collected, or are being considered for collection, that some stakeholders might consider offensive? For example, many customers claimed that a bank's purchase of additional profile information about them (income estimates, spending profiles) was a violation of privacy, although such an endeavor is perfectly legal. Insurance companies' collection of AIDS information offended many citizens, and many states eventually passed laws to

regulate such collection and use of information. In future years, insurance companies may face similar concerns if genetic test results become more widely available.

2. *Collection of information*. Are the methods in which information is being collected straightforward and honest? If not, executives must ask themselves whether the information is really required and whether revealing the true nature of the collection might yield a more positive situation while still managing to gather the same information. For example, one bank interviewee described a proposed computer system to be used on branch platforms. In the course of casual conversation with a new customer, platform personnel might gather information to be used later for marketing purposes. The platform worker might refer to pictures of his or her children on the desk and ask, "Do you have any kids?" The answer could be entered into the consumer profile after the consumer left the platform area. Many consumers in the study's sample felt great discomfort regarding such collection methods. A more forthright approach—explaining the need for the information and the potential benefits to all parties from providing the information—was viewed as much less likely to incite a potential backlash (although some consumers would decline to provide the information).

Executives should also question the surveillance of, and data collection about, their own employees. Alan Westin has described a paradigm shift in society's viewpoint regarding such practices: from an era of "employer prerogative," in the 1890s to the 1950s, to "employee rights recognition" in the 1960s to mid-1980s, to today's "socially mediated employment administration," which places debates about many data collection practices "in the troubled middle ground between total bans and total approvals."[42] Employers can therefore expect continued public argument and legislative attention to the ways in which they gather information about their own employees. Thus, they are well advised to audit their organizations' pre- and post-employment personnel approaches and to address any intrusive collection policies and practices.

In addition, executives should develop a climate in which employees can openly raise their concerns regarding information privacy. Just as many corporations have developed effective systems for resolving employee concerns in other areas,[43] an outlet must also be provided for questions regarding privacy.

3. *Accessing the information.* Who within the organization has access to each piece of personal information? Organizations' policies should restrict such access to the smallest set possible. At a bank, for example, tellers' access to personal information that is only needed under exceptional circumstances should be curtailed. At an insurance company, only those with a legitimate need to know should have access to medical information. Some keypunch operators at one health insurance company in this study saw applicants' answers to medical questions, even though their keypunch duties did not require their knowledge of such information.

One often hears the argument that "all our employees work for the same company, and there is no problem with letting them see the information, as long as it's kept inside the organization." Consumers are not so willing to accept this argument, however, and will question why certain individuals have access to information about them.

Closely related to the access issue is the use of data in testing new computer applications. Have appropriate sample databases been created, or are programmers forced to use the company's live data in testing new applications? The protection of printouts within the organization also relates to this issue. Have protections against unauthorized access been applied to hard copies as well as to their computerized counterparts?

4. *New uses of information.* Is information being used for purposes other than those for which the information was collected? This question can sometimes involve ambiguous distinctions, of course, since the purpose for collecting information can be open to debate. For example, a bank's customers might argue that the income and asset information on a loan application is intended strictly for processing the request for a loan. The bank might counterargue that the information is provided in order to create a relationship with the bank; hence, the information can legitimately be used to target specific products to the customer. Although such practices were not observed in this study, an insurance company might come under attack for using health claim histories in performing underwriting for life insurance policies.

In general, executives will profit from evaluating each piece of information in light of the question, "What might consumers *believe* is the purpose of this information?" Perception is reality in this situation, since consumer perception is the fact that executives must eventually address. This idea is consistent with one advocate's call for understanding the expectation of privacy that consumers carry into their marketplace relationships.

5. *Sharing of information.* Consumers are especially sensitive about one corporation's sharing information with another. If there are situations in which such sharing occurs, would consumers approve of such sharing if they knew about it? A common practice, of course, is the sharing of name and address mailing lists between organizations. It is sometimes difficult to determine, without additional knowledge, which consumers will find it helpful to receive mailings from related organizations and which will find it an invasion of their privacy. In addition, the particular information used in creating the lists (e.g., "known purchasers of pornographic materials") can be relevant to this question. As discussed later in this chapter, the best way to confront this dilemma is to allow customers to opt out of any such sharing. When this option is offered, it should be readily visible and customers should be clearly notified of their rights.

6. *Error detection and correction.* What are the policies for detecting and correcting errors in information? Are practices consistent with these policies? Approximately 40 percent of the respondents to the survey were concerned about the disparity between their organizations' official policies toward errors and the practices they observed in their organizations. Thus, there is evidently some inconsistency in procedures.

Compared with many other problems facing executives, this problem is often relatively easy to manage. It often entails merely a tightening of the management controls. In some more extreme situations, however, the error levels can be directly traced to specific policy decisions regarding checks and balances in the systems. In some cases, a careful evaluation will indicate a need for additional safeguards. Admittedly, such safeguards require trade-offs, because some mechanisms for reducing errors (for example, triple-checking all data entry exercises for accuracy), while theoretically possible, are prohibitively expensive. On the other hand, most consumers and lawmakers carry realistic expectations about the acceptable levels of errors, and executives should consider those expectations in their decisions. In addition, mechanisms for correcting errors as soon as they occur are crucial. Easily forgotten, but of paramount importance, are the trickle factors created by errors when information passes from one application or organization to another. There should be procedures for tracking all the points to which an error may have permeated, and those secondary uses of the information should all be addressed during the error correction process. For example, if an incorrect account balance has subsequently been used in a credit decision, the error correction process should take this mistake into account and trigger a reconsideration of the subsequent decision.

Preventing unauthorized access to and modification of an organization's databases—by either outsiders or employees—is, of course, a first step in addressing information errors. However, executives should be wary of accepting such efforts as sufficient in and of themselves. In fact, they should consider the entire information-handling process to determine whether the existing error-spotting and -correcting practices are sufficient.

7. *Reduced judgment.* Have processes that might require human judgment been automated to the point that such human judgment has been reduced? If so, would the new balance of human and automated judgment be acceptable to consumers? As many organizations move to a more automated decision-making environment, some consumers become upset—particularly if they sense that decisions about them are being made without sensitive consideration of all appropriate factors. Have adequate provisions for human handling of exceptions been made? Do the systems spot these exceptions and refer them to the appropriate personnel?

8. *Combining information.* Is the corporation contributing to a societal perception that information from several sources is being combined to create large databases of personal information? Many consumers become concerned by the idea that pieces of data, innocuous in themselves, are being combined to provide a larger profile of their lives and activities. Unlike the previous items, this item is usually not under the control of a single corporation; rather, all of society's organizational processes together fuel the consumers' perception. Nevertheless, executives should consider how their own corporations might be contributing to the situation.

Does the corporation contribute information to, or use information from, large databases that combine information from several sources? The consumer backlash for this item will not be directed to specific companies. Instead, it will produce a broad backlash against society's use of personal information. However, to the extent that a corporation is perceived to be involved in such activities, the corporation will ultimately suffer—as will American commerce in general—from this consumer backlash.

Organizations should consider these eight items carefully, since in most fields they are the ones with the highest probability of generating a negative reaction from consumers, the media, and legislators. If companies address these items appropriately on a voluntary basis, the need for a regulatory board will be greatly reduced. After conducting this audit of existing policies and practices, an organization will probably have a list of possible information privacy concerns for further investigation and action. In most cases, executives should take immediate action to change existing policies or practices or to tighten restrictions in certain areas. In a few cases, executives can opt to instigate studies of particular concerns; competitive analyses and studies of consumer perceptions will often be appropriate. If they choose to perform such studies, executives must be careful to streamline the studies and to make them action-oriented: time is of the essence.

Although the above list will be useful on an ongoing basis as a checklist for new proposals, its initial purpose is to set the base line for corporations that have not given these issues great consideration for some time.

Codification

After completing this initial effort, these organizations must codify their official policies. As we discussed earlier, most corporations allowed the privacy practices to be determined at a middle-management level during the drift period until some external crisis hit. Then the organization reacted by considering the set of practices in "batch mode," ultimately developing a new, official policy. But this approach suffers from several shortcomings, and in light of the extensive focus on privacy to be ensured by the Data Protection Board, it will be unacceptable for the future. Thus, executives should create a consolidated privacy policy for their organizations. The results of the initial audit can serve as useful input to the policy-making effort. This policy can be either the official, written codification of existing practices or, if appropriate, the official definition of new practices.

Before the policy itself is written, senior executives should make a strategic decision regarding the purpose of the policy. As noted during the discussion of CredCard's policy-making efforts, this decision can become pivotal. Should the policy merely reflect existing business approaches, or should it reflect goals for which the organization might strive in the future? The decision may not be clear-cut. The former path is akin to throwing a dart at the wall, then drawing a target around it. While the codification process may itself be useful, such an approach may not be as convincing an effort as one in which the corporate approaches undergo more scrutiny and questioning. This latter path carries its own danger, however. Once the policy is codified, the organization will then be held accountable and may later find itself in an embarrassing situation, if studies—perhaps by an external entity—reveal that the organization is not complying with its own dictates. Thus, if an organization's policy is to reflect goals rather than current realities, the only credible approach is to prepare, at the same time as the policy, a concrete list of action steps for achieving compliance. Executives should take care to couple the two entities—the policy and the action plan—in all discussions until compliance is achieved. In short, the organization should be prepared to implement any policy that it codifies.

Depending on its own values and habits, an organization might use a committee for this policy-making effort. Alternatively, the task might be assigned to a small group of responsible executives, a single executive (for example, the chief information officer [CIO]), or senior staff members.

In evaluating the current environment and creating a privacy policy, evaluators should adopt a questioning attitude and should assume the need to start from scratch. They should judge practices not in the context of organizational history but rather in their appropriateness for the future. After all, the Data Protection Board and other societal observers will be using this future-oriented outlook in making their evaluations. The use of focus groups including consumers and other stakeholders can be an excellent method for achieving this goal. Members of focus groups should be asked, "If we adopted this practice, how would you view it?" Based on this study's results, executives should find many of the results enlightening.

In addition, industry associations, in their new role as crafters of GAPPs, should have a good appreciation for current industry practices and possible changes in the legal environment. Consideration of these items can help executives to appraise their options for producing policies that will reduce the need for additional regulation. A word of warning may be appropriate, however. If executives look solely to other companies in their industry for guidance, they might miss two key opportunities: to be leaders themselves, and to gain any competitive benefits that might accrue from a first-mover position in privacy protection. Similarly, reliance solely on legislative boundaries is a dangerous practice because, as we have noted, consumers' interpretations are often stricter than the law.

The policy will undoubtedly require approval from a senior executive. Then the organization must consider how to publicize the new policy. At a minimum, the policy should be circulated within the organization so that all employees are aware of its contents. Distribution outside the organization may be open to debate, but the sunshine rule would dictate that few details of a noncompetitive nature should be kept secret from the consumers or other stakeholders. (Separating the information that might be helpful to competitors from the "safe" information can be a useful mechanism for organizing the policy statement.)

At this point, the organization will have a new, codified policy that reflects its official approach to handling personal information. This policy cannot be regarded as "final," however; it will need constant refinement and reevaluation over time. Thus, as the continual scrutiny of the Data Protection Board forces executives to stay on their guard with respect to privacy concerns, they will need to develop an appropriate long-term infrastructure within their organizations.

Long-Term Program

An executive must focus on four different areas in improving his or her organization's long-term information privacy environment. First, the executive must ensure a consistent focus on information collection, use, and protection within the organization. Second, the executive must engage the organization in an active campaign to educate its customers and other stakeholders regarding the policies and practices. Third, the executive must lead the organization to differentiate between its various customers and clients—whose perceptions of privacy and information use may differ substantially—and to allow some customers to opt out of practices they find distasteful. Fourth, the executive must ensure that the organization's data dictionary is sufficient to allow information policy questions to be easily answered.

Consistent Focus

The new societal mechanisms will undoubtedly get the attention of the organization from the *outside*. But it is equally important to create a mechanism that will cause the privacy issue to get continued attention *inside* the organization and to change the agenda among decision makers. Two important components of this long-term program of awareness are the establishment of an internal "responsible party" for privacy matters and of links to external parties that can provide additional input as needed.

The organization should create a responsible party for privacy matters. Like the "responsible person" of the Voluntary Control model,[44] such an entity would be responsible for organizational monitoring and compliance. While the specifics would vary by organization, the responsible party could be a single executive (for example, the CIO), a group of executives, a senior staff person, or a board composed of several executives. The involvement of the CIO could be important, as this mechanism would create an ideal leadership role; undoubtedly capable of understanding and influencing the policies, the CIO should be a strong candidate for a large role in this assignment. Whether as a member of a board or as the responsible executive, the CIO could provide great insight.

The purpose of the responsible party is to ensure a constant focus on privacy issues within the organization—to provide an impetus for considering privacy issues on an ongoing basis. This study revealed that many corporate interviewees felt their organizations had a policy vacuum around privacy issues. One executive said, "I wonder sometimes who is setting the *policies* about this information. . . . I have a scary feeling the answer is 'nobody.'" At HealthIns B, a new policy-making effort was about to begin, but an interviewee noted that "[the policy] probably needed [attention] several years earlier, but we didn't focus on it." An responsible party for privacy issues reduces the likelihood of such policy vacuums.

Ideally, the responsible party—whether an individual or a board—will answer directly to the chief operating officer of the organization. The responsible party can solicit regular input from other executives regarding the organization's collection, use, and protection of personal information; this input-soliciting process can also include questions about the appropriateness of such practices. The "internal audit" section above can be adapted as a checklist for these questions.

On a fairly regular basis (perhaps once per year), the responsible party should reconsider the official policy of the organization. Are there internal and external factors that suggest a rewriting of the policy's various sections? The internal factors should be apparent from the ongoing review of the functional units' practices, but uncovering the external factors requires more diligence. Thus, an additional task for the responsible party (or a designee) might be the continual scanning of the external environment. Sources like trade and general publications, legal briefs, and consumer advocates' publications,[45] can supply news of relevant environmental factors.

Even with this external scanning effort, however, some relevant items will be missed, due to two factors: the information available in the external publications, etc., is probably of a fairly general nature; and the scanning effort may be limited somewhat by the natural tendency to narrow a search along existing organizational dimensions. And even if the scanning effort were sufficient, the interpretation of both internal and external factors might sometimes be clouded by the organization's political and cultural histories. A real analysis requires objective opinions on information policies and practices, unbridled by organizational constraints. Such opinions can challenge rationalizations of new practices that might actually be questionable (e.g., "The customers cannot possibly complain about this, because it is legal"). As this study noted, consumers quite often disagree with corporate positions on privacy, but executives' assumptions do not always reflect an awareness of these disagreements. External input can mimic criticisms that could ultimately come from consumer advocates or legislators. Organizations are far better off learning of such potential objections in an environment controlled by their own management.

As needed, the responsible party should create links with external parties to gain additional input regarding privacy policies and practices. The objective is to understand the viewpoints of parties who feel they have a stake in the organizational decisions. Such input can be solicited through various mechanisms: focus groups composed of consumers; individual interviews with stakeholders (lawyers, legislative representatives, key customers, privacy experts, industry representatives, consumer advocates[46]); or—in somewhat more control-oriented option—an external advisory board. An external advisory board is based somewhat on the concept of an outside board of directors: it has an official membership and duties. Such a board should comprise informed individuals who represent the relevant stakeholder populations. The benefits of gathering input from an external board could be large: this approach would be more expeditious than conducting the individual interviews listed above, because a single board meeting would provide the opportunity for soliciting a number of varied opinions.

On a fairly regular basis (once a year would be sufficient for most organizations), the responsible executive should solicit opinions from the external parties. If an external board has been appointed, the executive should send its members a package of information that outlines the current practices, discussion items, etc. The external board members should be encouraged to express their observations on the organization's information policies and practices. If a company embraces the other mechanisms (focus groups, individual interviews) instead, the same questions about policies and practices can be asked. However, because the interviewees are unlikely to have an ongoing relationship with the corporation, more effort will be required to "bring them up to speed."

As they receive the input from external parties, executives may find a need for additional study of some items. This can be an ideal time for convening additional focus groups of consumers to discuss existing or proposed information practices. Alternatively, executives may wish to convene some short-term task forces to evaluate certain practices.

Education

The assumption of an informed consumer base undergirds theories of capitalism.[47] If a company has a coherent and thoughtful set of policies in place, it can benefit from a strategic, self-generated campaign to inform the marketplace of these policies. A corporation can ward off potential concerns by bringing its policies and practices to light and can ensure that its positions are presented in a reasonable context. Corporations that do not do so may be accused of trying to hide their activities; consumers may ask, "If they're not ashamed of it, why won't they talk about it?" Thus, one issue for careful discussion in privacy-intensive corporations should be the company's role in informing consumers of information collection, use, and protection policies and practices.

Corporations in privacy-intensive industries should consider campaigns to promote consumer understanding of their policies—provided, of course, that the preceding recommendations have already been implemented and that the policies are now in a position to withstand consumer scrutiny. This education campaign should inform consumers what information about them is in the corporation's databases; how that information is used within the corporation; what information, if any, is shared with outside entities; and what protections are in place. This last category might include the opportunity for consumers to inspect their own records for accuracy and to dispute any information with which they disagree.[48] Taking these steps voluntarily will allow corporations to argue with credibility that they have addressed privacy concerns on their own and do not need additional regulation.

There are several venues for communicating this information. Perhaps the cheapest option is to include the information in mailings that are regularly sent to the consumers (for example, monthly billing statements). Alternatively, the organization might contemplate a special mailing. Care should be taken to feature the information prominently, so that it easily catches the consumers' eyes, because the objective is to have the consumers actually read the information. This method is the antithesis of one adopted recently, in which a merchant mailed a notification of information practices as part of a special advertising package. The notice was buried in approximately one and a half inches of advertising circulars. Although the company could accurately claim that it had sent the information to all its customers, it had not done so in a credible fashion.

In addition to contacting the existing customers directly, executives may also wish to consider media exposure for their policies. Press releases that explain the corporation's commitment to information privacy and outline steps toward that goal could be quite useful in raising awareness. In addition, such publicity can create a competitive advantage if it causes consumers to look more favorably on the corporation. In some cases, positive media exposure could even prompt defections from competitors, if consumers perceive competitors' policies to be weaker.

Providing and publicizing toll-free telephone numbers that consumers can call to ask information policy questions might be appropriate in some instances. Alternatively, in many companies such questions could be fielded by the existing customer service units. In either case, representatives's answers must be thorough and honest.

These recommendations regarding education of consumers assume that the corporation is in a strong position to withstand consumer scrutiny. If that is not the case, executives would be well-advised to postpone consumer education activities until the privacy house is in order. As the consumer interviews in this study showed, much of the consumer complacency regarding privacy in the past has been the result of consumer ignorance. Making additional information about corporate practices available will not improve a corporate image unless the education can make consumers comfortable with the corporate activities. The optimal path for executives, then, is first to improve the corporate information privacy environment such that it can withstand consumer scrutiny and *then* to embrace a consumer education campaign.

Differentiating the Customer Base

As the customers become better informed about the policies, a clear distinction between customer types will likely become apparent. This study's focus groups and a recent survey[49] have revealed a lack of unanimity among consumers regarding which information practices they find appropriate and inappropriate. For example, some consumers readily accept the scrutiny of information regarding their life-styles and purchases if it brings them offers for products in which they are interested. Others find such scrutiny highly offensive. The task, then, becomes to differentiate between these two customer sets and develop appropriate treatment for each. Unless they manage to separate customers by their attitudes toward privacy, companies may eventually be forced to discontinue some information practices that many customers would accept as appropriate.

The education process can thus be coupled with an opportunity for consumers to opt out of, or opt into, various information practices. For example, consumers should choose whether or not to allow companies to exchange their names with other organizations, or to examine their purchase histories in order to determine their spending patterns. At present, some organizations, like CredCard, have flags in their computerized customer records indicating that the customer does not wish to be included in some practices. Executives in other organizations should consider implementing this system, which can be quite useful. Of foremost importance, however, is the mechanism through which customers learn of and exercise their options.

A differentiation system can rely on either negative customer responses or positive customer responses. In the negative response method, customers who do not notify the company otherwise are automatically included in the practices. This method assumes that if there is no evidence to the contrary, customers approve of the practice. The positive response method works in the opposite way: the company includes only those customers who state explicitly that they wish to be included. Of the two, negative response options are far more common. Some organizations' initial application forms include boxes for consumers to check if they wish to forego certain practices. Others provide postcards that customers can return to indicate their desire to be excluded from certain practices, and some accept phone requests to their customer service unit. Some instruct their telemarketing operators to make a computer entry if a customer they've called indicates displeasure with the contact.

But there are two problems with the current situation as implemented in many corporations: the public is often unaware of its ability to opt out, and the corporations do not provide the option for many practices that merit it. As an example of the former case, consider the selective use of information from consumers' credit files to create mailing lists. This practice has been common in the credit industry, for it allows potential creditors to make unsolicited credit offers based on customers' past histories. Some consumers approved of this use of their credit files; some did not.[50] The credit bureaus, which create the mailing lists, had provided flags in the credit records that allowed consumers to opt out of the practice. However, both the practice itself and the opt-out option were poorly publicized and hence poorly understood.[51] (The mechanism for opting out appeared to require writing a letter to each of the major credit bureaus. Even if consumers were aware that the practice existed, of course, most consumers did not know the names or addresses of the credit bureaus.) That corporations do not provide the negative response option for many practices that merit it is confirmed by the focus group results, which revealed many consumers' desires to avoid certain practices in the financial industry. Banks, in particular, have offered consumers few options for avoiding new uses of information.

It is tempting to suggest that moving to a positive response environment, in which companies assumed that consumers did *not* want to be included in the practices unless they indicated otherwise, would provide a good solution. However, this system would be quite costly and would probably exclude a number of individuals in the "undecided" category—people who would not object strongly to the practices but who would also not take the time to respond. To include them in the practices would probably benefit these consumers as well as the organizations. Thus, the assumption behind the negative response system is not necessarily invalid; rather, the implementation of the approach needs refinement. The approach must be systematic.

Thus, on a regular basis, the responsible party—whether a single executive or a board—should develop a comprehensive list of any information practices of the corporation that might be offensive to some consumers. (This move should alleviate the second problem from above.) Then, the educational materials discussed above should be distributed with at least one of two vehicles enabling consumers to opt out of practices they dislike: either an easy-to-complete, postage-paid card or a toll-free telephone number. The opt-out option must be *easy to effect* and *visible to all affected parties.* If monthly billing statements can be designed to focus attention on the option, organizations will probably prefer to include the option in these statements. In fact, an ideal solution might be a statement designed so that it can only be returned after the option card is torn off and placed back in the envelope. In industries where the relationship with the affected parties is quite distant (for example, credit bureaus that house files on individuals but communicate with merchants and creditors), both education and opt-out offers are more difficult. These companies might consider separate annual mailings to all individuals in the files, though this option would be expensive. A strong publicity campaign in both print and broadcast media, with "clip and mail" coupons and toll-free numbers, might be a reasonable alternative. Since customer perceptions can shift over time, the opt-out option must be provided on a regular basis. And, for customers who have previously opted out but now want back in, a reverse alternative should be provided.

If the opt-out option is implemented well, corporations will learn which of the individuals in their files choose to be involved in their information practices. The new, differentiated database will thus be more powerful.

Data Dictionary

In addition to considering the consistent focus, educational efforts, and differentiation mechanisms, executives should also evaluate the data management techniques they employ for sensitive personal information in their own organizations. In particular, it became apparent during the study that many organizations could not provide an accurate assessment of their existing information environments or manage the environments of the future because they did not have a working data dictionary. Many organizations cannot answer, without extensive effort, questions about which individuals in the organization can see which personal data elements, or which personal data elements are used for which purposes. Many organizations have hierarchical levels of access control for various *applications* that are based on one's need to know as well as the sensitivity of the information in the application;[52] and the ability to trace which *individuals* in each hierarchical level have access to each personal *data element* is also an important component of effective data management.

Organizations often control data access at an application or a file level and could probably produce a listing of which individuals have access and change privileges for each such application. However, the next step—determining which of the data elements is accessed by each application—can easily turn into an ad hoc investigative effort. This process often entails a visit to the developers of each application and relies on their own recollections or the documentation from the systems development effort. As organizational memories fade quickly with personnel changes and/or weak documentation efforts, this endeavor becomes more and more difficult. Should executives ever be asked on short notice to explain the organization's use of particular personal data elements, as they might in future years, such an approach will be unsatisfactory. In addition, the executives' own management of the information will suffer if a clear system is not available.

Thus, organizations should maintain a data dictionary for the personal data elements. This dictionary should cross-reference each data element of personal information with each application that reads, writes, or updates the data element. In addition to addressing the privacy concerns, such a data dictionary will provide many other benefits; in fact, it will serve as a good starting point for a strong information management architecture. Also, as computer-assisted software engineering (CASE) tools and systems become more widespread, the data dictionary will naturally become intertwined with the other parts of the system.

The systems development and maintenance process should include checkpoints to ensure that the data dictionary is updated with each release of application software that affects personal data. In addition, as new applications are purchased or developed, the data dictionary should be checked to ensure consistency with existing controls for accessing and updating the referenced data elements. If the new application causes any deviation from the existing privacy practices, this matter should be brought to the attention of the responsible party for a policy decision. Finally, the data dictionary should be linked with the access control tools—either technically or through procedures—so that the identity of all individuals who access or change each personal data element can be ascertained quickly.

Summary

I have made two groups of recommendations for U.S. corporations: a short-term audit to establish a base line, and a long-term program for maintaining a healthy information environment. The new pressure to be exerted by the Data Protection Board and consolidated through industry initiatives should provide executives with ample incentive for embracing these recommendations. However, if companies choose to continue on their present paths or to assume a more contentious posture with respect to privacy, legislators can turn to an attractive alternative: the addition of regulatory powers to the board's charter. To a great degree, the decision on how the country will address privacy problems in the future lies in corporate America's hands: will they voluntarily address the problems in a responsible fashion, or will they force legislators to do it for them? The decision is the executives' to make.

Concluding Remarks

This study examined some facets of the information privacy environment of the early 1990s. Perhaps the most interesting finding was the sensitivity of the topic in many industries. Executives were often unwilling to discuss their own companies' policies and practices—or to subject them to the scrutiny of research.

As U.S. society moves through the 1990s, with the technological "art of the possible" accelerating at an unprecedented rate, our infrastructure will inevitably be hard-pressed to handle the changes. Both individuals and institutions will struggle mightily with the distinction between right and wrong in the new environment. The three hands of our society's economic system, interlocked through their powers over one another, will either work together to face the new environment in a constructive manner or retreat into a set of antagonistic postures that adds nothing to the solution of the problems. As always, governmental regulation will be a ready alternative should the business community refuse to take proactive steps in confronting the issues. In addition, consumers may wield their economic power to effect changes in certain situations.

In 1989, the president of a leading-edge super-bureau,[53] enmeshed in several privacy battles in legislative arenas, said that "it's sometimes dangerous . . . to be a leader in this field."[54] He was right, of course, and that danger probably explains many executives' reticence in discussing this topic. But forward-thinking executives, who are pursuing the greatest strategic advantage for their firms, often cannot avoid being leaders in certain areas. They must confront potential practices before industry standards have been set, before the consuming populace is educated, and before the legislative process has had time to digest the new environment. They must make decisions that may have significant societal implications without the benefit of significant societal input. Then they must confront the societal response to their actions.

This is daunting challenge, particularly as it relates to the issue of personal privacy. Establishing rules for proper behavior in such an environment is an unenviable task but one that consumers, executives, and legislators must all confront.

Appendix

This appendix will explain the methodology used in this study. The study addressed three research questions:

1. What are the current corporate policies and practices with respect to uses of personal, private information?

2. How are corporate policies and practices regarding the use of personal, private information being created in American corporations? How do specific stakeholders' positions compare with those of the decision makers?

3. Within the studied companies, what are the corporate decision makers' and employees' perceptions of privacy concerns, policies, and practices?

Within this study, there were two interwoven phases: 1) a field-based research phase, in which I studied seven organizations and considered some stakeholders' positions, and 2) a field survey phase, which involved a written survey in four of the seven organizations.

The two phases both examined the three research questions. There was an overlap in the material covered by these phases and the questions: Phase 1 addressed questions 1 and 2; Phase 2 addressed question 3 directly but also added some evidence for the other questions.

Phase 1: Field-Based Work

In Phase 1, both questions 1 and 2 were addressed through a qualitative field research design that consisted of extensive, semistructured interviews of individuals at various hierarchical levels and in various functional areas: information systems, marketing, and others. The interviews were tailored to the individuals; there was a list of focusing probes (general questions that focused on the research sites) for the overall study. In addition, where possible and appropriate, written documentation was collected as additional evidence and as "triangulation"[1] for the interviews.

Sites and Interview Samples

The study targeted companies that handle personal and potentially sensitive information ("privacy-intensive" companies). Since the research was of an exploratory nature and part of a theory-building process, the study considered several different information types: financial information (banks), purchase histories (credit card issuer), and medical information (insurance companies). The depth of the study varied across the sites. In some cases, I was granted access to almost all levels and functional areas of the organization; in others, this access was more constrained. (Table A.1 lists the interviews conducted at each site.) Most initial interviews were conducted in person between December 1989 and November 1990; a number of follow-up interviews were later conducted by telephone.

Specifically, the sites and interview samples followed these patterns:

- At Bank A, the sample included individuals at almost all levels of the organization and in many different functional areas. The study had the strong sponsorship of the bank's CIO, and this sponsorship led to free access throughout most of the organization.

- At Bank B, the study was also sponsored by the CIO. Due to the bank's reorganization, the Bank B interview schedule was originally somewhat abbreviated outside the I/S organization, but within the I/S organization, the sample included individuals in all functions and at all levels. Follow-up interviews with lower-level employees and with some employees outside the I/S organization later provided additional insight.

- At Bank C, the original sample included a few high-level executives in the systems organization for interviews of moderate length (one to two hours). A limited number of follow-up interviews of lower-level employees were conducted later. Since the Bank C interviews were conducted after those at Banks A and B, I was able to streamline the Bank C interview process based on an evolving knowledge of banks' policies and practices.[2]

- At CredCard,[3] the original sample included interviews primarily at high organizational levels. Later I conducted follow-up interviews with some lower-level employees.

- A life/health insurance company had two subsidiary organizations in the study: LifeIns and HealthIns A. The organizations were distinct entities within the company, with very little interplay. At LifeIns, the sample included lengthy and informative discussions with a limited number of individuals in the underwriting organization. At HealthIns A, the sample included a number of individuals in various functional areas.

• At HealthIns B, a health insurer, the sample included individuals in various functional areas and at various levels.

Anonymity Agreement. When they were contacted for participation in the study, companies received assurances that their anonymity would be protected. Individuals at the companies are not quoted by name, and companies are not identified.

Studying Question 1

The interviews at each of the sites employed a set of focusing probes. These probes did not constitute an interview protocol per se; rather, they were intended to focus the overall study at the site. They are analogous to Robert Yin's concept of "study questions."[4] When an individual was interviewed, a short protocol was created for that particular interview, based on the individual's position in the hierarchy, function, etc. The probes for question 1 were:

a) What information regarding individuals resides in the company's files? What is the implied purpose of this information?

b) Are there pieces of information that could be stored in the files but that the company has refused to store?

c) Who can access and change each piece of information in the files? How is this matter decided?

d) In what forms, and under what conditions, is this information used for purposes other than that in a)?

e) In what forms, and under what conditions, is this information shared with other entities?

f) What are the policies for handling accidental errors in the information? What are the safeguards against deliberate errors?

g) What are the policies, if any, regarding the judgmental processes that must be applied to the use of this information?

h) What are the policies, if any, regarding the combining of several pieces of information into one larger record?

Table A.1. Interviews Conducted

Site	Interviews
Bank A	CIO (three times)
	Senior VP for mortgages
	Mortgage operations head
	Mortgage legal counsel
	Executive VP of marketing (twice)
	VP of marketing research (three times)
	Marketing VPs (3)
	VPs for direct mail (2)
	Data security officer
	Data security specialists (2)
	Senior auditor
	Junior auditors (3)
	Senior VP for systems development
	VP for systems development
	I/S project managers:
	Trust, consumer lending
	Platforms, ATMs
	Teller systems
	Deposit systems
	End user computing environment
	Consumer lending executive
	Bank operations executive
	Branch operations VP
	Branch operations incentive VP
	Private banking VP
	Programmers (2)
	Branch personnel (6)
	Marketing analysts (3)
Bank B	CIO
	Head of systems development
	I/S project managers:
	ATMs, IRAs
	Platforms, tellers
	Data management
	Data administration
	Data technicians (4)
	Retail assets (2)
	End user computing managers (2)

Table A.1. (continued)

Site	Interviews
	Senior I/S audit manager
	Senior auditors (2)
	Junior auditors (3)
	Marketing contact for platform system
	Mortgage group: VP and operations manager
	Security personnel (manager and two others)
	Private banking head
	Trust executive
	Mortgage officers (2)
	Branch personnel (3)
	Marketing analysts (2)
	Marketing manager
	Programmers (2)
Bank C	Systems group chairman
	Operations head
	Quality assurance head
	Systems head
	Data VP
	Credit corporation president
	Credit analysts (2)
	Marketing VP
	Auditor
	Marketing analysts (2)
	Programmers (2)
	Branch personnel (5)
CredCard	Senior credit executive
	Credit senior VP
	VP with special privacy assignment
	Marketing VP
	Data management VP
	Marketing database VP
	Systems director, operations director
	Credit collectors (2)
	Credit analysts (2)
	Marketing specialists (2)
	Programmer/analysts (3)

Table A.1. (continued)

Site	Interviews
LifeIns	Head of underwriting (three-hour interview)
	Head of confidentiality policies (four-hour interview)
	Underwriters (4)
	Staff physician
HealthIns A	Client consulting director
	Director, systems strategy
	Security director
	Claims system manager
	Group claim services executives (2)
	Monthly detail reports manager
	Claim analysis system head
	Claims support personnel (3)
	Marketing manager
	Marketing specialists (2)
HealthIns B	Director of planning
	I/S managers:
	Head of development
	Head of data security
	Head of telecommunications
	Systems manager for claims systems
	Lawyer for confidentiality issues
	VP, utilization review
	Utilization review specialists (4)
	Managers in utilization review area (3)
	Managers in underwriting services (2)
	Claims handling (operations) executive
	Personnel VP
	Marketing executives (customer service, administration) (2)
	Ombudsman (customer representative)
	Security head
	Membership services director
	Membership services specialists (3)
	Claims support personnel (3)
	Marketing specialists (2)

i) How do the executives compare their policies and practices with those of others in their industry?

j) Do the operating units' practices conform to these policies?

I attempted to get answers to all these questions at all the sites. The varied sample of interviewees—including those from marketing and information systems along with other executives and managers—provided different levels of awareness in addressing the questions. At some sites, all the questions could be answered in specific detail for almost all the operating units. At others, some questions could not be answered in great depth in certain units.

As additional support for the interviews, I often collected written documentation (e.g., policy statements, records of task forces). In addition, I solicited several interviews on each topic area so that different respondents' answers could be used for corroboration. According to Robert Yin, such collection of multiple sources of evidence develops converging lines of inquiry;[5] the findings thus become more convincing and accurate. Furthermore, this system addresses potential problems of construct validity (i.e., operational measures for the concepts being studied), because the multiple sources essentially provide multiple measures of the same phenomenon.

Studying Question 2

Question 2 traced the process of decision making through an examination of the relevant events and arguments that had led to the current policies. As with question 1, I relied primarily on interviews but also solicited documents for clarification and for triangulation.

Tracing the Process. As the set of policies and practices at each site became clear, I asked interviewees how the policies and practices had come into existence. Sometimes their recollections led to others in the organization who had served on a particular task force, participated in making a certain decision, or instigated a certain study. Those interviewees often provided direction to yet others in the organization. When I observed repetitious consistency in the interviewees' descriptions, I concluded the research on this question. The research process was an intuitive one—much more so than for question 1. It was also an approximate process, for the decisions were often embedded in the organizational psyche, and teasing them out was an indirect effort.

I used the following set of focusing probes to trace the process:

a) What were the company's historical positions regarding the use of the information? When were changes considered, if at all? How did that questioning process begin: by whom? in what form? Were there key events that led the company to think about how the information was used?

b) What were the trade-offs in the decisions?

c) What arguments were used in reaching decisions?

d) Did the questioning processes take any formal forms (e.g., task force)? (If a task force had been convened, I interviewed any available task force members.)

e) Were there any studies of probable consumer reaction to any new policy? of industry reaction? of reaction from others?

f) What was the involvement of the I/S community in the decision-making process? Did the I/S executives instigate any stakeholder analyses? How did this effort compare with those of other executives—for example, marketing executives?

g) How was the decision-making process ultimately concluded?

h) If the decision represented a change, how was it announced and codified?

i) What were the apparent management attitudes toward the tension between personal privacy and information needs?

j) How did the executives feel about potential challenges from privacy advocates?

Interview Methodology

The interviews in this study were semistructured. Before each interview I constructed a protocol, consisting of several questions to be answered by the interviewee. The specific list depended, of course, on the site in question, the individual's position in the organization, the individual's past experiences, etc. Through information gathered from either other interviewees or from my sponsor at each site, it was often possible for me to hone in on a particular interviewee's relevant knowledge before the interview and to tailor my questions accordingly. In addition, the interviewee's knowledge and observations often moved the interview into unanticipated territory. Not surprisingly, this sort of spontaneous exchange often produced the most useful data.

Because of the sensitivity of the topic under discussion, the interviews were not tape-recorded. However, except when interviewees requested otherwise, I took copious notes during the interviews and wrote down additional observations immediately after each interview. For key interviews, I transcribed these notes within a few hours of the interview.

I also made notes regarding the interview itself: did the interviewee appear open, honest, and candid? Did body language during the interview offer any clues? How did the interviewee's responses triangulate with others' in the organization? There were often obvious cues that led to conclusions about an interviewee's openness. When an interviewee prefaced his or her remarks with a comment like "Since this is anonymous, I'll level with you, but we don't even talk to a lot of the people around here about this," or blushed while openly discussing sensitive topics, I could feel reasonably sure that the answers were honest. On the other hand, some interviewees gave vague, "non-answer" answers to my questions; quoted published statements; toed the party line in their comments; or simply refused to discuss certain practices.

Occasionally, interviewees contradicted each other with respect to information practices within the corporation. Once, for example, a high-ranking interviewee said that "hard-copy printouts with personal information are carefully controlled." A few days later, though, another interviewee gave me a tour of the facility, during which she delighted in pointing out a large bin of such printouts in an unsecured area "where anybody can pick them up and walk out with them." A charitable interpretation, of course, would hold that the high-ranking interviewee is simply uninformed about the actual practices in the organization. Another interpretation would judge the high-ranking interviewee's remarks as less than candid. In all such cases where interviewees appeared less than honest or in which contradictions were noted, the interviewees' credibility diminished greatly.

Evaluating the Stakeholder Opinions

During Phase 1 I also used individual interviews and focus groups to investigate the opinions of various stakeholders with respect to the policy decisions. In each of these interchanges, I solicited the interviewee's opinions regarding the corporate policy. Did they agree or disagree with the policy? What were their reasons for feeling that way? I interviewed the following individuals:

• Twelve consumer/privacy advocates

• Three lawyers who were active in privacy issues

- The president of MIB, an insurance industry clearinghouse for medical information. MIB's president was interviewed twice and also provided me with useful documentation.

- The director of compliance at a midwestern insurance company. The director had performed a survey of insurance companies to determine some of their practices with respect to release of medical information.

- Three private physicians, one of whom was formerly a director of medical underwriting at a large insurance company

- A hospital medical records director, who often dealt with insurance companies

- A hospital's chief executive officer (also a physician)

- Lawyers who had represented gay and lesbian clients in AIDS-related matters, as well as two advocates who had been involved in protests regarding AIDS testing

- Outside observers for each industry in the study, including consultants, trade association representatives, former and present industry executives, etc. These interviews were often used as triangulation points for the findings at the sites; the observers were asked to confirm the findings based on their own sense of the industry. There were nine such interviews in the life/health insurance industry, six in the banking industry, and three in the credit card industry. Some additional interviews of external observers were also conducted outside the specific industries in the study (e.g., in the direct marketing industry and the credit industry).

- Individuals and focus groups. These interviews were conducted to determine private citizens' opinions regarding particular uses of information. These discussions were used as qualitative triangulation against the positions of the advocacy groups, which claim to represent individuals. As much as possible, these interviews involved a broad base of individuals: a group of five educated professionals in Boston, Massachusetts; six individuals, primarily employees of a service company, in Winston-Salem, North Carolina; and a group of seven salespeople, paralegals, and computer professionals in Raleigh, North Carolina.

- Present and former employees of the DIB in Stockholm, Sweden, and executives from Swedish companies.

In each stakeholder interview, I focused on the stakeholders' empirical definitions of the problem, their assumptions (especially regarding information ownership), and their argument in support of, or in opposition to, the corporate policy. After each interview I made notes regarding both whether the respondent(s) seemed informed and whether they seemed open. In evaluating openness, I used cues such as body language, revealing of self-incriminatory information, and responses to follow-up questions (for example, "Have you ever had a problem with that yourself?"). As noted earlier, the interviews at the corporate sites were not tape-recorded because of their sensitive nature. However, because the sensitivity was lower in the stakeholder interviews and focus groups, I sometimes tape-recorded these meetings.

Phase 2: Field Surveys

In the second phase of the research, a survey of employees in the studied companies was conducted. The purpose of this survey was, primarily, to answer question 3. However, it also provided some additional information for the other questions. The survey measured a) respondents' opinions regarding general privacy concerns; b) differences in concerns regarding various privacy issues and threats; c) perceptions regarding their own companies' approaches to privacy concerns; and d) perceptions regarding solutions in the privacy arena.

Basis and Pilot Tests. I used the 1989 Cambridge Reports[6] and 1981 Westin surveys[7] as a basis for the opinion questions. (See the relevant portions of the survey in the Addendum; other questions, which were included for future research purposes, are not included in the Addendum.)

Survey questions I-1 through I-3 were taken directly from the earlier surveys. For this instrument I also adapted the demographic data structure used in Westin's 1981 survey.[8] I developed additional questions based on this framework and pilot-tested the survey in two phases: 1) with peers at my university and with several other acquaintances (a total of about fifteen people) and 2) with contacts at the research sites (a total of about twenty-five people spread across the sites). Of the former group, about half were familiar with the framework. Those who understood the framework were expected to criticize the items for validity in measuring the desired constructs. With regard to the latter group, I administered some pilot tests in a focus group format at Bank B, and respondents talked about their answers after filling in the survey. As a result of these pilot tests and the focus group activity, I reworded several questions, modified the scales, and replaced one section.

Distribution of Surveys. The surveys were distributed by the corporations themselves. (Some modification of the survey was required to ensure that job titles, etc., conformed to each site's own language.) A cover letter, signed by an executive at the company, promised anonymity to respondents. (See the sample letter in Figure A.1.) The surveys were printed front and back on 6½-by-8½-inch paper and were enclosed in a printed cover. A postage-paid envelope was included so that respondents could mail the survey directly to me.

Sampling

Of course, distribution of the survey was subject to negotiation with the various sites. Four of the seven sites agreed to distribute the survey. In general, at each site a random sample was selected from the organization's roster of employees. To provide for a sufficient base of responses in testing certain propositions and to comply with some organizational constraints, I adopted the following modifications to this purely random methodology:

- At Bank A, surveys were sent to all members of the marketing organization to ensure an adequate base of marketing respondents. In all other areas (e.g., information systems, operations), sampling was purely random. However, at the time of the study, Bank A had several branch banking organizations, only one of which was sampled for this study. Within that organization, sampling was purely random.

- At HealthIns B, three-fourths of the sample was selected from the employee roster on a purely random basis. This sample contained employees at all levels of the hierarchy. The remaining fourth of the sample was selected from the supervisory ranks of the company, again on a purely random basis. This sample contained only supervisors, managers, and executives.

- CredCard had more than one credit organization, but only one of those organizations was used in this study's sample. In addition, approximately twenty surveys were distributed to headquarters personnel. Consequently, because the sample is only partial, it would be inappropriate to make inferences regarding the entire CredCard organization. Instead, results should be interpreted in light of this sample.

Figure A.1. Sample Cover Letter

Dear [company name] employee:

[Company name] is currently participating in a . . . study regarding information privacy. One part of this multi-industry study entails an assessment of different individuals' opinions regarding privacy. Your name has been randomly selected for this mailing.

Attached is a short survey—which will take about ten minutes to complete—that asks for your opinions. I would appreciate your completing this survey and returning it to [the researcher] in the attached, self-addressed business reply envelope. Your responses will be completely anonymous.

So that the results can be tabulated quickly, it would be helpful if you could return the survey *within the next ten days.*

Thank you for taking the time to help with this important project.

The distribution of the surveys is shown in Table A.2. Overall, there were 704 responses from 1,103 distributed surveys, for a response rate of 63.8 percent. The responses can be broken down by the functional areas and hierarchical levels reported by the respondents, as shown in Table A.3.

Study Generalizability

This study was exploratory, with an asymmetric design. Because it relied on access to real-world corporations, the study was necessarily constrained by the willingness of corporations to cooperate. The interview summary and survey distribution data clearly illustrate that different industries and corporations received different levels of coverage. For example, the study involved three banks and two health insurers, but only one life insurer and one credit card issuer agreed to par-

Table A.2. Distribution of Surveys

Site	Number of surveys distributed	Number of surveys returned	Response rate
Bank A	373	213	57.1%
LifeIns	100	68	68.0%
CredCard	180	121	67.2%
HealthIns	450	302	67.1%

ticipate. The written survey was not distributed at all sites, and its distribution at CredCard was relatively constrained. Interviews were easily obtainable at almost all levels of some corporations (such as Bank A) but were more restricted in others (such as Bank C). As chapter 2 explained, the difficulty of even gaining access to organizations made the use of personal contacts very important in this research; however, such an approach also meant that the sites were *not* randomly selected. While there is no reason to think that this methodology led to any inherent bias in the site selection—in fact, it may have increased the openness with which the study sites ultimately did embrace the research process—this study certainly differs from many controlled experimental designs in which subject selection is rigorously qualified. Such is the nature of real-world research, in which a researcher must be sensitive to the comfort level of the organizations involved and accommodate their requirements.

To check the validity of the study's findings under these constraints, I employed a few—albeit imperfect—techniques. One was the use of industry observers, with whom the results were checked. As I explained above, these observers were asked to comment on the findings and to note areas where, in their experience, convergence and divergence were evident in the industry. In many cases, their comments took this form: "Well, I've never really thought about it, but now that you mention it, I think they are pretty representative in their approach." In the very few cases where they felt the sites' experiences diverged from the main (e.g., LifeIns's late embracing of AIDS testing), the text above has noted their observations. Another technique was after-the-fact reviews and discussions of some findings with selected individuals at the study sites. While these reviews were not possible for all findings at all sites, they did provide an opportunity for me to clarify some points of confusion. A final technique—one demonstrated throughout the book—is the combining of qualitative and quantitative data collection techniques. Many times, the written survey results were used to

Table A.3. Respondent Breakdown

Site	Functional areas of returned surveys (self-reported)		Hierarchical levels of returned surveys (self-reported)	
Bank A	Audit	8	Executive	8
	Branch banking	31	Division head	10
	Corporate	10	Middle manager	68
	Finance	11	Line manager	54
	I/S	58	Staff	66
	Line operations	52	Missing IDs	7
	Marketing	27	Total	213
	Other	9		
	Missing IDs	7		
	Total	213		
LifeIns	Underwriting	68	Manager	18
			Underwriter	37
			Clerical	8
			Missing IDs	5
			Total	68
CredCard	Credit	101	Senior/middle manager	19
	Finance	2	Line manager	17
	I/S	2	Staff	73
	Line operations	4	Missing IDs	12
	Missing IDs	12	Total	121
	Total	121		
HealthIns	Claims	45	Senior manager (executive)	29
	Finance	46	Manager	48
	HMO	55	Supervisor	61
	Health care affairs	28	Staff	148
	I/S	59	Missing IDs	16
	Marketing	29	Total	302
	Other	24		
	Missing IDs	16		
	Total	302		

verify and confirm the interview data. In addition, the written survey was used to determine whether the corporate employees were different in any appreciable way from Americans as a whole with respect to their privacy attitudes. As Table A.4 shows, three questions that had been presented to the U.S. public in early 1989 were used a few months later in the written survey distributed to the corporate employees. For the most part, the attitudes of the general public and the corporate employees are fairly similar. One notable difference does appear between the two samples: on the last item in Table A.4, the respondents to this study's survey—employees of corporations that deal with sensitive personal information—viewed this trend as a more serious threat than did the respondents in the general public survey. This difference may be due either to the employees' greater awareness of the power of the technology and the prevailing practices in the industries or to the context in which the survey was administered (sanctioned by executives of the employees' corporations). Otherwise, the corporate employees are apparently not unlike Americans as a whole. Thus, when we find them expressing opinions about their corporate policies and practices, discussing their own emotional dissonance at their corporations, etc., we can safely assume that most Americans, if exposed to the same environment, would probably express similar feelings.

Other differences between the results from this survey and those from the Cambridge Reports survey probably stem from differences between the surveys themselves. The Cambridge Reports survey consisted of in-person interviews with approximately 1,500 people selected to represent the U.S. population of eighteen years or older. This study's survey, on the other hand, was administered in a written format to employees at four of the studied sites. However, the precedent for using such items in a written format was successfully established by Ronald Lee Esquerra.[9] One might argue, for example, that nonresponse bias under this study's methodology would be more significant than in the Cambridge Reports survey. Such a bias, if it existed, would likely bias the percentages *upward*, since it is reasonable to assume that individuals who do not feel strongly about privacy matters might be less likely to return the survey. However, the response rates on this study's survey were reasonably high, dampening the danger from nonresponse bias. In addition, I conducted an approximate test for such nonresponse bias: I assumed that the characteristics of nonresponders were more like those of late responders than early responders. Therefore, I separated surveys that were received within fifteen days of distribution from those returned later, then conducted statistical tests to measure the differences between these two groups regarding attitudes for numerous survey items. A testable proposition that there

Table A.4. Survey Comparisons

Survey item	Answer options	% this survey	% general public
Compared with other subjects on your mind, how important is personal privacy?	Very important	63.2%	67%
	Somewhat important	30.4%	24%
	Not too important	5.6%	4%
	Not important at all	.7%	3%
How concerned are you about the invasion of personal privacy in the United States today?[1]	Very concerned	45.1%	44%
	Somewhat concerned	44.2%	32%
	Only a little concerned	9.7%	17%
	Not concerned at all	1.0%	6%
As computer usage increases in business and the general society, more and more information on individual consumers is being acquired and stored in various computers. How serious a threat to personal privacy is this development?	Very serious threat	29.8%	22%
	Somewhat serious threat	48.5%	33%
	Only slightly serious threat	17.6%	23%
	Not a serious threat at all	4.1%	17%

Note: "% this survey" refers to the responses in this administration of the survey. "% general public" refers to the administration of the items in the Cambridge Reports survey, *Technology and Consumers: Jobs, Education, Privacy*, Bulletin on Consumer Opinion no. 157 (Cambridge, Mass., 1989).

1. In the Cambridge Reports survey, this item referred to "the invasion of *your* [my emphasis] personal privacy in the United States today."

were significant differences between the two groups failed to find support at the (very liberal) .20 level of significance.[10]

The use of these three techniques for validation of the results—interviews with industry observers, reviews with site personnel, cross-checks between qualitative and quantitative data—provide some measure of assurance that the study results are accurate. Even so, the study's design has some inherent constraints that should be considered. What does this mean in terms of the study results? Clearly, a qualification is in order. Because only a few sites were covered in any one industry, we cannot conclude that "all banks [or insurance companies, or credit card issuers] operate in this fashion." Obviously, differences in the larger population must exist. What we can say is that *some* banks, insurers, and credit card issuers operate like those in this study; that finding in and of itself leads to some reasonable concerns about ambiguity in the overall privacy domain. Conversion across multiple sites—like the similarities this study discovered among the banks and the insurers—increases the generalizability of the industry findings. And when a phenomenon like the drift–external threat–reaction cycle is observed to some degree in *all* the sites, regardless of industry, that finding has great credibility and can reasonably serve as a basis for public policy-making. Nevertheless, the study results should not be considered exhaustive ones, as a need for further research is also clearly indicated. In sum, while the study design does not provide for conclusive answers to all questions, it provides enough credible evidence to suggest that changes in the privacy domain are appropriate and necessary.

Addendum: Survey Used for This Study

We are interested in your own personal opinions about the issue of privacy. Your responses will be held in complete anonymity.

Section I: General Privacy Questions

This section contains some general questions about personal privacy in our society today.

1. Compared with other subjects on your mind, how important is personal privacy? (Please check one answer.)
   Very important   _____
   Somewhat important   _____
   Not too important   _____
   Not important at all   _____

2. How concerned are you about the invasion of personal privacy in the United States today?
   Very concerned   _____
   Somewhat concerned   _____
   Only a little concerned   _____
   Not concerned at all   _____

3. As computer usage increases in business and the general society, more and more information on individual consumers is being acquired and

stored in various computers. How serious a threat to personal privacy is this development?

Very serious threat   _____

Somewhat serious threat   _____

Only slightly serious threat _____

Not a serious threat at all   _____

4. There are several different ways in which personal privacy could be protected in the United States. For each of the following, indicate whether you agree or disagree with the statement by circling the appropriate number.

a. The best way to protect personal privacy would be through stronger laws.

Strongly agree			Neutral			Strongly disagree
7	6	5	4	3	2	1

b. The best way to protect personal privacy would be through technological safeguards (for example, password protection on computer databases).

Strongly agree			Neutral			Strongly disagree
7	6	5	4	3	2	1

c. The best way to protect personal privacy would be through corporate policies, which the corporations would develop themselves.

Strongly agree			Neutral			Strongly disagree
7	6	5	4	3	2	1

5. Here are some statements about personal privacy that have been made by others. We would like to know your opinions.

a. "There are certain kinds of information that are very sensitive and should never be stored in a computer database."

From the perspective of personal privacy, how concerned are you about the *kinds of information* that are stored in computer databases? (Please circle a number to indicate your answer.)

Very concerned			Neutral			Not concerned at all
7	6	5	4	3	2	1

b. "When you supply personal information to a particular business for a particular purpose, the business sometimes uses the information *internally* for *another purpose*."

From the perspective of personal privacy, how concerned are you that businesses might use personal information *internally* for *new purposes*?

Very concerned			Neutral			Not concerned at all
7	6	5	4	3	2	1

c. "When you supply personal information to a particular business for a particular purpose, the business sometimes *shares or sells* the information *externally* so that other businesses can use it for other purposes."

From the perspective of personal privacy, how concerned are you that businesses might *share or sell* personal information *externally* in these ways?

Very concerned			Neutral			Not concerned at all
7	6	5	4	3	2	1

d. "Deliberate errors may occur in computer databases. For example, an unauthorized person may access the database, or someone may intentionally modify the data without authorization."

From the perspective of personal privacy, how concerned are you about *deliberate errors*?

Very concerned			Neutral			Not concerned at all
7	6	5	4	3	2	1

e. "Accidental errors may occur in computer databases. For example, data may be entered improperly or classified incorrectly."

From the perspective of personal privacy, how concerned are you about *accidental errors*?

Very concerned			Neutral			Not concerned at all
7	6	5	4	3	2	1

Section II: About Your Company

Now we would like to ask for your opinions regarding your own company's approach to personal privacy as it handles sensitive information about your clients [nomenclature modified based on the company]. Please remember that your responses will be held in complete anonymity.

Does your company have *official policies* regarding the handling of sensitive information about your clients?

Yes   _____

No   _____

If yes . . .

1. In your opinion, how adequate are these policies?

Very adequate			Neutral			Not very adequate
7	6	5	4	3	2	1

2. Sometimes, the way that sensitive information is actually handled in a company does not match the company's official policies. In your opinion, how well do the *actual practices and operations* in your company match the official policies regarding handling of sensitive information about your clients?

Match very well			Neutral			Match very poorly
7	6	5	4	3	2	1

In what areas do these mismatches between official policies and actual practices/operations occur? (Check all that apply.)

Kinds of information in databases   _____

Who can access the databases   _____

Error detection and correction   _____

How decisions about clients are made   _____

How people handle information in the office _____

How information is shared with others   _____

Other (please specify):

Section III: About You

We would like to know a little about you personally. These responses will not be used to identify you in any way. They will be used only for aggregating responses.

1. How long have you worked for [name of company]?

   _____ years

2. How would you describe your present job? [choices modified based on the company]

   Corporate executive _____

   Division head _____

   Middle manager _____

   Line manager _____

   Staff _____

   Other (please specify):

3. In which functional area do you work? [choices modified based on the company]

   Audit _____

   Community banking _____

   Corporate _____

   Finance _____

   Information systems _____

   Line operations _____

   Marketing _____

   Private banking _____

   Other (please specify):

4. Your age?

   _____ years

5. Highest level of education completed?

   Eighth grade or less _____

   High school _____

   College _____

   Graduate school _____

6. Your sex?

    Male   _____

    Female   _____

Please use the space below for any additional comments.

Notes

Chapter 1

1. Quoted in Josh Kratka, *For Their Eyes Only: The Insurance Industry and Consumer Privacy* (Boston: Massachusetts Public Interest Research Group [MassPIRG], April 1990): 1.

2. Quoted in Jeffrey Rothfeder, "Is Nothing Private?," *Business Week* (September 4, 1989): 74–82.

3. Deborah G. Johnson, "The Public-Private Status of Transactions in Computer Networks," in *The Information Web: Ethical and Social Implications of Computer Networking*, edited by Carol C. Gould (Boulder: Westview Press, 1989): 37–55.

4. For an interesting discussion of alternative definitions of privacy, from which this one is adapted, see Ferdinand Schoeman, ed., *Philosophical Dimensions of Privacy* (Cambridge: Cambridge University Press, 1984): 1–33.

5. Michael W. Miller, "Lotus Is Likely to Abandon Consumer-Data Project," *Wall Street Journal* (January 23, 1991): B1.

6. Michael W. Miller, "Coming Soon to Your Local Video Store: Big Brother," *Wall Street Journal* (December 26, 1990): 10. Also see Michael W. Miller, "Blockbuster Contradicts Official, Saying It Won't Sell Rental Data," *Wall Street Journal* (January 2, 1991): B6.

7. Consumers Union, "Smile—You're on Corporate Camera!," *Consumer Reports* (June 1989): 423.

8. U.S. House of Representatives, "Fair Credit Reporting Act," Hearing before the Subcommittee on Consumer Affairs and Coinage of the Committee on Banking, Finance, and Urban Affairs (September 13, 1989), serial number 101–50. Also see U.S. House of Representatives, "Amendments to the Fair Credit Reporting Act," Hearing before the Subcommittee on Consumer Affairs and Coinage of the Committee on Banking, Finance, and Urban Affairs, (June 12, 1990), serial number 101–132.

9. Mitch Betts, "States File Suit against TRW," *Computerworld* (July 15, 1991): 4.

10. Michael W. Miller, "Six States Sue TRW Over Credit-Reporting Practices," *Wall Street Journal* (July 10, 1991): B1, B2. Also see Evan I. Schwartz, "Credit Bureaus: Consumers Are Stewing—And Suing," *Business Week* (July 29, 1991): 69, 70.

11. Michael W. Miller, "Equifax to Stop Selling Its Data to Junk-Mailers," *Wall Street Journal* (August 9, 1991): B1, B2.

12. "FTC Charges Trans Union On Lists; TRW Agrees To Limit Credit Data," *DM News* (January 18, 1993): 1, 2. See also Paul M. Alberta and Ray Schultz, "Trans Union Challenges FTC Ruling," *DM News* (October 4, 1993): 1, 3.

13. "Zooming In on You," *Privacy Journal* (June 1991): 7.

14. See John Hoerr, "Privacy," *Business Week* (March 28, 1988): 61–68; and Jeffrey Rothfeder, "Is Nothing Private?," *Business Week* (September 4, 1989): 74–82.

15. Alan F. Westin, "Consumer Privacy Issues in the Nineties," in Equifax Inc., *The Equifax Report on Consumers in the Information Age* (Atlanta, Ga.: Equifax Inc., 1990): xviii–xxviii. Quote appears on p. xix.

16. In the "Evening Magazine" exposé, a reporter—using only a couple's drivers' license numbers—was able to create an extensive portfolio of credit, health, and life-style information. WBZ-TV, Boston, Mass. (December 5, 1988).

17. For example, see Dan Rea (reporter), "Is Nothing Private?," special news feature, WBZ-TV, Boston, Mass. (May 21–22, 1990).

18. See Mitch Betts, "Focus Turns to Consumer Rights," *Computerworld* (May 14, 1990): 1, 127.

19. David F. Linowes, *Privacy in America: Is Your Private Life in the Public Eye?* (Urbana: University of Illinois Press, 1989).

20. Jeffrey Rothfeder, *Privacy for Sale: How Computerization Has Made Everyone's Private Life An Open Secret* (New York: Simon and Schuster, 1992).

21. Michael W. Miller, "Credit-Report Firms Face Greater Pressure; Ask Norwich, Vt., Why," *The Wall Street Journal* (September 23, 1991): A1, A6.

22. Michael W. Miller, "TRW Agrees to Overhaul Its Credit-Reporting Business," *The Wall Street Journal* (December 11, 1991): B1, B10.

23. See Evan Hendricks, "Here We Go Again! Torres, 16 Others Sponsor FCRA Bill," *Privacy Times* (February 24, 1993): 1, 2. For background, see also Robert Ellis Smith, "In Congress—Fair Credit Reporting Act," *Privacy Journal* (June 1992): 6.

24. Peter Pae, "American Express Co. Discloses It Gives Merchants Data on Cardholders' Habits," *New York Times* (May 14, 1992): A4.

25. Michael Autrey, "Federal Judge Rules Ban On Junk Phone Calls Unconstitutional," *Privacy Times* (June 4, 1993): 5.

26. Robert Ellis Smith, "Telemarketing Bill Signed Into Law," *Privacy Journal* (January 1992): 3.

27. Richard O. Mason, "Four Ethical Issues of the Information Age," *MIS Quarterly* (March 1986): 4–12.

28. Equifax Inc., *Harris-Equifax Consumer Privacy Survey 1992*, 4.

29. See Benn R. Konsynski and F. Warren McFarlan, "Information Partnerships—Shared Data, Shared Scale," *Harvard Business Review* (September-October 1990): 114–20, for a discussion of this trend.

30. See James I. Cash, Jr., F. Warren McFarlan, and James L. McKenney, *Corporate Information Systems Management: The Issues Facing Senior Executives*, 3d ed. (Homewood, Ill.: Irwin Press, 1992): 111–14, for an introduction to some aspects of the "islands" problem.

31. See Al Gore, "Infrastructure for the Global Village," *Scientific American* 265, no. 3 (September 1991): 150–53.

32. See Kenneth C. Laudon and Jane Price Laudon, *Business Information Systems: A*

Problem-Solving Approach, 2d ed. (Fort Worth, Tex.: Dryden Press, 1993): 94–95, for a discussion of "downsizing" and its ramifications.

33. Howard Gleckman, John Carey, Russell Mitchell, Tim Smart, and Chris Roush, "The Technology Payoff," *Business Week* (June 14, 1993): 57–68.

34. See Mitch Betts, "Romancing the Segment of One," *Computerworld* (March 5, 1990): 63–65; David Churbuck, "Smart Mail," *Forbes* (January 22, 1990): 107–8; and Pierre Passavant, "The Strategic Database," *Direct Marketing* (May 1990): 41–44.

35. See Betts, "Romancing the Segment of One."

36. James E. Krier and Edmund Ursin, in their book *Pollution and Policy: A Case Study on California and Federal Experience with Motor Vehicle Air Pollution, 1940–1975* (Berkeley: University of California Press, 1977), have referred to the concept of a "crisis" in setting environmental policy.

37. David H. Flaherty, *Protecting Privacy in Surveillance Societies* (Chapel Hill: University of North Carolina Press, 1989): 309.

38. Paul M. Alberta, "Congresswoman Makes Third Bid To Set Up a U.S. Privacy Board," *DM News* (February 15, 1993): 1, 36.

39. Evan Hendricks, "Capital Insights," *Privacy Times* (April 8, 1992): 1.

40. Evan Hendricks, "Despite Flexibility, New EC Proposal Still Too Tough for US," *Privacy Times* (October 21, 1992): 2–4; Patrick Oster, "Firms Look Askance at EC Plan to Tighten Privacy," *Washington Post* (July 25, 1991): 89. Also see John Markoff, "Europe's Plans to Protect Privacy Worry Business," *New York Times* (April 10, 1991): A1, D6; and Evan Hendricks, "U.S.-E.C. Complete Cordial First Round; Major Differences Unresolved," *Privacy Times* 11, no. 14 (August 5, 1991): 1–3. For a lucid analysis of international privacy regulation in the financial sector, see Joel R. Reidenberg, "The Privacy Obstacle Course: Hurdling Barriers to Transnational Financial Services," *Fordham Law Review* 60, no. 6 (May 1992): S137–S177.

41. See Krier and Ursin, *Pollution and Policy*.

Chapter 2

1. This chapter and those that follow utilize a concept called "anchor" organizations. In each industry, one site has been chosen based on access to relevant information. Deviations in the other organizations, where observed and where deemed important, are noted. The anchor organizations are: for banking, Bank A; for health insurance, HealthIns B; for life insurance, LifeIns; and for credit cards, CredCard. In some cases, to preserve anonymity, quotes have been attributed to individuals who are not identified as being associated with any particular site. In such situations, the individuals are not necessarily employed by the sites listed above.

2. R. Edward Freeman, *Strategic Management: A Stakeholder Approach* (Boston: Pitman, 1984): 25.

3. J. William Bowen, "The Changing Face of Consumer Banking," *Journal of Retail Banking* (Fall 1990): 9–18.

4. Steve Bergsman, "Money Centers Rediscover Retail Banking," *Bankers Monthly* (June 1989): 75–78.

5. Bowen, "The Changing Face of Consumer Banking," 9.

6. Ibid., 14.

7. Ibid., 9.

8. "Interstate Banking: The Genesis" and "Regional Interstate Banking: The Reality," *Industry Surveys* (July 26, 1990): B26, B27.

9. "Where Will It End?," *Industry Surveys* (June 26, 1990): B27.

10. "The Mighty Fallen," *The Economist* (July 27, 1991): 68–69.

11. Bergsman, "Money Centers Rediscover Retail Banking," 75.

12. Note that Banks A, B, and C may or may not appear in Table 2.1.

13. Bowen, "The Changing Face of Consumer Banking."

14. Jackey Gold, "Don't Look Back," *FW* (December 10, 1991): 38–39.

15. Bergsman, "Money Centers Rediscover Retail Banking," 77; and Charles E. Bartling, "Distribution Strategy Is a Many-Faceted Thing," *Bank Marketing* (August 1988): 29–31.

16. Michael Blanden, "Stars in Their Eyes," *The Banker* (June 1990): 7–11.

17. Stanley M. Huggins, "What You Should Know about Regulatory Enforcement Actions," *ABA Banking Journal* (February 1992): 18–20.

18. Ibid., 18.

19. L. Richard Fischer, *The Law of Financial Privacy: A Compliance Guide* (Boston: Warren, Gorham, & Lamont, 1991): 1.1–1.265.

20. Ibid., 7.1–7.24.

21. Ibid., 4.1–4.272.

22. Ibid., 2.4, 2.5.

23. Colin J. Bennett, *Regulating Privacy* (Ithaca: Cornell University Press, 1992): 174.

24. Fischer, *The Law of Financial Privacy*, 2.5.

25. Ibid., 2.1–4.272.

26. Note that these access prohibitions address, for the most part, entry from *outside* the organization by, say, computer "hackers." They do not address the access rights given to various individuals who work for the organization.

27. Fischer, *The Law of Financial Privacy*, 6.1–6.125.

28. Rick Young, "The Fantastic Future of EFT," *Bankers Monthly* (April 1988): 53–55.

29. Ibid., 54.

30. Shimon-Craig Van Collie, "The Technological Thrift of Tomorrow," *Bankers Monthly* (March 1990): 44–48.

31. Michael Violano, "Banks Bet the Ranch on the Branch," *Bankers Monthly* (November 1990): 39–42.

32. Ibid., 39.

33. Ibid., 42.

34. Thomas P. Fitch, "Teaching Computers to Be Bankers," *Bankers Monthly* (May 1988): 51–54.

35. "Life and Health Insurance: Long-Term Outlook Uncertain," *Industry Surveys* (July 12, 1990): I-28.

36. Ibid., I-33.

37. J. Chris Lehner, "The Workplace in the '90s: Benefits and Labor Trends," *Rural Telecommunications* (September/October 1991): 38–48, reports that 34 million Americans are lacking such coverage. With a national population of approximately 240 million, this represents a coverage ratio of about 86 percent.

38. "Life and Health Insurance: Long-Term Outlook Uncertain," I-28.

39. Ibid., I-33.

40. Christine Woolsey, "Life/Health Industry Sound: Analysts," *Business Insurance* (March 16, 1992): 3, 28.

41. Lehner, "The Workplace in the '90s: Benefits and Labor Trends," 40.

42. Donna DiBlase, "Group Health Bills Equal a Third of Profits," *Business Insurance* (May 29, 1989): 1, 38, 39.

43. "Life and Health Insurance: Long-Term Outlook Uncertain," I-33.

44. DiBlase, "Group Health Bills Equal a Third of Profits," 1.

45. Burton A. Weisbrod, "The Health Care Quadrilemma: An Essay on Technological Change, Insurance, Quality of Care, and Cost Containment," *Journal of Economic Literature* (June 1991): 523–52. Quote appears on p. 531.

46. Thomas M. Burton, "Second Opinion: Firms That Promise Lower Medical Bills May Increase Them," *Wall Street Journal* (July 28, 1992): A1, A9.

47. Employee Benefit Research Institute (EBRI), "EBRI Databook on Employee Benefits," 2d ed. (Washington, D.C.: EBRI-ERF [Education and Research Fund], 1992): 281.

48. Ibid., 281.

49. Amy Katz, "HMO Profits on Upswing Despite Flat Enrollment," *Business Insurance* (July 29, 1991): 38, 39.

50. Joanne Wojcik, "Plans Go Open-Ended: Interstudy," and Christine Woolsey, "Firms Seeking PPOs, New Options: Hewitt," *Business Insurance* (March 11, 1991): 3, 28.

51. Lehner, "The Workplace in the '90s: Benefits and Labor Trends," 40.

52. Ibid.

53. Chuck Jones, "Small-Group Reform at Core of Bush Health Plan," *LAN* (March 1992): 26–30.

54. Cynthia K. Hosay, "Congressional Interest Rises to Aid Non-Insured Americans," *Pension World* (October 1991): 44–46.

55. Marybeth Burke, "Anxious for Reform, Congress Targets Health Insurance Industry," *Hospitals* (June 20, 1991): 38–40.

56. "Accident and Health Insurance—1990," *Best's Review* (December 1991): 60–66.

57. Sidney E. Harris and Joseph L. Katz, "Firm Size and Information Technology Investment Intensity of Life Insurers," *MIS Quarterly* (September 1991): 333–52.

58. "The 500 Leading Life Companies in Total Premium Income," *Best's Review* (July 1991): 19–24.

59. Note that LifeIns, HealthInsA, and HealthIns B may or may not appear in Table 2.2.

60. MIB background information from MIB documents and from interviews.

61. Data regarding SEARCH provided by an Equifax spokesperson.

62. Dana Priest, "In W. Va., an Insurance Safety Net Unravels," *Washington Post* (August 3, 1992): A1, A6.

63. See Mark A. Hofmann, "State Oversight Working: Regulator," *Business Insurance* (December 9, 1991): 26; and Rhonda J. Ruch, "Insurers Urged to Brace for a Decade of Difficulties," *Best's Review* (December 1991): 124–26.

64. More than half of LifeIns's agents sold only for LifeIns.

65. The list included the necessary examinations for various coverage amounts and applicant ages.

66. However, LifeIns was considering the addition of an expert system that would assist underwriters by giving clues for further investigation. Should the system be adopted, the medical information would be entered into the computer.

67. Nicholas D. Latrenta, "Privacy and Fair Information Practices Principles in the Life Insurance Business: A Modern Historical Review," American Council of Life Insurance Legal Section Meeting (November 12–14, 1990): 51.

68. Ibid., 20–21.

69. Ibid., 79–80.

70. For an in-depth overview of the Model Privacy Act, see ibid., 79–134.

71. Harold Skipper, Jr., "An Analysis of the NAIC Model Privacy Act—Part II," *Best's Review* (September 1980): 25–29.

72. EBRI, "EBRI's Benefit Outlook" (June 1992): 9.

73. The Americans Disabilities Act became law on July 26, 1992, and provided an additional level of protection for those with disabilities. See Robert H. Woods and Raphael R. Kavanaugh, "Here Comes the ADA—Are You Ready? (Part I)," *Cornell H.R.A. Quarterly* (February 1992): 24–32.

74. Sidney E. Harris and Joseph L. Katz, "Firm Size and the Information Technology Investment Intensity of Life Insurers," *MIS Quarterly* (September 1991): 333–52.

75. Jennifer Cranford Rankin, "Insurers Sound Off on Field Computing," *Best's Review* (November 1991): 102–8.

76. Ibid., 108.

77. Grover Norwood, "Providing Better Client Service," *Managers Magazine* (February 1992): 32.

78. Maryfran Johnson, "Service Delivers Painless Insurance Claims," *Computerworld* (July 15, 1991): 27.

79. These and other interesting tales of credit cards' history are detailed in Nancy Shepherdson, "Credit Card America," *American Heritage* (November 1991): 125–32.

80. Ibid., 132.

81. "The Big Squeeze," *The Economist* (November 2, 1991): 69–70.

82. Ibid., 69.

83. Eric J. Savitz, "Fate Worse Than Debt: Competition Is Rearing Its Ugly Head in Credit Cards," *Barron's* (February 18, 1991): 12–14. Quote appears on p. 12.

84. Most cards do not charge interest on purchases if they are paid off in the month charged. However, this is not uniform across the industry, and a few issuers offer no such grace period.

85. Arthur P. Hall and J. Marc Wheat, "Do Credit Cards Need Interest Rate Caps?," *Consumers' Research* (February 1992): 28–31.

86. Shepherdson, "Credit Card America," 132.

87. "The Big Squeeze," 70.

88. Ibid.

89. Peter Pae, "AT&T to Offer Debt Defectors a No-Fee Card," *Wall Street Journal* (February 23, 1992): B1, B6.

90. "The Big Squeeze," 69.

91. "Banks Get a Break, But Cardholders Don't," *Changing Times* (May 1991): 70.

92. Lawrence M. Ausubel, "The Failure of Competition in the Credit Card Market," *American Economic Review* (March 1991): 50–81.

93. Jeffrey M. Laderman, "The Street's Fear: 'The Crazy Things Congress Might Do,'" *Business Week* (December 2, 1991): 15.

94. Pae, "AT&T to Offer Debt Defectors a No-Fee Card," B1.

95. Nancy Linnon, "Cards That Try Harder," *U.S. News and World Report* (January 21, 1991): 77–80.

96. Ausubel, "The Failure of Competition in the Credit Card Market."

97. Although Banks A, B, and C also issued credit cards, their credit card activities are not necessarily included in this study. In many banks, credit card units are separate and distinct organizations. At most (or all) of the banks in this study, access to the credit card units' employees was not available because of organizational sensitivity, geographic dispersion, and/or political reasons. Thus, while CredCard might be associated with Bank A, Bank B, or Bank C, this is not necessarily the case. Note that CredCard may or may not appear in Table 2.3.

98. Michael Quint, "Suits Pushing Banks to Obey State Laws on Credit Card Fees," *New York Times* (February 23, 1992): 1, 24.

99. "Your Credit Muscle," *Changing Times* (June 1989): 90.

100. Shepherdson, "Credit Card America," 130.

101. "Preapproved Credit, For Real," *Changing Times* (July 1990): 72.

102. A crude estimate of data storage at CredCard could be constructed as follows: (total disk storage) divided by (number of cards) equaled approximately 54,000 bytes per card. Actual number of cards and size of disk storage are being withheld to preserve CredCard's anonymity.

103. Peter Coy, "Now Your Credit Card Can Get An Instant O.K.," *Business Week* (August 20, 1990): 88C.

104. Most of this information is taken from "Cash and Credit Cards Will Soon Be Obsolete, But How Brainy Are the New Smart Cards?," *Omni* (June 1991): 59–62.

105. "Cash and Credit Cards Will Soon Be Obsolete," 60.

106. The attorney's comments were related by a spokesperson at the corporation.

Chapter 3

1. The concept of a crisis as a prod for societal attention has been documented by James E. Krier and Edmund Ursin, *Pollution and Policy: A Case Study on California and Federal Experience with Motor Vehicle Air Pollution, 1940–1975* (Berkeley: University of California Press, 1977).

2. Various models for corporate reactions in societal settings are reviewed by Elizabeth Gatewood and Archie B. Carroll, "The Anatomy of Corporate Social Response: The Rely, Firestone 500, and Pinto Cases," *Business Horizons* (September/October 1981): 9-16. See also William H. Starbuck, "Why Organizations Run Into Crises . . . and Sometimes Survive Them," in Kenneth C. Laudon and Jon A. Turner, eds., *Information Technology and Management Strategy* (Englewood Cliffs, N.J.: Prentice-Hall, 1989): 11–33; and Charles E. Lindblom, "The Science of 'Muddling Through,'" *Public Administration Review* 19 (1959): 79–88.

3. A hospital administrator, interviewed separately, described a similar campaign in which hospital employees were urged to tug on their ears when they heard others engaged in inappropriate discussions of patient information.

4. A similar phenomenon was noted at LifeIns, where situations but not names were discussed.

5. David F. Linowes, *Privacy in America: Is Your Private Life in the Public Eye?* (Urbana: University of Illinois Press, 1989), 28.

6. Ibid., 42.

7. For frameworks which draw this distinction quite clearly, see James I. Cash, Jr., F. Warren McFarlan, and James L. McKenney, *Corporate Information Systems Management: The Issues Facing Senior Executives*, 3d ed. (Homewood, Ill.: Richard D. Irwin, 1992).

8. By 1992, some state legislation that appeared to restrict such uses of customer information, without express consent, was being considered. See John Ward Anderson, "Va. Bill Would Curb Abuse of Computerized Mail Lists," *Washington Post* (February 5, 1992): C1, C2.

9. Kenneth C. Laudon, *Dossier Society: Value Choices in the Design of National Information Systems* (New York: Columbia University Press, 1986).

10. Robert Jackall, *Moral Mazes: The World of Corporate Managers* (New York: Oxford University Press, 1988).

11. Equifax Inc., *The Equifax Report on Consumers in the Information Age* (Atlanta, Ga.: Equifax Inc., 1990).

12. Jackall, *Moral Mazes*.

13. A research proposition, stated before the fact, predicted that technical and corporate approaches would be preferred to legal approaches.

14. Equifax Inc., *The Equifax Report on Consumers in the Information Age*.

15. Steven D. Murch, "Big Brother Meets Public Opinion: The Cancellation of Lotus MarketPlace," Harvard Business School class paper (April 25, 1991). Also see Mary J. Culnan, "The Lessons of the Lotus MarketPlace: Implications for Consumer Privacy in the 1990s," working paper, Georgetown University (1991).

16. For an interesting discussion of this phenomenon, see Michael R. Vitale, "The Growing Risks of Information Systems Success," Harvard Business School note (1986), number 187–067.

Chapter 4

1. Jeffrey Rothfeder and Michele Galen, "Is Your Boss Spying on You?," *Business Week* (January 15, 1990): 74–75.

2. Privacy Protection Study Commission (PPSC), *Personal Privacy in an Information Society: Report of the Privacy Protection Study Commission* (Washington, D.C.: U.S. Government Printing Office, 1977).

3. United States Department of Health, Education, and Welfare (HEW), *Records, Computers, and the Rights of Citizens: Report of the Secretary's Advisory Committee on Automated Personal Data Systems* (Washington: U.S. Government Printing Office, 1973).

4. Although MIB was not a study site in the strict sense (for example, I did not observe their operations), its policies—as described by its president and as presented in some of the documents that were shared with me—are sometimes referenced in this section. In general, MIB appeared to embrace a more formal and conservative approach to access and use of its data than did the study sites.

5. Many people would of course debate this statement and argue with the distinctions insurance companies' underwriting processes make. Such debate is interesting, but this discussion assumes the validity of the underwriting distinctions.

6. Of course, both the banks' and CredCard's credit decisions were subject to the Equal Credit Opportunity Act, which prohibited credit discrimination on the basis of race, color, religion, national origin, sex, marital status, welfare payments, or age. See Robert Ellis Smith, *Compilation of State and Federal Privacy Laws* (Providence, R.I.: Privacy Journal, 1992) for more details.

7. HEW, *Records, Computers, and the Rights of Citizens.*

8. Note that the bank would not always have access to an individual's income. This information would be provided on loan applications, but not all customers had loans with the bank. The next section ("Sharing Information") discusses another source of income information being utilized by banks.

9. John Ladd, "Computers and Moral Responsibility: A Framework for an Ethical Analysis," in *The Information Web: Ethical and Social Implications of Computer Networking* (Boulder: Westview Press, 1989).

10. Dictated, for the most part, by the Right to Financial Privacy Act of 1978. However, actual practices may deviate from legal requirements. See PPSC, *Personal Privacy in an Information Society*, pp. 345–91, and Linowes, *Privacy in America*, 106–8.

11. HEW, *Records, Computers, and the Rights of Citizens.*

12. Robert Ellis Smith, *War Stories* (Providence, R.I.: Privacy Journal, 1990).

13. PPSC, *Personal Privacy in an Information Society*, 45–46.

14. Linowes, *Privacy in America*, 102–12.

15. These categories of "deliberate errors" and "accidental errors" correspond roughly to the database concepts of *security* and *integrity*. C. J. Date distinguishes between the two as follows: "Security means protecting the database against unauthorized users . . . and integrity means protecting it against authorized users. . . . Security involves ensuring that users are *allowed* to do the things they are trying to do. Integrity involves ensuring that the

things they are trying to do are *correct*." See C. J. Date, *An Introduction to Database Systems*, 4th ed. (Reading, Mass.: Addison-Wesley Publishing Company, 1986), 453, 437.

16. Consumers Union, "What Are They Saying About Me?" (April 29, 1991), special news release.

17. Consumers Union, "What Price Privacy?" *Consumer Reports* (May 1991): 354–60.

18. Charles Perrow, *Normal Accidents: Living with High-Risk Technologies* (New York: Basic Books, 1984).

19. Rob Kling, "Value Conflicts and Social Choice in Electronic Funds Transfer Systems Developments," *Communications of the ACM* 21, no. 8 (August 1978): 642–57.

20. Laudon, *Dossier Society*.

21. Ibid.

22. See Robert Ellis Smith, "A Hit and an Error," *Privacy Journal* (April 1987): 1.

23. Until mid-1990, MIB's normal policy was to release the records only to the individual's physician. However, the policy was being modified to allow release of most information directly to the individual.

24. Such edits would include, for example, ensuring that a zip code entered on a computer screen was in a valid format.

25. See Richard M. Cyert and James G. March, *A Behavioral Theory of the Firm* (New York: Prentice-Hall, 1963). Also see Herbert Simon, *Administrative Behavior* (New York: Free Press, 1976).

26. Robert Ellis Smith, *Compilation of State and Federal Privacy Laws* (Washington, D.C.: Privacy Journal, 1988), v.

27. Laudon, *Dossier Society*.

28. Abbe Mowshowitz, *The Conquest of Will: Information Processing in Human Affairs* (Reading, Mass.: Addison-Wesley, 1976): 120.

29. John Ladd, "Computers and Moral Responsibility."

30. Robert Ellis Smith, *War Stories*.

31. Ibid.

32. PPSC, *Personal Privacy in an Information Society*, 8–11.

33. H. Jeff Smith, "National Credit Information Network," Harvard Business School case (1989), number 190–043. See also H. Jeff Smith, "Note on the Credit Bureau Industry and the Fair Credit Reporting Act (FCRA)," Harvard Business School case, (1989), number 190–044.

34. Simson Garfinkel, "The Age of the 'Super Bureaus,'" *Privacy Journal* (March 1989): 1, 5–6.

35. Arthur Miller, "Computers and Privacy," in *Ethics and the Management of Computer Technology*, edited by W. Michael Hoffman and Jennifer Mills Moore (Cambridge, Mass.: Oelgeschlager, Gunn, and Hain, 1982), 96.

36. Equifax Inc., *The Equifax Report on Consumers in the Information Age*, 11.

37. Ibid., 18.

38. *Communications of the ACM* 23, no. 7 (July 1980): 425 (item EC5.2).

39. A few states required that patients be allowed to see their own records except in cases where it might be detrimental to their treatment.

40. On IBM computers, these safeguards usually included implementation of either the Remote Access Control Facility (RACF) or the ACF2 software on the mainframe.

41. This finding is based on Banks A and B and HealthIns A and B.

42. The reference at HealthIns B read "Employees may disclose to another employee . . . any information about a member which the other employee needs in the regular course of work." Restrictions on the use of, and access to, printed MIB reports were quite explicit. Reports could only be kept in coded form, access to the MIB code book (required to understand the reports) was to be strictly controlled, etc.

43. See Linowes, *Privacy in America*, 175. One might construe Linowes's references to Citicorp's policy statement as addressing this item.

Chapter 5

1. Some liberties have been taken with Potter's original nomenclature.

2. Ralph B. Potter, *War and Moral Discourse* (Richmond: John Knox Press, 1969).

3. See Robert Ellis Smith, *Compilation of State and Federal Privacy Laws* (Providence, R.I.: Privacy Journal, 1992).

4. Day letter to Act Up.

5. Josh Kratka, *For Their Eyes Only: The Insurance Industry and Consumer Privacy* (Boston: Massachusetts Public Interest Research Group [MassPIRG], April 1990).

6. Neil Day, "Notes by Neil Day of MIB, Inc., for Submission to Insurance Departments, Legislative Committees, and Study Commissions" (July 1989).

7. Kratka, *For Their Eyes Only*, 4–5.

8. During one focus group interview, a consumer yelled out "so *that's* how they got my phone number!"

9. In 1977 the PPSC reported that many individuals' fear that their medical records will be reviewed by outsiders keeps them from seeking treatment for their illnesses, especially if the illness is psychiatric in character. A psychiatrist who was interviewed for this study confirmed that he often advises patients who can afford to pay their own bills to avoid claiming the charges on their health insurance, so that they can avoid any stigma attached to psychiatric care. See PPSC, *Personal Privacy in an Information Society: Report of the Privacy Protection Study Commission* (Washington, D.C.: U.S. Government Printing Office, 1977).

10. It should be noted that HealthIns B executives also revealed a commitment to confidentiality, which had occasionally been expressed in the rejection of some employers' requests for medical information, even when this had led to a cancellation of the account, with a negative impact on profitability. However, this seemed to be an unusual occurrence.

11. Alan F. Westin, "How the American Public Views Consumer Privacy Issues in the Early 90's—and Why," testimony before the Subcommittee on Government Information, Justice, and Agriculture of the Committee on Government Operations, U.S. House of Representatives, Washington, D.C., April 10, 1991.

12. James E. Tobin, letter to *Privacy Times*, reproduced in July 1, 1992 issue.

13. Paul M. Alberta, "Equifax Inc. Consents to Rework Its Credit-Reporting in 18 States," *DM News* (July 6, 1992): 3.

14. Evan Hendricks, "Equifax Reaches Agreement With 18 State AGs on Credit Reports," *Privacy Times* (July 1, 1992): 3.

15. D. Van Skilling, TRW executive vice president, quoted in Evan Hendricks, "TRW Settles FTC, Multi-State Suit on Credit Reports; Vermont Not Satisfied," *Privacy Times* (December 17, 1991): 2–3.

16. Under that plan, pieces of information were gleaned from credit report files and placed in a separate database. The new database was used in generating lists of likely candidates for various offers, especially those for pre-approved credit offers. For example, a credit grantor might buy a list of "individuals in the Southeast with at least three credit cards and no outstanding credit balances over 60 days old."

17. Alberta, "Equifax Inc. Consents to Rework Its Credit-Reporting in 18 States," 3.

18. One notable exception was Equifax's use of consumer focus groups during the development of the Lotus MarketPlace: Households product. However, given the ultimate withdrawal of the product before its release, it is unclear how effective the use of focus groups was in this situation.

Chapter 6

1. "Lotus, Equifax Cancel Shipment of Lotus MarketPlace: Households," news release (January 23, 1991).

2. For a lucid discussion of privacy's origins, see Alan F. Westin, *Privacy and Freedom* (New York: Atheneum, 1970).

3. David H. Flaherty, *Privacy in Colonial New England* (Charlottesville: University Press of Virginia, 1972): 7.

4. These four "functions of individual privacy" were established by Westin (1967): 32–39.

5. Flaherty, *Privacy in Colonial New England*, 3–21.

6. Ibid., 219–41.

7. Robert Ellis Smith, *The Law of Privacy in a Nutshell* (Providence, R.I.: Privacy Journal, 1993): 8.

8. John Perry Barlow, address to the Computers, Freedom, and Privacy conference, San Francisco, Calif., March 1993.

9. Robert Ellis Smith, *The Law of Privacy in a Nutshell*, 4–5.

10. See "Privacy Protection in the United States," prepared by Ronald L. Plesser and Emilio W. Cividanes for Piper and Marbury [law firm], Washington, D.C., May 1991. Also see Robert L. Sherman for the Direct Marketing Association, "Statement of the Direct Marketing Association Before the New York State Consumer Protection Board," June 11, 1992; and David F. Linowes, *Privacy in America* (Urbana: University of Illinois Press, 1989): 13.

11. Samuel Warren and Louis Brandeis, "The Right to Privacy," *Harvard Law Review* 4 (1890): 193–220.

12. Edward J. Kionka, *Torts in a Nutshell*, 2d ed. (St. Paul, Minn.: West Publishing, 1992): 399–403.

13. For a good overview of existing laws at both a state and federal level, see Robert Ellis Smith, *Compilation of State and Federal Privacy Laws* (Providence, R.I.: Privacy Journal, 1992). The broad theories undergirding U.S. privacy law are ably discussed by Joel R. Reidenberg, "Privacy in the Information Economy: A Fortress or Frontier for Individual Rights?," *Federal Communications Law Journal* 44, no. 2 (March 1992): 195–243.

14. Direct Marketing Association (DMA), *1991–92 Compendium of Government Issues Affecting Direct Marketing* (New York and Washington: Direct Marketing Association, 1992).

15. Robert Ellis Smith, *The Law of Privacy in a Nutshell*, 37.

16. For summaries of competing views of privacy and philosophical disputes associated with those views, see Ferdinand David Schoeman, ed., *Philosophical Dimensions of Privacy* (Cambridge: Cambridge University Press, 1984). See also James B. Rule, Douglas McAdam, Linda Stearns, and David Uglow, *The Politics of Privacy: Planning for Personal Data Systems as Powerful Technologies* (New York: Elsevier, 1980). Although the following discussion focuses mainly on tensions in the commercial sector, good syntheses of the tensions between efficiency and rights in the governmental sector can be found in David Burnham, *The Rise of the Computer State* (New York: Random House, 1983) and *A Law unto Itself: Power, Politics, and the IRS* (New York: Random House, 1989).

17. Equifax Inc., *The Equifax Report on Consumers in the Information Age* (Atlanta, Ga.: Equifax Inc., 1990): Table 1–5, p. 7.

18. See Robert Ellis Smith, "House Kills Credit-Reporting Reforms, After 'Preemption' Vote," *Privacy Journal* (September 1992): 1.

19. Kenneth E. Goodpaster, "The Concept of Corporate Responsibility," in *Just Business: New Introductory Essays in Business Ethics*, edited by Tom Regan (New York: Random House, 1984). See also Kenneth E. Goodpaster and John B. Matthews, Jr., "Can a Corporation Have a Conscience?," *Harvard Business Review* (January–February 1982): 132–41.

20. Milton Friedman, "The Social Responsibility of Business Is to Increase Its Profits," *New York Times Magazine* (September 13, 1970): 32–33, 122, 124, 126.

21. This phenomenon was observed in the Lotus MarketPlace: Households incident, in the Blockbuster Video incident, and in numerous comments by executives during the Fair Credit Reporting Acts (FCRA) hearings in Congress in 1990–92.

22. Max D. Hopper, "Rattling SABRE: New Ways to Compete on Information," *Harvard Business Review* (May-June 1990): 119.

23. International Business Machines (IBM) Corporation, *Benefits from Technology*, IBM Form G505–0071–01.

24. The author is indebted to Dick MacKinnon, manager, IBM Cambridge Scientific Center, for this term.

25. This section is primarily based on Harvey M. Deitel, *An Introduction to Operating Systems* (Reading, Mass.: Addison-Wesley, 1984). However, I have added additional observations—particularly as an update to Deitel's fourth generation. Additional informa-

tion available in C. C. Gotlieb, *The Economics of Computers: Costs, Benefits, Policies, and Strategies* (Englewood Cliffs, N.J.: Prentice-Hall, 1985).

26. Globecon Group, Ltd., *Electronic Data Interchange and Corporate Trade Payments* (Morristown, N.J.: Financial Executives Research Foundation, 1988).

27. Robert Ellis Smith, *Compilation of State and Federal Privacy Laws* (Washington, D.C.: Privacy Journal, 1988), v.

28. Deborah G. Johnson, *Computer Ethics* (Englewood Cliffs, N.J.: Prentice-Hall, 1985), 2.

29. John Ladd, "Computers and Moral Responsibility: A Framework for an Ethical Analysis," in *The Information Web: Ethical and Social Implications of Computer Networking*, edited by Carol Gould (Boulder: Westview Press, 1989): 207–27.

30. Deborah G. Johnson, "The Public-Private Status of Transactions in Computer Networks," in *The Information Web: Ethical and Social Implications of Computer Networking*, edited by Carol C. Gould (Boulder: Westview Press, 1989): 37–55.

31. Evan Hendricks, "AT&T 800 Number Directory Spawns Business Backlash," *Privacy Times* (September 10, 1991): 3–4.

32. Terry Brennan, "CADM Releases Its Unanimous Objection to AT&T 800 Directory," *DM News* (October 7, 1991): 1, 2.

33. Michael W. Miller, "Citicorp Creates Controversy with Plan to Sell Data on Credit-Card Purchases," *Wall Street Journal* (August 22, 1991): B1, B7.

34. Alan F. Westin, "Consumer Privacy Protection: Ten Predictions," *Mobius* (February 1992).

35. Alberta, "Credit List 'Opt-In' Measure Beaten," 1, 3.

36. Jerrold Ballinger, "N.Y. Mulls Opt-In for Bank Card Files," *DM News* (December 9, 1991): 1.

37. John Ward Anderson, "Va. Bill Would Curb Abuse Of Computerized Mail Lists," *Washington Post* (February 5, 1992): C1, C2. See also DMA, *Washington Update*, (February 24, 1992): 4, and Evan Hendricks, "Virginia Passes Privacy Statute for Transactional Data Held By 'Merchants,'" *Privacy Times* (April 22, 1992): 4.

38. "Europe Parliament Recommends a New Data-Protection Measure," *DM News* (March 23, 1992): 1, 8.

39. "DMA Joins FCC in Opposition to National Do-Not-Call Database," *DM News* (July 13, 1992): 3.

40. Evan Hendricks, "Capital Insights," *Privacy Times* (April 8, 1992): 1.

41. "New Bill Would Require NCOA Opt-Out Provision," *DM News* (June 1, 1992): 1, 3.

42. "Technology Pits Privacy vs. Information Age," *San Diego Union* (June 7, 1992), as reproduced in RISKS Digest computer conference.

43. Michael W. Miller, "Data Mills Delve Deep to Find Information about U.S. Consumers," *Wall Street Journal* (March 14, 1991): A1, A8.

44. Ray Schultz, "FBI Said to Seek Compiled Lists for Use in Its Field Investigations," *DM News* (April 20, 1992): 1, 8, 48, and Evan Hendricks, "FBI Relies on Direct Marketer's Database; May Seek to Expand Use," *Privacy Times* (May 7, 1992): 4.

45. Michael W. Miller, "Credit-Report Firms Face Greater Pressure; Ask Norwich, Vt., Why," *Wall Street Journal* (September 23, 1991): A1, A6.

46. Ibid.

47. Consumers Union, "What Are They Saying About Me?" (April 29, 1991), and Consumers Union, "What Price Privacy?," *Consumer Reports* (May 1991): 354–60.

48. See Mary J. Culnan, "In Credit Reports, 'Free' Isn't the Issue," *New York Times* (December 8, 1991): F15.

49. Walecia Konrad, "Credit Reports—With a Smile," *Business Week* (October 21, 1991): 100–102.

50. Peter Kerr, "Credit-Data Settlement for Equifax," *New York Times* (July 1, 1992): D3.

51. Jeffrey Rothfeder, "Is Nothing Private?," *Business Week* (September 4, 1989): 74–82.

52. "Evening Magazine," WBZ-TV, Boston, Mass. (December 5, 1988).

53. See H. Jeff Smith, "National Credit Information Network," Harvard Business School case (1989), number 190–043. For a later update, see Jeanne Sadler, "Three Credit Data Firms Agree to Try to Keep Clients from Misusing Reports," *Wall Street Journal* (August 19, 1992): A2.

54. The American Council of Life Insurance and The Health Insurance Association of America (co-sponsors), "Report of the ACLI-HIAA Task Force on Genetic Testing" (1991). Much of the information in this discussion is taken from this report and from David Brown, "Individual 'Genetic Privacy' Seen as Threatened," *Washington Post* (October 20, 1991): A6.

55. Summarized from Brown, "Individual 'Genetic Privacy' Seen as Threatened."

56. Summarized from The American Council of Life Insurance and The Health Insurance Association of America (co-sponsors), "Report of the ACLI-HIAA Task Force on Genetic Testing."

57. Quoted in Brown, "Individual 'Genetic Privacy' Seen as Threatened."

58. Debbie Chase, "Genetic Testing Legislation: Here's a State-by-State Summary," *Council Review* (journal of the American Council of Life Insurance) (July 1992): 7–8.

59. Michael W. Miller, "Patients' Records Are Treasure Trove for Budding Industry," *Wall Street Journal* (February 27, 1992): A1, A6.

60. Michael W. Miller, "Congress, AMA Move to Protect Patient Records," *Wall Street Journal* (July 10, 1992): B2.

61. Ibid.

62. U.S. Senate Congressional Record (June 23, 1992): S8659–S8668.

63. Jeffrey Rothfeder, "Is Your Boss Spying on You?," *Business Week* (January 15, 1990): 74–75.

64. Karen Nussbaum, "Workers under Surveillance," *Computerworld* (January 6, 1992): 21.

65. Mitch Betts, "VDT Monitoring under Stress," *Computerworld* (January 21, 1991): 1, 14.

66. See Gary T. Marx, "The Case of the Omniscient Organization," *Harvard Business*

Review (March-April 1990): 4–12; and Ronald Corbett and Gary T. Marx, "No Soul in the New Machine: Technofallacies in the Electronic Monitoring Movement," *Justice Quarterly* 8, no. 3 (September 1991): 399–414.

67. Amy Kuebelbeck, "Getting the Message," *Los Angeles Times* (September 4, 1991): E1, E2; and Ernest A. Kallman and Sanford Sherizen, "Private Matters," *Computerworld* (November 23, 1992): 86–87.

68. Kuebelbeck, "Getting the Message," and Kallman and Sherizen, "Private Matters."

69. Michael W. Miller, "Historians Crusade to Preserve 'E-Mail,' " *Wall Street Journal* (March 31, 1992): B1.

70. For the specifics of states' approaches to the Caller ID debates, see *Privacy Journal* and *Privacy Times* issues from 1989 through 1992. Also see Milo Geyelin and Mary Lu Carnevale, "Caller ID Service Is Ruled Illegal in Pennsylvania," *Wall Street Journal* (March 20, 1992): B1, B10.

71. Edmund L. Andrews, "Telephone Companies to Get Right to Transmit Television," *New York Times* (July 16, 1992): A1, D17.

Chapter 7

1. Alan F. Westin and Michael A. Baker, *Databanks in a Free Society* (New York: Quadrangle Books, 1972): 249.

2. James E. Krier and Edmund Ursin, *Pollution and Policy: A Case Study on California and Federal Experience with Motor Vehicle Air Pollution, 1940–1975* (Berkeley: University of California Press, 1977).

3. Christopher D. Stone, *Where the Law Ends* (New York: Harper and Row, 1975): 88–118; and Kenneth E. Goodpaster and John B. Matthews, Jr., "Can a Corporation Have a Conscience?," *Harvard Business Review* (January–February 1982): 132–41.

4. Stone, *Where the Law Ends*, 35–57 and 93–110.

5. Ibid., 88–92.

6. For a discussion of this phenomenon, see N. Craig Smith, *Morality and the Market: Consumer Pressure for Corporate Accountability* (London: Routledge, 1989).

7. Stone, *Where the Law Ends*, 35–110.

8. Summarized from Colin J. Bennett, *Regulating Privacy: Data Protection and Public Policy in Europe and the United States* (Ithaca: Cornell University Press, 1992): 153–61. See also David H. Flaherty, *Protecting Privacy in Surveillance Societies* (Chapel Hill: University of North Carolina Press, 1989) for a very thorough treatment of several countries' privacy protection experiences.

9. Bennett, *Regulating Privacy*, 161–92.

10. The following commentary relies to some degree on the excellent analyses of the various models in ibid., 155–61.

11. See Stone, *Where the Law Ends*, 88–92.

12. Bennett, *Regulating Privacy*, 173.

13. Priscilla M. Regan, "Public Uses of Private Information: A Comparison of Person-

al Information Policies in the United States and Britain (Ph.D. diss., Cornell University, 1981): 114, as quoted in Bennett, *Regulating Privacy*, 158.

14. Equifax Inc., *The Equifax Report on Computers in the Information Age* (Atlanta, Ga.: Equifax Inc., 1990).

15. Of course, the U.S. government has at times embraced such a mechanism. When corporations continued to subvert environmental controls, for example, the Environmental Protection Agency (EPA) was created. (See Krier and Ursin, *Pollution and Privacy*, for additional details.) As discussed later in this chapter, models of greater governmental control do stand as viable options should corporations refuse to cooperate on privacy issues.

16. Flaherty, *Protecting Privacy in Surveillance Societies*, 93-162.

17. See Priscilla Regan, "Protecting Privacy and Controlling Bureaucracies: Constraints of British Constitutional Principles," *Governance* (January 1990): 33–54.

18. Bennett, *Regulating Privacy*, 189.

19. Flaherty, *Protecting Privacy in Surveillance Societies*, 21.

20. Ibid., 27.

21. Bennett, *Regulating Privacy*, 182–83.

22. Alan F. Westin, "Consumer Privacy Protection: Ten Predictions," *Mobius*, February 1992, 11. Dr. Westin is the source of the term "privacy-intensive," used later in this book.

23. Marc Rotenberg, "In Support of a Data Protection Board in the United States," *Government Information Quarterly* 8, no. 1 (1991): 79–93.

24. John R. White, "President's Letter," *Communications of the ACM* (May 1991): 15–16. See also Association for Computing Machinery (ACM), "ACM Urges Government Action to Protect Privacy," *ACMemberNet*, a supplement to *Communications of the ACM* 34, no. 7 (July 1991): 1, 9.

25. Flaherty, *Protecting Privacy in Surveillance Societies*, 305.

26. Bennett, *Regulating Privacy*, 170–72.

27. Ibid., 172, with references to David H. Flaherty, "The Need for an American Privacy Protection Commission," *Government Information Quarterly* 1 (1984): 235–58.

28. H.R. 3669, 101st Cong., 2d sess.

29. Richard A. Barton, "Privacy and Direct Marketing: Issues for the 1990s," *Directions* (DMA publication; November/December 1990): 4–6, 13.

30. Ibid., 13.

31. John Baker, testimony before the Subcommittee on Government Information, Justice, and Agriculture of the Committee on Government Operations, U.S. House of Representatives, Washington, D.C. (April 10, 1991).

32. Equifax Inc., *The Equifax Report on Consumers in the Information Age*, 106.

33. Some studies in other fields (e.g., personnel research) have found that individuals display varying thresholds of sensitivity toward different types of information (see, for example, Richard W. Woodman, Daniel C. Ganster, Jerome Adams, Michael McCuddy, Paul Tolchinsky, and Howard Fromkin, "A Survey of Employee Perceptions of Information Privacy in Organizations," *Academy of Management Journal* 25, no. 3 [1982]: 647–63). Such work should be extended into the policy domain, where consistency with corporate approaches can be measured.

34. An example of such a study can be found in H. Jeff Smith and Ernest A. Kallman, "Privacy Attitudes and Practices: An Empirical Study of Medical Record Directors' Perceptions," *Journal of Health Information Management Research* 1, no. 2 (Fall/Winter 1992): 9–31.

35. Such an instrument has been addressed by H. Jeff Smith, Sandra J. Milberg, and Sandra J. Burke, "Development of an Instrument for Measuring Information Privacy Concerns," unpublished working paper, Georgetown University School of Business Administration, 1993.

36. Tom M. Plank and Douglas L. Blensly, *Accounting Desk Book: The Accountant's Everyday Instant Answer Book* (Englewood Cliffs, N.J.: Prentice-Hall, 1989).

37. See Terrence H. Witkowski, "Self-Regulation Will Suppress Direct Marketing's Dark Side," *Marketing News* 23, no. 9 (April 24, 1989): 4.

38. Jerrold Ballinger, "DMA Seeks Privacy Effort Funds, Gitlitz Announces at Spring Session," *DM News*, April 6, 1992, pp. 6, 18.

39. Robert Ellis Smith, "If It's a Privacy Bill, Direct Marketing Group's Fingerprints Are on It," *Privacy Journal* (May 1992): 5.

40. Some have questioned the extent to which the DMA's self-regulation initiatives have been adopted. See, for example, Mary J. Culnan, " 'How Did They Get My Name?': An Exploratory Study of Consumer Attitudes Toward Secondary Information Use," *MIS Quarterly* 17, no. 3 (September 1993): 341–63.

41. I am grateful to Jane Linder for the suggestion of this terminology. See Richard E. Walton, "Establishing and Maintaining High Commitment Work Systems," in *Organizational Life Cycle*, edited by John R. Kimberly and Robert H. Miles (San Francisco: Jossey-Bass, 1980): 208–90, for a discussion of this dichotomy.

42. Alan F. Westin, "Past and Future in Employment Testing: A Socio-Political Overview," *University of Chicago Legal Forum* (1988): 93–111.

43. See David W. Ewing, *Justice On the Job* (Boston: Harvard Business School Press, 1989) and Douglas M. McCabe, *Corporate Nonunion Complaint Procedures and Systems* (New York: Praeger Publishers, 1988).

44. Bennett, *Regulating Privacy*, 155.

45. For example, the *Privacy Journal* and *Privacy Times* are excellent sources of information regarding consumer advocates' concerns.

46. In some industries, suppliers of information might also be logical candidates.

47. Jack N. Behrman, *Essays on Ethics in Business and the Professions* (Englewood Cliffs, N.J.: Prentice-Hall, 1988).

48. Note that this is mandated by federal law for many credit-related activities.

49. Equifax, *The Equifax Report on Consumers in the Information Age*.

50. See ibid.

51. See U.S. House of Representatives, "Fair Credit Reporting Act," Hearing before the Subcommittee on Consumer Affairs and Coinage of the Committee on Banking, Finance, and Urban Affairs (June 6, 1991), serial number 102–45.

52. Organizations without such a hierarchy may want to consider instituting it as a technique for addressing the appropriate access to personal information. See item 3 in the "Initial Audit" checklist.

53. It will be recalled that super-bureaus tie together several databases through front-end computer systems. They often provide access to several credit bureaus' databases as well as drivers' registration records, motor vehicle records, etc. In a sense, they can be viewed as "one-stop shopping depots" for personal information.

54. H. Jeff Smith, "National Credit Information Network," Harvard Business School case (1989), number 190–043.

Appendix

1. See Yvonna S. Lincoln and Egon G. Guba, *Naturalistic Inquiry* (Beverly Hills, Calif.: Sage Publications, 1985). Also see Robert K. Yin, *Case Study Research: Design and Methods* (Beverly Hills, Calif.: Sage Publications, 1984).

2. See Lincoln and Guba, *Naturalistic Inquiry*, for a discussion of this "emergent paradigm" research methodology.

3. To protect the identity of CredCard, it is not being disclosed whether the firm is a) a corporation that issues credit cards as its primary business or b) a bank's division that issues bank-branded Visa and/or MasterCards.

4. Yin, *Case Study Research: Design and Methods*.

5. Ibid.

6. *Technology and Consumers: Jobs, Education, Privacy*, Bulletin on Consumer Opinion no. 157 (Cambridge, Mass.: Cambridge Reports, 1989).

7. Alan Westin, *The Dimensions of Privacy: A National Opinion Research Survey of Attitudes Toward Privacy*, conducted by Louis Harris and Associates and Alan F. Westin (New York: Garland, 1981).

8. Ibid.

9. Ronald Lee Esquerra, "Personal Privacy in a Computer Information Society," Ph.D. diss., University of Arizona, 1982.

10. Note, however, that this procedure does not test a rival, ironic conjecture that individuals who are more concerned about privacy will be less likely to return a written survey. The assumption regarding late responders and nonresponders would not hold for this group of individuals.

Index